THE COMPLETE COMPANIC
TEACHING AND LEADING
IN THE EARLY YEARS

Previously published as *The Early Years Professional's Complete Companion*, this new edition has been thoroughly updated and is the essential resource for aspiring and existing leaders of early years practice.

Covering a wide range of theoretical and practical concepts, this book helps the reader consider how they can develop excellent practice within their unique setting. Divided into three distinct sections, the book begins by exploring the origins of early years practice, before discussing principles in development, social policy and child protection. The second section considers what constitutes high-quality practice, and reflects on the role of emotional security, environment and adults in shaping children's learning and development. The third and final section examines how activities associated with continued professional development impact on teaching standards, before finishing with a discussion on international perspectives on early years practice.

Key features include:

- New chapters on safeguarding, children's rights, continuing professional development and international perspectives on early years practice.
- Chapter objectives, tasks and links to the Early Years Foundation Stage.
- Case studies with questions for reflection to promote critical thinking.
- New developments in the early years practice arena are outlined, including the emergence of Early Years Teacher Status (EYTS).

This book is an essential text for those working towards qualifications in early years teaching and leading practice, and provides a flexible basis for tutors, trainers, assessors and mentors to further develop programmes of education and training. It will also appeal to teachers and practitioners interested in considering potential routes for continuing their professional development.

Pam Jarvis is both a chartered psychologist and a historian, and her key research focus is the development of social policy for children, young people and their families. She has 20 years of experience of creating and teaching developmental, social science and social policy modules for Education/Child Development programmes in higher education.

Jane George has extensive experience in the voluntary sector and working in socially deprived areas with ethnically diverse groups. She is Head of Faculty, Social Care and Community Practice at Bradford College

Wendy Holland has experience of teaching in mainstream nurseries, primary and special schools for over 30 years. From the 1970s onwards, her focus has been around inclusive provision and practice for children from birth to eight years.

Jonathan Doherty has worked in a number of roles in early years and education in school and higher education. Prior to his appointment as Head of Primary Education at Leeds Trinity University, he was Head of Early Childhood Education at Leeds Metropolitan University and then Head of Early Years and Childhood Studies at Manchester Metropolitan University.

THE COMPLETE COMPANION FOR TEACHING AND LEADING PRACTICE IN THE EARLY YEARS

Third edition

Pam Jarvis, Jane George, Wendy Holland
and Jonathan Doherty

Routledge
Taylor & Francis Group

LONDON AND NEW YORK

First published 2016
by Routledge
2 Park Square, Milton Park, Abingdon, Oxon OX14 4RN

and by Routledge
711 Third Avenue, New York, NY 10017

Routledge is an imprint of the Taylor & Francis Group, an informa business

British Library Cataloguing in Publication Data
A catalogue record for this book is available from the British Library

Library of Congress Cataloging in Publication Data
A catalog record for this book has been requested

ISBN: 978-1-138-82392-1 (hbk)
ISBN: 978-1-138-82459-1 (pbk)
ISBN: 978-1-315-74059-1 (ebk)

Typeset in Interstate and Celeste
by Saxon Graphics Ltd, Derby

For Lennon, Frankie and all their fellow millennium babies: this book is dedicated to you, in the hope that it helps your carers and educators to nurture your dreams, which are our future.

Pam Jarvis

To my children, Sarah and Graham. As babies, you sparked my interest in child development and now you have developed into amazing human beings!

Jane George

To all those young children it has been my delight to know and share with the 'awe and wonder' that is early childhood, especially to my grandchildren Joseph, George and Alice.

Wendy Holland

To Katherine, who supported me through the journey of this book. Thank you.

Jonathan Doherty

CONTENTS

ABOUT THE AUTHORS

Pam Jarvis is both a chartered psychologist and a historian, and her key research focus is the development of social policy for children, young people and their families. She has 20 years of experience of creating and teaching developmental, social science and social policy modules for Education/Child Development programmes in higher education. Pam currently leads the BA(Hons) in Child and Family Welfare at Leeds Trinity University. She has Qualified Teacher Status, an MA in history and an MEd, and was awarded a PhD by Leeds Metropolitan University in 2005 for her thesis 'The Role of Rough and Tumble Play in Children's Social and Gender Role Development in the Early Years of Primary School'. Pam is a member of the academic advisory team for the National Save Childhood Movement and 'Too Much, Too Soon' campaign. Her recent publications include:

- Jarvis, P. and Liebovich, B. (2015) British nurseries, head and heart: McMillan, Owen and the genesis of the education/care dichotomy. *Women's History Review*. 24(6). Available at: www.tandfonline.com/doi/abs/10.1080/09612025.2015.1025662?journalCode=rwhr 20#.VUZripPff4U
- Jarvis, P., Newman, S. and Swiniarski, L. (2014) On 'becoming social': the importance of collaborative free play in childhood. *International Journal of Play*. 3(1), 53–68. Available at: www.tandfonline.com/doi/pdf/10.1080/21594937.2013.863440
- Brock, A., Jarvis, P. and Olusoga, Y. (2014) *Perspectives on Play: Learning for life* (2nd Edn). Abingdon: Routledge.

Jane George (MEd) has extensive experience in the voluntary sector, in toddler groups and playgroups and managing and teaching for the Pre-School Learning Alliance. She has worked in community education developing and delivering Parent and Toddler at Play classes in areas of social deprivation and to various cultural groups. Working in colleges across West Yorkshire, she has developed and delivered a variety of early years programmes across further and higher education. She was awarded an MEd in 2002. In her current role of Head of Faculty for Social Care and Community Practice (Higher Education) at Bradford College she manages a curriculum which includes social work, youth work, health and social care and counselling as well as early years. She is an External Examiner for early years and keeps up to date with policy and practice thorough her role as Community Trustee in a Primary Academy Trust and as Chair of Governors at one of the Schools in the Trust. Her recent publications include:

- Jarvis, P., Newman, S., Holland, W. and George, J. (2012) *Research in the Early Years Setting: A step by step guide*. Harlow: Pearson Longman.
- Jarvis, P. and George, J. (2010) Thinking it through: rough and tumble play, pp. 164-78 in J. Moyles (Ed.) *Thinking it Through: Reflecting on playful pedagogy in the early years*. Buckingham: Open University Press.

Wendy Holland (MA) has experience of teaching in mainstream nurseries, primary and special schools for over 30 years. From the 1970s onwards, her focus has been around inclusive provision and practice for children from birth to eight years. Through the establishment of mother and toddler groups and playgroups for children with particular needs, integrated mainstream provision for hearing and hearing impaired nursery and primary aged children, she has pursued her particular interests around the inclusion of parents/carers in the caring and educative process. The importance of the role of the reflective practitioner as an agent for change in early years practice is another of her interests. She is also currently working in the teaching, health and care sector at Bradford College, developing and producing modules for the BA(Hons) with Qualified Teacher Status degree and the BA(Hons) Educational Studies degree, alongside supporting students engaged in a range of undergraduate and masters level programmes. Her recent publications include:

- Holland, W. (2009) The patchwork quilt, pp. 25-32 in G. Murphy and M. Power (Eds) *A Story to Tell*. Stoke-on-Trent: Trentham Books.
- Jarvis, P. and Holland, W. (2011) The early years professional and the children's centre: at the hub of the 'Big Society'?, pp. 79-92 in A. Brock and C. Rankin (Eds) *Making it Work for the Child: Professionalism for the early years interdisciplinary team*. London: Continuum.
- Jarvis, P., Newman, S., Holland, W. and George, J. (2012) *Research in the Early Years Setting: A step by step guide*. Harlow: Pearson Longman.
- Jarvis, P., George, J. and Holland, W. (2012) *The Early Years Professional's Complete Companion* (2nd Edn). Harlow: Pearson Longman.

Jonathan Doherty has worked in a number of roles in early years and education in school and higher education. Prior to his appointment as Head of Primary Education at Leeds Trinity University, he was Head of Early Childhood Education at Leeds Metropolitan University and then Head of Early Years and Childhood Studies at Manchester Metropolitan University. He has worked as an Early Years Foundation Stage Regional Adviser for the National Strategies with responsibility for birth to five years provision in settings and schools in the North West of England. After the Strategies contract ended, Jonathan set up and became a Co-Director with Ann Langston in a consultancy business offering support and advice to settings and schools, before joining Wakefield Local Authority as a School Improvement and Transformation Adviser.

Jonathan's research interests are in inclusion, pedagogy and educational achievement and he is passionate about improving outcomes for children and supporting all children by giving them the very best start in life. He has much experience of working with practitioners and teachers developing action research projects relating to curriculum and teaching and learning. In the past he has served on a number of national groups informing education debate. He has presented his research to national and international audiences and authored eight books and a number of articles in academic and professional journals. Recent publications include:

- Cooper, L. and Doherty, J. (2010) *Supporting Development in the Early Years Foundation Stage: Physical development.* London: Continuum.
- Langston, A. and Doherty, J. (2012) *The Revised EYFS in Practice: Thinking, reflecting and doing.* London: Featherstone.
- Doherty, J. and Hughes, M. (2013) *Child Development: Theory and practice 0-11* (2nd Edn). Harlow: Pearson Education Publishers.

Sue Elmer is an Associate Principal Lecturer in the Institute of Childhood and Education, Leeds Trinity University. She is Head of Undergraduate Programmes and Leader of the MA in Family Support. She also supervises PhD students.

She is a Health and Care Professions Council (HPCP) registered social worker, Relate trained counsellor and full member and Director of the British Association of Play Therapists (BAPT). She is experienced in teaching and training students registered on professional awards as part of their continuing professional development (CPD), including professionals in the teaching, health and social care sectors. Her research interests include social work play therapy, domestic abuse, integrated practice and practitioner research. She is currently researching creative strategies in higher education.

FOREWORD

It's a great honour to be asked to write the Foreword for a book as comprehensive, well-researched, practical and fundamentally *wise* as this one – especially since I'm not actually an early years expert myself. However, as a writer on child development (and grandmother of a three-year-old), I'm well aware of the complicated juggling act early years practitioners must perform every day. Caring for young children is an immense responsibility and it's by no means easy to focus on the best interests of each individual child, whilst simultaneously attending to innumerable professional and statutory duties.

In this respect, the *Complete Companion* is an invaluable aid for any practitioner, as it performs that same juggling act on paper, pulling together all the essential principles and policies of which the profession must be aware, yet always 'keeping the child in the centre'. So, along with a masterly overview of developmentally appropriate, rights-respecting practice, the *Companion* provides a source of 'ready reference' for professional knowledge and regulatory detail that practitioners are likely to need on a daily basis.

Here and now

The book also outlines – and for some readers this may not at first seem relevant – the historical and international context in which this professional knowledge and regulatory detail has been amassed. For anyone working with young children, there's so much to learn, remember and then *do* every day, that harking back to the past and/or considering what people do in other parts of the world may seem unnecessarily time-consuming. But the many ethical problems that beset early years practitioners in the UK today – and which this book resolutely tackles – can't be solved from the narrow perspective of the here and now.

In terms of the early years juggling act, it's clear that the single most important ball to keep in the air is 'the individual child'. And in one way, 'keeping the child in the centre' is extremely simple. When a child is there in front of you he or she is clearly central – a living breathing human being to whose immediate needs you feel obliged to attend. But what if those needs are at odds with what the regulatory details require you to do?

Here's an example from my own area of professional interest – literacy. What if a four-year-old child is lying sprawled across a table feebly whimpering 'I can't do it!'. Or what if he's thrown his group's pencil container across the room and is now huddled under the teacher's desk howling like a dog? I've come across both these scenarios in recent years and many more like them. The regulatory detail in question is statutory guidance in the Early Years Foundation Stage (EYFS) that, by five, children will 'write simple sentences which can be read by themselves and others'. In many Reception classrooms there's considerable pressure from senior management to ensure that this guidance is followed, resulting in regular incidents like those above. Unfortunately, this pressure often extends downwards into nursery and pre-school settings and thus affects the social and emotional development of extremely young children.

It might therefore be helpful for today's practitioners to know that the EYFS guidance concerned was drawn up – very hurriedly – in the early years of this century, that the politicians who commissioned it wanted children to crack on with schoolwork at the age of five because that's when school starts in the UK, that five was chosen as the school starting age by Victorian politicians for economic (not educational) reasons, and that in non-English-speaking countries children aren't beset by such regulations because – in 86% of countries worldwide – school doesn't start till they're six or seven (I've just helped launch a campaign in Scotland to delay formal schooling till seven there, so if you want more details on the background to these assertions, please visit www.upstart.scot).

The problem of small children who can't or won't write is only one of many dilemmas likely to confront English early years practitioners regarding the vexed question of 'school readiness' – and about which they may have to justify their eventual decisions to primary senior management. So the better informed they are about the historical and political context in which those dilemmas arise, the better they'll be able to argue their case. From the first chapter of the *Complete Companion* (the history of early years practice) to Chapter 10 (international perspectives) this context is clearly outlined. In my opinion, this greatly enhances the discussions of principles and practice in the two major sections of the book.

First do no harm

'School readiness' is by no means the only area of early childhood care and education where ethical considerations are likely to crop up. The *Complete Companion* includes many case studies and questions for 'reflection' that exemplify problems practitioners in twenty-first-century Britain may face. Indeed, issues such as child protection and parental rights raise ethical questions in every part of the world, making international guidelines such as the UN Convention on the Rights of the Child extremely important. But the historical and political context of early years policy-making in the UK adds an extra layer of complexity.

These policies have been devised (and continually revised) at break-neck speed compared with those in many other countries. This too is due, to some extent, to the UK's early school starting age because widespread demand for state-funded pre-school care and education didn't become a political priority here until the 1990s. In countries such as Finland and Sweden, where children were traditionally at home with their mums for *seven* years before starting school, pressure on government to provide pre-school day care began in the 1970s, so policy was devised at a more leisurely rate (and before competitive consumerism became the guiding light of western political thought). In all mainland European countries the influence of well-established European early years authorities such as Froebel, Montessori and Piaget tends to have more impact on public (and therefore political) perceptions of early childhood than in an off-shore island where children have traditionally been 'seen but not heard' and packed off to formal education at four or five years of age.

UK practitioners, therefore, have some very particular problems when attempting to follow the age-old ethical maxim 'First do no harm'. There are serious conflicts between established principles of early years practice and some of the guidance provided by government agencies. These conflicts are often fudged in professional discourse – including training courses and manuals – which doesn't help practitioners at all in performing their day-by-day juggling act. Nor does it help leading practitioners when trying to facilitate professional development in their own settings.

Perhaps this is my main reason for admiring the *Complete Companion*. It doesn't hesitate to identify and address these areas of conflict head on. It doesn't present any easy answers either, because there are none. But it does encourage informed reflection and the sharing of experience and understanding with colleagues, which are the most effective tools for any professional confronting an ethical dilemma. That's why, if the staff in my granddaughter's nursery had only one book in their professional library, I'd want it to be this one.

The most important job in the world

I've so far managed to resist trotting out the well-worn phrase about early years practitioners doing 'the most important job in the world'. It's now been said by so many politicians and public figures, whose actual behaviour shows they don't value the efforts and expertise of the profession in the least, that many practitioners I know raise their eyes to heaven when they hear it – and I don't blame them. Lip service is both patronising and intensely frustrating.

Nevertheless, the fact that the phrase is often used ignorantly or insincerely doesn't make it any less true. There *can* be no more important job – from the point of view of the individual children concerned, their families, and the society those children and families inhabit – than the care and education of the under-sevens. The significance of these years in human development has been acknowledged by philosophers throughout history, explained over the last two centuries by the 'early years pioneers' described in Chapter 1, and confirmed in the last couple of decades by neuroscientific research.

As a literacy specialist, I'm in no doubt whatsoever that primary children's ability to read and write depends on physical, social, emotional and cognitive foundations laid down during the pre-school years. As someone approaching three score years and ten, I've seen how the personality and character of every child I've watched grow up was forged through their early experiences and relationships. And as a researcher in the field of child development for the last 15 years, I'm convinced (by everything I've read and every expert I've interviewed) that the long-term health and well-being of individual children – and thus the society those children eventually inherit – depends on how they're cared for before they're seven years old.

The current generation of politicians and public figures was reared in a culture that places little value on small children and their carers, so it may take some time before early years practitioners are granted more than lip service for the important work they do. However, the better equipped they are to do that work well, the sooner that time is likely to come. I therefore congratulate you on having found the *Complete Companion* and hope it helps you not only to negotiate through the choppy waters of contemporary childcare practice, but also to enjoy thinking about that practice.

Enjoy...!

I was so busy worrying about dilemmas that I'd forgotten to mention 'enjoyment' until now. That's what happens when human beings try to juggle a lot of complicated ideas – they can rapidly forget the reason they were engaging with the ideas in the first place. And, of course, the reason practitioners choose to work with little children is that (most of the time) they are such a joy to be with. Unless something has gone seriously awry, children instinctively know how to *love* and *play*, which are the twin sources of human joy.

So in the end, it's the joy children bring that helps us adults keep them in the centre, do them no harm and remember why caring for them is the most important job in the world. Hold fast to that joy, use informed reflection and shared professionalism to deal with the dilemmas, keep your *Companion* by your side, and even the choppy waters may turn out to be fun!

Sue Palmer, author of *Toxic Childhood*
Edinburgh, 2015
(P.S. An updated version of *Toxic Childhood* was published this year!)

ACKNOWLEDGEMENTS

Pam Jarvis

As always, my first acknowledgements are to my family who put up with me while I write and edit. Many thanks are offered to all the people who have participated in my research over the years, various aspects of which are referred to throughout the chapters of this book. We would also like to thank Chris Jarvis, Dr Simon George and Dr Sarah George who patiently proofread the first edition of this book. I would like to thank Dr Jonathan Doherty who came to the writing team quite late in the process of putting this version of the book together, and hit the ground running at Olympic speed, adding a huge amount of value in a very short time. Many thanks also go to Dr Sue Elmer, who contributed her considerable expertise on safeguarding to the team, and patiently bore my repeated 'is your chapter done yet?' nagging! I would also like to acknowledge all the students I have taught on Early Years Professional and Early Years Teacher pathways over the years: you have all taught me at least as much as I have taught you! Finally, my thanks go to my long-term collaborators Jane George and Wendy Holland; if the next generation of early years practitioners are as talented, dedicated and knowledgeable as you both, then the millennium generation and beyond will be in very safe hands.

Jane George

To my husband, Simon, always patient when I am distracted by work and writing. To all the children and families I have worked with, you have influenced my thinking and my practice. To my colleagues at Bradford College, to former colleagues in other organisations, and to my co-authors – you challenge me to challenge myself.

Wendy Holland

The very nature of early years practice is founded on good teamwork, and I would like to acknowledge all the help and support and inspiration I've received from the dedicated early years teams I have worked with both in mainstream and special school settings here in Yorkshire and in Lancashire. I would also like to express the immense gratitude I feel to those parents and carers of young children, who have welcomed me into their homes and worked with me, sometimes in very difficult circumstances, to enhance the lives of children. To Barry Miller and Maggie Smith, a huge thank you for having the initial vision to see what a difference the Early Years Professional Status programme could mean for future early years practice, and Jane Guilfoyle along with the tutors, mentors and assessors for turning that vision into the reality of a very effective Early Years Professional Status programme at Bradford College. To Dr Clive Opie, my sincere thanks for his enthusiastic support and encouragement of a once fledgling programme that now commands wide recognition and respect. Finally, my thanks go to all my collaborators in this book for giving of their time, and sharing their knowledge and expertise to create something so uniquely knowledgeable and diverse for the early years professionals of the future.

Jonathan Doherty

I would like to acknowledge the tremendous support given to me by my wife Katherine in compiling this book.

Introduction

The Complete Companion for Teaching and Leading Practice in the Early Years

Welcome to *The Complete Companion for Teaching and Leading Practice in the Early Years*. This book provides a companion handbook for candidates currently engaged in academic study and professional training that focuses upon teaching and leading practice for children in the early years of development and learning (birth to seven). It aims to support teachers and practitioners in training/early career to reflect upon and develop their practice, and to consider potential routes for continuing professional development.

The book takes a holistic 'developmental' approach, initially exploring the origins of early years professional practice in Chapter 1, and the theoretical background to practice in the early years in Chapter 2. Chapter 3 considers the core principles of safeguarding within early years settings, and Chapter 4 summarises the development of social policy for children and families in England, comparing this with examples drawn from other nations. This format will also be used in the three practice-focused chapters that follow, which explore teaching and learning, emotional support/behaviour management, and enabling environments within early years settings.

We use the global term 'setting' to encompass the various professional environments in which children from birth to seven are housed, for example including classrooms, daycare settings and nurseries, carefully signposting where we are focusing on a specific early years environment. In general, however, we take the position that children's learning and development is best supported by environments which are designed to nurture their holistic well-being and meet their individual needs.

We use the term 'Early Years Teacher' (EYT) throughout the book to refer to all of those whose principal professional role is designated primarily as teaching, and 'Early Years Graduate Practitioner' (EYGP) for those who are not in a designated teaching role, but who have some responsibility for leading practice, in the sense of modelling best practice within the setting. Issues relating specifically to management are addressed in Chapter 8, which additionally encompasses the management of partnerships with parents and families. In Chapter 9, we discuss continuing professional development (CPD) and present some effective ways for the early years workforce to continue their professional learning in today's fast-moving climate of educational change; here we also clarify the recent, somewhat confusing distinction which has arisen in England between 'Early Years Teachers' who work with children between birth and five, and those with 'Qualified Teacher Status: Early Years', who work with children aged three to seven. In our final chapter, we consider early years practice across a wider international arena, highlighting similarities to and differences from early years practice in England. Within each chapter, ideas for practical activities and further reading are suggested, and the text is interspersed with boxes outlining examples of practice, accompanied by reflection and advice.

Chapter summaries

Introduction

Introducing early years practice.

Chapter 1. Wendy Holland and Pam Jarvis: The history of early years practice

This chapter will explore the core question 'What is early years practice?', considering how and why specifically early years education/educare developed through the influence of the following key pioneers and their concepts of early years care, teaching and learning: Pestalozzi, Owen, Froebel, Steiner, Montessori, McMillan, Isaacs, Malaguzzi (Reggio Emilia). The current relevance of their ideas to contemporary practice will be considered. Readers will be prompted throughout the chapter to apply concepts and ideas to their own personal practice

Section 1: The children's agenda: principles in children's development, social policy and inclusion

Chapter 2. Pam Jarvis and Jane George: Principles in childcare and education

This chapter will explore major theories in child development across physical, intellectual, social, emotional and language development, with frequent examples of theory applied to practice, in particular through the English Early Years Foundation Stage (EYFS), with some comparisons to early years frameworks in other nations. There will be an introduction to the observational skills that are so important in early years practice. Readers will be frequently prompted to apply their own practice to the theories cited within the text and to develop these further, particularly in the light of highlighted further reading opportunities at the end of the chapter.

Chapter 3. Sue Elmer: Safeguarding, child protection and children in need in the early years

This chapter will explore the complex issue of safeguarding and protecting children in the modern early years care and education environment. It will consider current legislation and policy initiatives, with reference to relevant current research findings and serious case reviews. The responsibilities of practice leaders in English early years settings will be discussed, in particular the requirements of current statutory frameworks including the EYFS. The brief history of the national Child Assessment Framework and its later local variants will be reviewed, with particular reference to the emergence of 'Early Help' for children in need. The chapter will contain some interactive activities to help readers explore leadership responsibilities within safeguarding practice, including a worked step-by-step example of the creation of a child protection policy for an early years setting.

Chapter 4. Pam Jarvis: Families and the state: the ongoing development of social policy

This chapter will follow the development of English social policy for children and families, additionally considering the creation of the United Nations Convention on the Rights of the Child (UNCRC) international guidelines and how these relate to policy in England today. Some recent developments in the UK nations will be considered; for example, the English Children and Families Bill (2014). Readers will be encouraged to view social policy as a continually evolving arena, in which policy for children and families is developed as a compromise that is reached with respect to wider national and international interests. In particular, the issue of 'children as human capital' will be explored.

Section 2: Leading practice in the early years setting

Chapter 5. Wendy Holland and Jonathan Doherty: Leading high-quality practice in children's learning and development from birth to seven years

This chapter will explore ideas around what constitutes high-quality practice when leading continuous provision for children from birth to seven years in the varied and various settings and classrooms of early years provision in the UK. The chapter will focus especially on consideration of the individual needs of the child; for example, ethnicity, gender and additional needs. The use of provocation, differentiation and an inclusive approach to practice that is the hallmark of high-quality provision will be examined. Some reference to planning and assessment procedures within the English EYFS and Primary Key Stage 1 will be made, but in the frame of critical evaluation, with some comparison with the practices of other nations and frameworks. The growing impact of a 'school readiness' approach will be considered.

Chapter 6. Wendy Holland and Jonathan Doherty: Promoting emotional security and positive behaviour

This chapter will cover the aspect of children's confidence and 'well-being' in care and education settings. The focus will therefore be on the provision of constructive feedback to young children, through the use of a range of strategies, such as sustained shared thinking, modelling and positive behaviour management. The importance of listening to the child's and the family's 'voice' will be considered, and the need to be aware of children's family, cultural and societal backgrounds in order to fully understand (and potentially deal with) troubling behaviours.

Chapter 7. Wendy Holland and Jonathan Doherty: Creating environments for play and learning

This chapter will cover in more detail the areas of planning, particularly with regard to individual needs, and the impact of environments upon children's learning and development. The aspect of the 'school readiness' agenda will be further explored in the issues involved in balancing this with children's individual needs and consequent impacts upon the delivery of play-based learning. Some investigation of how this situation has impacted upon the quality of provision and practice will be included. Provision for children with additional needs and their families will also be considered.

Chapter 8. Jane George, Pam Jarvis and Wendy Holland: Partnership and leadership in early years

This chapter will cover the importance of working with, managing and leading other adult stakeholders in early years practice. It will begin by focusing upon the important topic of working with parents and families, with some discussion of the impact of the statutory Two Year Progress Check in England. The chapter will then move on to focus upon leading multi-agency working in the early years, building upon some aspects of multi-agency practice initially raised in Chapter 3. It will also consider issues relating to leading teams within early years settings, particularly in the context of contemporary democratic environments and distributed responsibility.

Section 3: Wider perspectives in early years leadership

Chapter 9. Jonathan Doherty and Pam Jarvis: Continuing professional development

This chapter will consider the historical context of continuing professional development (CPD) in general, moving on to consider the background to CPD and 'professional learning' specifically for early years leaders/early years teachers, dispelling the notion of early years as a 'poor relation' in both the care and education sectors. It will then briefly explore New Labour's attempts to 'upskill the children's workforce', considering the professionalism versus professionalisation debate. The dissonance of recent government agendas versus public recognition of early years professionalism is also addressed. Recent routes in CPD will be unpicked and discussed in the frame of vocational routes, with a focus upon the Early Years Graduate Practitioner, Early Years Teacher Status and Qualified Teacher Status (Early Years). Some brief comparisons with international professional roles will be made. The chapter will then turn to practical issues surrounding CPD, including a thorough exploration of action research, and the use of journaling, which will include online and interactive portfolios and blogs.

Chapter 10. Pam Jarvis: The child, the family and the state: international perspectives

This chapter will briefly consider the orientations of various nations to early years practice, in particular through a comparison of the Anglo-American 'child as human capital' agenda with the Nordic 'child as citizen' concept. The chapter will explore opportunities and threats emerging from internationalist approaches, and the role of teachers and graduate practitioners in different cultural 'frames'. Readers will be asked for their own reflections at several points in the chapter, and directed towards sources of information on the practices/policies of different nations, particularly as they are outlined within English language sources which are regularly updated on the World Wide Web.

Conclusion

The Complete Companion for Teaching and Leading Practice in the Early Years is the successor to a text that has been thoroughly updated for all currently in training or early career, whose sole focus is upon the early years. It is an extensively revised edition of a book that has already been very effective in this arena; now expanded to take into account international perspectives, including many comparisons between the UK nations, who, following the 2015 General Election, have been set on a pathway where a highly diverse range of early years practices are likely to emerge. It draws upon the carefully co-ordinated training programme initially developed for training early years professionals by this highly effective team of teacher-authors, and has been subsequently updated to take recent developments in the early years practice arena into account, including the emergence of Early Years Teacher Status (EYTS). It is designed to become a key text for the growing number of early years teachers and graduate professionals within early years practice in the UK and internationally. It will also provide a flexible basis for tutors, trainers, assessors and mentors to further develop programmes of education and training for those wishing to become teachers and graduate practitioners in early years education and care.

1　The history of early years practice

Wendy Holland and Pam Jarvis

CHAPTER OVERVIEW

This chapter will introduce the reader to eight people in history who pioneered different ways of providing collective education and care for young children, and whose ideas have been taken forward into current early years education and care practices. It will address the following questions:

✔ Who were the 'pioneers' and what is their place in the history of early years practice?
✔ Where did each pioneer stand on the question of curriculum, assessment and the role of the adult in children's learning?
✔ What relevance do the pioneers have to current practice in the early years?

The recommended reading list at the end of this chapter will introduce readers to a range of texts and online resources in which to read further on these topics.

Introduction: who were the 'pioneers' and what is their place in the history of early years practice?

For many generations, most children in western nations did not experience a childhood as we understand the concept today, but rather infancy followed by a quick entry into adult responsibilities. Literacy and numeracy skills (in the sense that we use them today) were not essential in order to operate as a full adult in society. The concept of original sin was strong within the Christian west, particularly in Protestant nations. Children were raised from the perspective that they were tainted from birth in this way, and that the principal role for the adult was to teach them to control their sinful urges. However, starting in the mid-seventeenth century, Europe began to experience what is now referred to as an age of 'Enlightenment'. Scientists began to make important discoveries that explained how many natural phenomena actually 'worked', and this in turn led to developments in sociological and political thought, which eventually reached the area of child development. The philosopher Jean-Jacques Rousseau (1712–78) strongly criticised the traditional attitude to childhood. He said in *Émile ou de l'Éducation (Émile, or on Education)*:

> Love childhood, indulge its sports, its pleasures, its delightful instincts. Who has not sometimes regretted that age when laughter was ever on the lips, and when the heart was ever at peace? Why rob these innocents of the joys which pass so quickly, of that precious gift which they cannot abuse?
>
> Why fill with bitterness the fleeting days of early childhood, days which will no more return for them than for you? Fathers, can you tell when death will call your children to him? Do not lay up sorrow for yourselves by robbing them of the short span which nature has allotted to them. As soon as they are aware of the joy of life, let them rejoice in it, so that whenever God calls them they may not die without having tasted the joy of life.
>
> (Rousseau, 1762, online)

In Switzerland, **Johann Heinrich Pestalozzi (1746–1827)** studied Rousseau's philosophy of education, and then determined to engage in the practical implementation of a Rousseau-inspired pedagogy. He was convinced that rather than being 'talked at', as was the custom at that time, children should learn through activity and through interactions with the physical world in situations where they were free to experiment and draw their own conclusions. He believed that the younger the child, the more open s/he would be to learning, an idea we know now to be absolutely correct with respect to neuronal development (see chapter 2). Pestalozzi founded several schools at different times to pioneer these ideas. However, the situation both in the time and place he was located – during the Napoleonic wars, in Switzerland, which was occupied several times – meant that although he had some clear successes, his ventures, the two most famous being located in Yverdon and Burgdorf, often came to abrupt and untimely ends (Bruhlmeier, 2010). However, his fame spread and endured, and even today in Switzerland the name 'Pestalozzi' is not only connected with education, but with boundless charity, rather like the name of Barnardo in Britain (Rubi, 2014).

Early British industrialist **Robert Owen (1771–1858)** met with Pestalozzi in 1818. Owen's father-in-law, factory owner David Dale, had started a school for his young workers in Lanark, Scotland, to ensure that they had sufficient literacy and numeracy skills to cope with the requirements of their working role. On marrying Dale's daughter, and taking over major responsibility for the Lanark enterprise, Owen carried out careful research to discover the most progressive, current pedagogical ideas. While Dale's motives for educating his workforce had been overwhelmingly pragmatic, Owen was searching for a more fully articulated pedagogy, underpinned by philosophical concepts (Davis and O'Hagan, 2010). Owen was much in agreement with Pestalozzi's focus on children's emotional well-being and their sense of civic responsibility, and with his emphasis on vocationalism and learning through 'hands-on' interactions with physical objects, rather than simply through listening. However, he did not share Pestalozzi's religious and somewhat mystical approach, thinking it impractical and over-romanticised.

Influenced by the ideas of Pestalozzi, German **Friedrich Froebel (1785-1852)** developed one of the first comprehensive pedagogical frameworks for young children: a child-centred approach, with the emphasis upon active learning. He was the originator of the term 'kindergarten' (children's garden) for the Play and Activity Institute he founded in 1837 at Bad Blankenburg in Germany. Froebel challenged many conventions of his time, one of which was the giving of inappropriately delicate and complicated toys to children. Children at this time were still considered to be adults in the making, a concept which Froebel rejected. His design of open-ended learning materials (often referred to as 'Gifts') can be linked to today's ideas around play with educational toys; for example, block play. At the time, Froebel saw such play in a more spiritual sense than we regard it today, as a means to helping children discover the interrelatedness of things. Unfortunately, he, like Pestalozzi, met with social and political challenges that meant that he did not see the blossoming of his children's garden; in 1851 the Prussian court banned kindergartens (Le Blanc, nd). Froebel's ideas, however, did survive and began to permeate more widely through Europe, with various pioneers re-interpreting them to fit their own cultural niche, as we will see below.

Pestalozzi's sense of the mystical was reproduced in the pedagogy of **Rudolph Steiner (1861-1925)**, who had been an established scientist, thinker and published scholar before becoming involved in education. His humanist views were well known, and after the chaos and devastation of World War I, he began a tour giving lectures under the title of 'Social Three-Folding' to factory workers, on the topic of a restructuring of society. Such restructuring involved the independent operation of economics, government and culture whereby no one area could dominate. Steiner also introduced the concepts of Anthroposophy (a focus on individual freedom through spiritual development) and Eurythmy (communication through movement and gesture) to the early years education environment (Anthroposophical Society, 2015).

After one of Steiner's lectures to workers at the Waldorf-Astoria cigarette factory in Stuttgart, requests came from both the factory workers and the factory owner, Emil Mott, for Steiner to found a school based on his humanist principles. Steiner agreed, and developed a pioneering institution which disregarded many of the conventions of the time, most prominently introducing principles of co-education – boys and girls educated together. It was also inclusive, being open to children of any background and of all ages from pre-school to high school. Steiner recognised the importance of parents in children's learning and development and welcomed their participation. The other essential ingredient Steiner thought important was the independence of education from any centralised control or interference (Pope Edwards, 2002). This last aspect was one to which the 1933–45 Nazi regime was opposed; they also objected to Steiner's emphasis on passive humanitarianism; this was seen as dangerously subversive within Hitler's National Socialism, and resulted in the closure of Steiner schools in Nazi-occupied Europe for the duration of World War II.

The pedagogy of **Margaret McMillan (1860-1931)** sprang, like Pestalozzi's, from firm religious beliefs, but in her philosophy, these were blended with political conviction: Christian Socialism. In the last decade of the nineteenth century, McMillan took an indirect route into early years education, from her beginnings as a highly effective socialist orator. From this basis, she was elected to the Bradford School Board as a representative of the Independent Labour Party in November 1894, and in this role she became a remarkably active and extremely practical social reformer, instigating medical inspections and free school meals in all Bradford schools and securing the installation of bathing facilities for children in some of the schools in the district. In 1906, in collaboration with her sister Rachel, McMillan led a deputation to Parliament to lobby for the compulsory medical inspection of school children. When this aim was realised in the Education (Administrative Procedures) Bill of 1907, Margaret and Rachel received sufficient charitable donations to open a school clinic in the socially deprived district of Deptford in South London. When they realised that children regularly came and went from the clinic due to constant re-infection caused by their poor living conditions, the sisters set up an experimental overnight camp in their small but well-kept garden in which children between seven and 12 were provided with sleeping and washing facilities under a canvas shelter, fresh air, play time and good food (Jarvis and Liebovich, 2015).

When one of the local girls was permitted to bring her ailing little sister along, and the child died a few months later, Margaret proposed 'We must open our doors to the toddlers ... we must plan the right kind of environment for them and give them sunshine, fresh air and good food *before* they become rickety and diseased' (Stevinson, 1954, p. 8). In 1914, the McMillans acquired premises from the London County Council for a dedicated nursery in Deptford. They soon established a familiar regime: cleanliness, sunshine, fresh air, good food and open access to an abundant garden. The nursery was a great local success during the war years of 1914-18, but sadly Rachel McMillan died in 1917. Following the Armistice, national and international interest began to coalesce around the newly christened 'Rachel McMillan Open Air Nursery School' and its holistic, outdoor-oriented regime (Jarvis and Liebovich, 2015).

Maria Montessori (1870-1952) was born in Italy in 1870, as the only child of middle-class, devoutly Roman Catholic parents. Montessori showed her strong convictions and beliefs early on by flouting conventional wisdom, a trait she would demonstrate for the rest of her life. At 13 she enrolled in a technical school mainly attended by boys, determined to become an engineer. This later changed into a wish to become a doctor, a profession that in nineteenth-century Italy was not thought suitable for a woman. True to her early feminist beliefs, she endured considerable prejudice, qualifying as Italy's first female Doctor of Medicine in 1896 (Hainstock, 1997). However, her first appointment was not of her choosing, as an Assistant Doctor at a psychiatric clinic in the University of Rome. One of her tasks was to travel round asylums selecting children for treatment at the clinic. As she observed these children, institutionalised and traumatised as many were, Montessori came to the conclusion that it was not the children or the 'labels' they had been given that were the core problem, but the way that they had been treated by society. She initiated the technique that was to become a mainstay of her pedagogic method: close observations of her charges, through which she determined that, given the right kind of stimulation, the children would develop and learn. This ignited a need to strengthen her pedagogic knowledge, and for this, she turned to the work of two pioneers in the field of special education: Jean-Marc Itard (1774–1838) and Edouard Seguin (1812-80), even travelling to London and Paris in order to document their methods for herself, such was her need for scientific scrutiny. Not content with this, she returned to university study, attending courses in anthropology, philosophy and psychology. This effort was rewarded in 1904, when she was appointed Lecturer in

Pedagogical Anthropology. In 1907 she was given the opportunity to work with children of slum workers by opening a children's centre in a deprived district in Rome. This became the first *Casa dei Bambini* or 'House of Children' (American Montessori Society, 2015, online), and the beginning of a pioneering method of childhood education. There have been and continue to be critics of Montessori's method, yet it has survived almost unchanged in its essential features for over a century.

Susan Isaacs (1885-1948) was both a trained teacher and a psychoanalyst. She undertook teacher training at Manchester University under Grace Owen, who had trained in Froebelian methods at the Blackheath Kindergarten Training College and at the University of Columbia in the US (Jarvis and Liebovich, 2015). Later in her career Isaacs undertook psychoanalytic training. She may have been initially drawn to psychoanalysis due to personal issues relating to the early death of her mother and the subsequent failure of her first marriage; however, by this time Isaacs was not only a teacher, but an educational researcher, and it is likely that she felt that a depth of understanding in this area would be of benefit to her in both her teaching practice and her research (Graham, 2009, p. 71). She went on to write a highly practical guide to child development entitled *The Nursery Years* (in 1929) which became a bestseller to both parents and teachers, winning the 1937 outstanding book of the year medal awarded by *Parents Magazine* (M. Almy, in Isaacs, 1968). Between 1929 and 1933 she worked as a teacher-researcher at the Malting House School, publishing her detailed observations and analyses in *Social Development in Young Children* (1933). While some of Isaacs' analyses would be seen as highly contentious today, given the heavy influence of Freudian psychology upon them, her key contribution to early years practice is her emphasis upon the requirement for detailed observation of young children, to inform practitioners' in-depth, holistic knowledge of the child, not only to indicate 'next steps' in learning, but also in the diagnosis of emotional problems which may be creating barriers to learning and healthy development.

Loris Malaguzzi (1920-94) originated a Rousseau-influenced curriculum in his native northern Italy in the Region of Emilia (Reggio Emilia). Like Pestalozzi, Froebel and Steiner, Malaguzzi saw the child as rich in potential and capable of thinking for themselves, of being the 'co-constructors' of their own learning and development. Like Steiner, his vision of education followed a period of political and social unrest which had led to the catalyst of war. He was moved to action in the late 1940s, on learning of a community of women who were rebuilding their lives and their schools in the Reggio Emilia region of northern Italy. The pre-school first established by the people of Reggio Emilia was paid for by the sale of leftover armaments from World War II. In true 'guns to ploughshares' spirit, the parents of these children were determined to create a different post-war *structure* in education that encouraged non-conformity, and the ability to think critically and to work collaboratively (Dahlberg *et al.*, 1999). They were adamant that their children's education should be independent of centralist government, as a reaction to living under the oppression of a nationalistic, fascist regime.

Where did each pioneer stand on the question of curriculum, assessment and the role of the adult in children's learning?

Theory of childhood

Steiner's theory of child development was based within a belief in natural, dynamic and self-righting forces within children, that enabled them to become the authors of their own learning and development. Like Piaget (see chapter 2), Steiner believed in a cycle of stages with a seven-year interval (0–7 yrs, 7–14 yrs, 14–21 yrs). However, in its emphasis on human emotion, his theory was perhaps more similar to the Freudian theory of Erik Erikson (Erikson, 1950), which is based in psychoanalysis; this would in turn indicate some similarity to Susan Isaacs' approach. Where Steiner clearly links with Piaget is in his emphasis upon the importance of imaginary, imitative and symbolic play in a child's development, and his insistence upon the need for a stimulating environment which allows and encourages children to explore independently (Bruce, 2005).

Montessori also believed in a stage theory. For her, children developed through a series of six-year periods (echoes here of Steiner's seven-year intervals, and again, Piaget's four stages). During each period, she proposed that the child was 'sensitised' to a particular kind of learning, and all these stages were characterised by a constructivist perspective. Children were constructed as eager to learn through exploring reality, play and work. The earliest phase, from birth to three years, she called the 'unconscious absorbent mind'. She proposed that children between three and six years subsequently entered a '*conscious* absorbent mind' phase. Both these periods, in practice, construct the child as in need of some kind of order in which to explore sensory experiences, freedom to follow their interests and uninterrupted time to explore them. This can be seen in the three-hour session of the Montessori nursery that is standard practice with children from three years of age, where a child's 'work' or interests are given time to unfold without adult interruption.

Montessori's understanding of child development reflects the concerns of earlier educational philosophers such as Rousseau and Pestalozzi. It was a holistic view of the child that embraced the child's natural intelligence as well as rational, empirical and spiritual aspects of their development. She also saw the role of parents as crucial to this development, describing them as the child's first educator. The need to form a trusting partnership with parents was embedded in her philosophy, which was based in the essential elements of this triangular relationship between the child, the parent and the school. The holistic view of the child was also very much shared by Owen, although he had a rather more pragmatic view of the child's eventual destination, which underpinned his emphasis on vocationalism. Here we meet the social construction of children as human capital, a perspective you will meet again in chapters 4 and 10.

Case study: the concept of 'human capital'

In the web magazine *New Republic* Elizabeth Stoker Bruenig comments:

> Human capital is one of the more odious terms in the capitalist lexicon. The phrase advances a couple of key confusions: First, that human value arises from an ability to produce wealth; second, that there is no distinction between labor (the work that humans do) and capital (sources of wealth that passively generate income).
>
> (Stoker Bruenig, 2015, online)

You will discover throughout this book that the debate on this topic is quite complex. Robert Owen was highly focused upon the education of children for industry, and he appeared to believe that this was a charitable endeavour. You can find a short discussion of this issue online at www.bl.uk/learning/histcitizen/21cc/utopia/model1/model.html.

Reflection

What do you think? Should we educate children with a focus upon the types of job that we have attempted to predict that they are likely to do when they grow up, or should we focus more on giving them a general education rooted in 'learning to learn'? You will find this topic further discussed within this book, with reference to current policy and practice, particularly in Chapter 10.

Froebel, through his deeply held Christian faith, saw children as nature's most creative beings, and the freedom of children's play as the ultimate expression of that creativity. This view of the child challenged the conventions of his era, where children under the age of seven were typically not considered capable of social or intellectual thought. Froebel, however, along with all his fellow pioneers, believed that early childhood experience was vitally important as the foundation of intellectual, exploratory skills and social competences that would serve as foundations for later development and understanding (Bruce, 2012).

Isaacs' theory of childhood was by contrast based on Freudian theory, with the child moving through a set of 'psychosexual' stages to full emotional competence. In summary, the Freudian psyche is divided into three separate entities who continually negotiate for balance between gratification and restraint. These entities are:

- The Id: Babies are *all* Id. They have no idea of waiting for gratification; if they want something, they simply scream until they get it. They may not be aware of exactly what it is they want, but if hunger or discomfort is felt they scream until someone comes and takes the unpleasant feeling away. Adults are also motivated by the 'wanting' of the Id, but they have other psychic entities who negotiate with the Id to allow the person to live realistically and (relatively!) peacefully within the world (see below).
- The Ego: This tells us what is physically possible and is formed from living in the real world. Children very soon learn, for example, that it is simply not possible to fly like a bird. This is an Ego-based understanding.
- The Superego: This is formed as the result of the Oedipus complex (see below) and is basically a conscience/internal parent who tells us what is morally and socially

acceptable. It may be quite physically possible to walk around the street naked on a hot summer day – but very few of us do so, because we know that such an action is just not possible, due to social and moral (not physical) constraints.

Freud believed that people were born with an internal energy he called libido. This is now commonly used as a word to describe the adult sex-drive, but this is not exactly what Freud meant by the term. He proposed that this energy was rooted into different behaviours over the course of child development, *finally ending up* as the energy behind the adult sex-drive. The libido is said, in Freudian terms, to be the energy behind feeding in babies of 0–18 months (the oral stage) and evacuation in children of 18 months to approximately three years, the usual age of toilet training (the anal stage).

The next stage, the phallic stage, is slightly more complicated, and is the basis for the development of the superego. Once the anal stage is over and toilet training is accomplished, the child is thought to develop a romantic fixation upon the parent (or parental figure) of the opposite sex. This results in a jealousy of the parent of the same sex, combined with a wish to replace him/her. As Freud's theories were male oriented he called this the *Oedipus complex* after an ancient Greek legend about a man who fell in love with his mother, and killed his father. The child slowly moves through this stage over the next two to four years, and during this time psychologically internalises the parent of the same sex by striving to become him/her.

In this way, proposed Freud, we take in both gender-appropriate behaviour and all the values and morals of the same-sex parent, thereby developing an internal parent we constantly carry with us throughout our lives to 'police' our behaviour – the superego. The phallic stage typically occurs between three and five, but may last until seven years of age. Freud also proposed that there were major differences between the superego development of boys and girls, meaning that girls do not develop such a powerful superego. He thus claimed that women were not as inherently moral as men. Freud's postulation was that boys internalised the disciplinary aspect of the father's role, creating more fear relating to disapproval from the superego. He also proposed that girls suffer from something called 'penis envy' during this stage, feeling that boys have something that they do not; however, this is one of the most contentious parts of his theory and has been called both misguided and sexist. Karen Horney, a mid-twentieth-century Freudian theorist, proposed that, in the Victorian society Freud inhabited, it wasn't the penis that girls envied, but the social advantages that went along with being male (Feminist Voices, 2015).

Eventually, within the Freudian model, the child resolves the Oedipus complex by reluctantly realising that the same-sex parent is bigger, stronger and can out-think him/her, so this is a contest s/he is never going to win. With the resolution of the Oedipus complex the basis for the adult personality is complete. Freudian therapeutic analysis will always involve an in-depth investigation of the way that the patient was parented before the age of seven, with a view to initiating 're-parenting' in problematic areas.

After the resolution of the Oedipus complex, the child, now between five and seven years of age, tends to become far more involved in the world away from home, where the libido is channelled into activities such as school work, friendship groups and playing sports. Freud suggests that this widening of social activity prepares the ground for the independence which comes with adolescence and sexual maturity, at which time the child enters the genital stage, the last and adult stage within Freudian theory, where the libido is channelled into adult sexual behaviour. Further discussion about Freud's developmental theory can be found at www.personalityresearch.org/papers/beystehner.html

This theory of childhood marks Isaacs out as rather different to the other pioneers; however, she shared their emphasis on play-based learning, although for her, coming from this Freudian base, the main purpose of this practice was for children to learn to deal with and independently channel their emotions.

While **McMillan** was certainly not a Freudian, she shared Isaacs' concern for children's social and emotional development; however, for McMillan, these were dependent upon their physical needs being met. She felt that the grinding poverty in which many inner-city children lived during the early twentieth century was responsible for both unhealthy bodies and minds. Unlike Isaacs, however, she did not subscribe to a complex theory to explain this, but to a more simple emphasis on healthy nutrition, exercise, fresh air and sunlight, a popular cultural concept at the time, which became known as 'health and efficiency'. This difference is rather similar to the philosophical difference between Pestalozzi and Owen – while they might have agreed on a pedagogical regime, their underlying reasons for doing so were very different, with one taking a far more deeply philosophically embedded position than the other.

Case study: theories of childhood

Current researchers and practitioners have far more theoretical and empirical information at their disposal, particularly from the modern understanding of the developmental process embedded in the human genome, and the construction of the physical brain throughout childhood and adolescence. However, time and again, as neuroscience expands our understanding and knowledge we return to these original pioneers, realising that their intuitive intelligence highlighted areas of learning and development that are still relevant today. Contemporary theories of childhood, supported by a clearer understanding of brain function, increasingly demonstrate the intricate, multi-directional relationship between nature and nurture within human development in childhood and adolescence, including the central importance of interaction with others, both peers and adults (Jarvis, 2015).

Recent biological research into stress-coping (see chapter 2) has resulted in general agreement that young human beings need to develop secure attachments, and that failure to achieve this can have long-lasting consequences. There is also now more general acceptance amongst those who specialise in child development that there is a need for the young child to initiate and lead their own learning. Children's natural biological development requires that they actively *build* neural pathways by cognitively and socially constructing and further refining concepts. Pestalozzi, the original pioneer, had long ago intuited that passively absorbing didactic adult instruction does not lead to deep or enduring learning. However, we now have concrete, biological evidence to confirm that the young brain contains limitless capacity to build and refine cognitive representations of the world 'out there'. Children build neuronal connections in active, independent interaction with both the physical and social world; they are not passive, empty vessels that need filling.

In the current early years international environment, this 'rich' child is reflected in the approach of the Reggio Emilia infant/toddler and pre-schools of northern Italy and in Scandinavian pre-schools and kindergartens, where children are, most importantly, given *time* to develop and learn. However, Anglo-American practice currently tends to restrict children too closely to adult-mediated activity, designed to mechanically develop academic skills such as literacy and numeracy, which does not effectively address young children's need to engage in holistic learning, encompassing their emotional, social, linguistic and physical development (see chapter 10).

Modern children have access to technologies that were never dreamed of within the cultures of the past inhabited by the early pioneers, which also agitates the situation. For example, contemporary Early Years Teachers (EYTs) and Early Years Graduate Practitioners (EYGPs) must engage with the battle to protect and safeguard children from the dangers inherent in modern marketing strategies to which they are exposed through television, social media and the internet; for example, media representations of 'celebrities' and consequent 'too much, too young' issues that arise, including exposure to adult behaviours that they are too young to understand, and insidious marketing of products that are unsuitable for children. A more extended discussion of this topic can be accessed in Jarvis *et al.* (2014).

Reflection

It would be useful to briefly research contemporary social constructions of childhood, using resources from the recommended reading list below, and consider how they compare with the concepts of childhood held by each pioneer.

Concept of 'curriculum'

The 'curriculum' of the early theorists, **Pestalozzi** and **Froebel** was principally drawn from Rousseau, and as such, a reaction against the 'talking at' method of teaching that was most common within the schools of their time. **Owen** brought some pragmatism into his practice; child-centred though it might be, he did attempt to focus upon skills that children would need to fill the employment roles for which they were destined. However, this was not the narrow goal-setting we find in some modern curricula. Davis and O'Hagan (2010, p. 93) propose that

> as well as emphasising reading, writing and accounts ... the stress on knowledge of some one useful manufacture, trade or occupation is highlighted for its contribution to self-fulfilment as well as to employability, undertaken by the pupil for the improvement of his mental and physical powers.

In particular, Owen was opposed to mechanical, skills-based approaches to literacy instruction 'to avoid literacy becoming an end in its own right, to ensure that the ability to decode and print text was wedded to the capacity to comprehend and derive satisfaction from the act of reading' (Davis and O'Hagan, 2010, p. 94).

Steiner's 'curriculum' reflects the three cycles of his theory of development, with children up to the age of seven attending kindergarten or nursery; the mixed age group here would be from three until seven, rather than five as we find in the current English early years system. In Steiner's nursery, *play*, as Montessori famously said, was seen as the child's *work*. The educational focus both in Steiner's original conception, and in modern Steiner pre-schools, is upon physical, intellectual, emotional and social development. The environment provides a wide range of different opportunities for creative play. A balance is encouraged to ensure there is a rhythm to the day's activities. As well as free play, times are set aside during the day for communal activities, such as bread making or singing songs, and listening to stories that are narrated rather than read. **Malaguzzi**, as he was introducing what was to become known as the Reggio Emilia approach, drew some of its central tenets from the Rousseau Institute and Piaget's Ecole des Petits in Geneva (Malaguzzi, 1997). He also researched the ideas of Vygotsky, Dewey, Erikson and Bruner. These influences helped him shape his pedagogical philosophy for the Reggio Emilia infant and pre-schools.

Like Steiner, **Montessori** was a great believer in the benefits of having a mixed age group. She believed that such an arrangement provided encouragement for younger children to imitate older students, and for the more able, the opportunity to explain and support others' learning. Such a process, she emphasised, helped embed new knowledge more securely. A further similarity to Steiner is her belief in the importance of the environment; aesthetically pleasing 'workplace' classrooms and outside spaces are now 'traditional' in Montessori schools. Again, like Steiner, Montessori believed in an integrated curriculum, in which subjects were not taught discretely, but encountered as children pursued their interests, so, for example, an historical interest in the pyramids could lead on to a discussion involving mathematical ideas around shape and size, or the scientific arguments around gravity, density and the use of pulleys. Montessori believed that this mode of learning was particularly suitable for children aged between six and 12.

Graham (2009, pp. 113-14) states that **Isaacs**' Malting House School was very different from other schools because 'there were no lessons ... there was an emphasis on activity undertaken spontaneously'. Her emphasis on children being able to freely express their emotions led some visitors to criticise her school as completely undisciplined: 'all that appears to happen is that [the children] are allowed to do whatever they like' (Graham, 2009, p. 119). However, Isaacs herself reported that the children became less aggressive after a settling-in period, and some visitors confirmed this, proposing that the children seemed happier than in other schools; additionally, some of the children themselves later wrote in adulthood about how much they had enjoyed attending the school (Graham, 2009).

McMillan wrote little about 'curriculum' as such; her focus was principally on resourcing, particularly with regard to the natural outdoor environment, what today might be termed enabling environments. The children were routinely housed in 'shelters', which she had attached to the main buildings; most of their days were spent in these, including the periods in which they napped and ate, and they ran around in the open air in all weathers. A short film of the children at the McMillan Nursery in the late 1930s can be viewed on this link: www.britishpathe.com/video/nursery-days

Case study: the development of curriculum

In the modern era, using the term 'curriculum' supposes an established and agreed framework through which children are expected to gain knowledge and understanding as well development in all other domains (social, emotional and physical). Underpinning these 'curricula' are themes and principles of practice that emphasise particular philosophical perspectives. Such perspectives usually have historical and often political drivers. The age at which curriculum begins to have an impact also varies vastly between nations. Most do not prescribe frameworks for children between birth and three years; some begin at three, while yet others do not make any specifications for pedagogy until children are five, six or seven years old. Many do not have national frameworks at all, but rely on different regional governments to administer education systems. Given this complexity, comparisons are sometimes difficult to make.

What can be compared to some degree are the philosophies or drivers for such curricula. In New Zealand, Te Whariki ('the woven mat for all to stand upon') attempts to encompass a culturally relative approach, with roots in the narrative of 'Learning Stories' that capture the differing needs of ethnically diverse communities (New Zealand Ministry of Education, 1996). Swedish early years programmes support the rights and independence of the child to learn through play (see chapter 10). The Perry pre-schools/HighScope programme in the US (Epstein, 2015) was born out of a desire to support and re-integrate disillusioned and disadvantaged communities and had at its base an economic driver of engagement with the mainstream, to bring people back into employment. The current English early years provision, with its outcomes-based approach, also has economic drivers at its core; in this we can trace it back to Owen and the pursuit of vocationalism.

In the UK, and England in particular, successive governments' emphasis upon children's earlier entry into collective education and care facilities is rooted within a drive to facilitate parents' paid employment. An increasing focus on children's transition to a more formal curriculum that is subject specific and focused on later 'employability' has proved problematic (see chapters 4 and 10). In particular, the issue around what support needs to be in place for children who do not achieve stated 'Early Learning Goals' has yet to be sufficiently resolved (see chapter 5).

Reflection

Having considered the information above relating to curriculum, consider the complex collection of motivations for modern governments with regard to the education of children between birth and seven and compare these with the concepts of teaching, learning and 'curriculum' that were present in the philosophies and practices of the early years pioneers.

Role of assessment

While **Pestalozzi**, **Owen**, **Isaacs** and **McMillan** were all recorded in the commentary of the time in which they practised as producing positive results, little precise information is available to indicate how or even *if* they formally assessed their pupils. It is unlikely that **Isaacs** would have been supportive of a formal assessment regime. **McMillan**'s nursery was well known in the Deptford area for positive results, in its production of pupils who went on to higher academic achievements than those in the district who did not attend the school.

In terms of assessment, **Steiner** schools have not historically gone down the route of focused outcomes for children, relying instead on the testimonials of parents and graduates themselves as evidence of 'success'. However, with the introduction of government funding for some **Steine**r schools (free schools in particular) this has now become an issue. Some aspects of the English Early Years Foundation Stage (EYFS) (DfE, 2014), for example the need to teach and subsequently assess phonics, literacy and numeracy with children under seven, is counter to the Steiner philosophy, while the giving of grades or marks contradicts the Steiner approach with its emphasis on intrinsic motivation gained from the enjoyment of a task or interest itself. Results for Steiner pupils against SATs and GCSE examinations in the UK tend to vary, with some in the lower percentile (Woods *et al.*, 2005). Research is currently being undertaken into the possible revision of some assessments to take into account the different focus of Steiner education and practice. The difficulty however persists, as a result of Ofsted's requirement for children to be assessed in an ongoing manner that is counter to traditional Steiner practice. Another issue that has caused concern with this partial integration of Steiner schools into mainstream education is the unique Steiner philosophy, Anthroposophy, which underpins a highly spiritual approach to education (British Humanist Association, 2014). However, **Steiner** schools continue to thrive, and the current impetus towards the establishment of free schools in England may make this increasingly likely in the future.

Froebelian methods of assessment rely upon the careful observation of children's play, the type of formative assessment of children's play that underpins good practice within the EYFS (see chapter 5). This in turn supports the means of assessment provided by learning journeys as a method of ongoing assessment of children within all seven areas of learning and development, a method of self-assessment for individual children and a means of informing and communicating with parents. All of the above processes have been adapted by the EYFS from Froebelian approaches to the integral importance of play in children's learning. The use of a mosaic approach, listening and transcribing children's own thoughts and ideas not present within the EYFS are also closely linked to Froebel's perceptions of the intrinsic importance of play to children (Bruce, 2005).

Methods of assessment in **Montessori** schools are mainly formative. Montessori stated that her use of 'scientific' observation, with self-correcting, or auto-didactic resources, provided feedback to the child and knowledge for the teacher in terms of an individual student's stage of knowledge in any particular area. The use of an end-of-year journal for older children reflecting the integrated approach taken is a loosely summative account of the child's learning to date. Montessori schools do not grade or rank cohorts of children against prescribed criteria, or against each other. The stress is upon the achievements of the unique, individual child. In America, the American Montessori Association (2015) has issued a paper on learning and assessment that recommends procedures for assessment should include presentations, portfolios and increased use of technology in multi-media end-of-year projects, rather than fixed question-and-answer tests. The American Montessori Association also sponsors a Teachers' Research Network. This encourages teacher reflection both in their classroom practice, and as part of ongoing research into finding valid and authentic ways of establishing and conducting assessments of children's learning. Montessori claimed her theory was 'scientific', based on her focused observations of a child's learning. Her critics, particularly in America, called this 'shoddy' science (Kilpatrick, cited in Beck, 1961), when compared with the more precise and summative assessments used by developmental psychologists such as Piaget. Ironically, it is contemporary research in the US (Lillard, 2008) that now links Montessori's sensory approach to breakthroughs in neuroscience. There are currently approximately 20,000 Montessori schools and nurseries worldwide.

Malaguzzi is again in agreement with both Steiner and Montessori with regard to assessment procedures. Children's development and learning in the Reggio Emilia approach are not measured or assessed using the conventional grading systems so commonly used in England and the US. Additionally, there is no commitment on the part of Reggio teachers to keep detailed records of children's outcomes against a set of nationally or regionally set criteria. In Reggio schools there is no predesigned curriculum. Rather it evolves, as children follow their interests which may lead into more extended projects, through questioning, hypotheses, observations, reflections and interpretations. Teachers in Reggio schools engage in detailed documentation of this process which is a cooperative practice between teachers. There are usually two 'pedagogistas' (class teachers) per group of 20 children, one 'atelierista' (artist in residence) in every Reggio school and a visiting municipal teacher, responsible for a number of schools, who supports teachers' professional development through research and dialogue. Parents are also actively involved in the planning of teaching and learning as are the children themselves. Every Reggio school's timetable sets aside a minimum of six hours each week for teacher meetings, preparing the environment for children, parent meetings and in-service training (Hendrick, 2003). This establishes a less didactic role for the teacher, one that is almost alien to the type of 'transmit and test' teaching cultures that have recently evolved in England and the US. The Reggio teacher is not afraid to make mistakes alongside the children. They are open to new learning, willing to research and 'learn as they go', precisely as Malaguzzi himself suggested.

The role of the adult in children's learning

The role of the adult in a **Steiner** nursery involves engaging in everyday domestic tasks, such as preparing the lunchtime meal, baking bread, gardening or providing an active role model for the children to imitate. From seven to 14, learning becomes more formalised and more structured, but there is still a multisensory, integrated approach without the use of formal textbooks. There is as a result more reliance on listening and memory; children create their own learning artefacts and journals of their learning experiences through various media. Children stay with the same teacher all the way through this cycle, forming a close knit group, not having to negotiate the yearly transitions that are a feature of primary education in maintained schools in the UK. As previously indicated, strong partnership with parents is sought, and contemporary Steiner schools regularly invite parents to join in on specific days. This cooperative relationship starts with the infants and toddlers who have yet to join the kindergarten, and reinforces a strong sense of community.

The role of the teacher in the Reggio Emila is to achieve a balance between engagement and observation. The use of formative observations is an essential element, the detailed recording of each child's interests and learning, which both adult and child review and reflect upon constantly, to provide self-esteem at individual achievement, and progress in future learning projects. In this, there are echoes of Montessori's 'scientific observations'. **Malaguzzi** particularly valued the 'researcher and facilitator' aspects of the teacher's role. Through organising an environment rich in provocations and possibilities, the teacher supports the child's natural curiosity and helps extend this need to explore, to solve problems, to destroy and create, to cooperate with others and engage in democratic debate. Malaguzzi and the parents of Reggio Emilia focused upon building a wholly *democratic* education system – the phoenix arising from the rubble left by a war undertaken to remove a fascist regime.

Montessori's views on the role of the adult differed to some degree. She believed in the unobtrusive facilitator, but combined that with a focus upon critical moments in a child's learning where the adult may lead and demonstrate. The ability to identify this readiness is only achieved after numerous detailed child observations over time. Adult-led sessions are also supported by specific learning resources, which Montessori herself developed, to support tactile and active learning. The concept of Vygotsky's zone of proximal development can be linked to this practice (see chapter 2).

The triangular relationship of child, teacher and parent is also reflected in both the Steiner and Montessori approaches, but not as centrally as in the Reggio Emilia programmes that Malaguzzi established. For Malaguzzi, there is a fourth element, that of the community. To some degree, it could be said his philosophy of education which he called 'education based on relationships' is less about the individual child and more about the child's reciprocal relationships with other children, family, teachers, society and the environment (Malaguzzi, 1993). The influence of Bronfenbrenner here (see chapter 2) can be seen in Malaguzzi's view of the child as 'producer of culture, values and rights' (Malaguzzi, 1997). He strongly believed that children had rights rather than simply needs (see chapter 4 for a more comprehensive overview of children's rights). The lack of a prescribed curriculum with set learning outcomes supports this open-ended, flexible approach, which in turn promotes reflective practice and helps the educators themselves to more thoroughly understand the needs and responses of children and other stakeholders involved in the Reggio approach.

In spite of the lack of statistical data for other communities of educators to measure the outcomes and impact of the Reggio schools, the influence of Malaguzzi's ideas has had repercussions worldwide. Whereas Steiner and Montessori schools can be counted, the exact number of schools across the world influenced by the Reggio approach is difficult to estimate, but the practice within the Infant and Toddler centres and pre-schools in Reggio Emilia has had a resonance across the world.

Malaguzzi rejected staged theories such as the one underpinning Piaget's meticulous constructivist view of academic learning as too limiting and focused on individualism; the Reggio model of the child emphasises sociability from birth. Although Malaguzzi would have firmly rejected a model of the teacher as a 'transmitter', viewing the teacher's role as a more experienced facilitator supporting children's self-initiated activities, this does evoke some similarity to Vygotsky's social constructivist theory. However, there is no element of transmission of a pre-designed curriculum in Reggio pedagogy. In this aspect Malaguzzi is in accord with Steiner and Montessori, who both rejected the idea of narrowly targeted pedagogical regimes.

For **Froebel, McMillan** and **Isaacs**, the role of the adult was very much as a facilitator, to provide what we would nowadays term 'enabling environments' (see Chapter 7) which would become the principal educator of the child. This is a pedagogical approach we would nowadays think of as Piagetian at root (see Chapter 2). Indeed, Piaget spent some time in Isaacs' Malting House School in March 1927, when he was developing his theory.

> Susan Isaacs pointed out [that] the adult–child relationships were more as fellow-workers and playmates, accompanying them in their real and imaginary experiences than as teachers and pupils.
>
> (Graham, 2009, p. 115)

While McMillan tended to see herself more as a benefactor than a playmate, her instinct was to support the children to learn through play within a natural environment, rather than to directly instruct. She raised the idea of children being the future of 'the race', by which she meant healthy and educated people going forward in life to become the British parents and workers of the future, not quite a human capital approach, but sharing some of the same concerns.

For **Pestalozzi** and **Owen**, the greater rigidity of the culture of their era determined that the relationship between child and adult would be one of teacher and learner, but both clearly strove to provide the child with more self-motivation and independence, albeit in the case of Owen, within a human capital frame, while Pestalozzi's focus was, above all, the translation of Rousseau's child-centred philosophy into a practical pedagogy. These early practices laid the foundations for more radical reformers such as Isaacs and Malaguzzi to develop their highly liberal pedagogies.

What relevance do the pioneers have to current practice in the early years?

From the late eighteenth to the mid-twentieth century, pioneers in children's education and development were, to a great extent, speaking in unison in their mission to make early years practice more child-centred. Yet their voices, many would argue, have still to be effectively heard, in particular by Anglo-American governments. Another common denominator between the pioneers lies in their ability to create something positive and lasting out of difficult and sometimes traumatic situations for children. For **Steiner** and **Malaguzzi** the impetus sprang from devastating international warfare. Their idealism lay in the belief that, given a democratic developmental environment in the early years, humankind could create a peaceful existence free from violence, particularly the violence of war. For **Owen** and **McMillan**, the impetus sprang from issues arising from industrialisation, in the pursuit of blunting its potential for crushing the human spirit. At the beginning of the process, Owen hoped that education would be the answer, that it would be able to humanise industrial communities. Nearly a century later, McMillan had no such illusions; her impetus was to nurture the bodies, minds and spirits of children at the earliest possible point in development, in an attempt to give them the resilience to cope with working class adult lives in such an industrial society.

Isaacs' impetus was possibly more personal; many of her motives and problems appear to have resonance in the early death of her mother, and her upbringing by a stern Victorian father (Graham, 2009). Her exploration of this through psychoanalysis probably had much to do with the regime she went on to develop for her Malting House School. From this example, we can see how Freud's theory had a significant effect on the way that the post-nineteenth-century western milieu constructs its model of a human being, immersed in complex and sometimes contradictory motivations. This is not only relevant to educators, but also to those working with children and families in the health and social care arenas. For **Pestalozzi**, the original pioneer, the core impetus for his work came from Rousseau's insistence that the human spirit was essentially noble and benevolent, rather than shameful and sinful, a focus shared by **Froebel**. At the centre of their idealistic vision of humanity lies a view of the child as rich in natural resources and potential, who is the author of his/her own individual development and learning, a child who has natural human rights and deserves respect. The role of teacher or pedagogue moves towards that of a facilitator, who works alongside the child, and whose responsibility it is to provide an aesthetically and intellectually stimulating environment to support the child's holistic development. McMillan shared a similar impetus, rooted within her Christian Socialist convictions.

The **Froebelian**, **Steinerian**, **Montessorian** and **Reggio Emilia** approaches are all still alive and well today, recognised as important alternatives to mainstream education and seen as sources of inspiration for progressive educational reform. Unfortunately, however, the increasingly dominant view underlying Anglo-American early years agendas is that of a didactic process, focused upon making younger and younger children school (and thence employment) ready. Within England, for example, the move to begin a more structured educational approach for the youngest in society has already begun with the proposed introduction of two-year-olds into maintained schools (see chapter 10). This seems light years away from the nurturing and learning environment created in the Reggio Infant and Toddler schools. There is also a growing impetus to bring outcome-based assessment, in the shape of Early Learning Goals, to the very youngest children in England. Coupled with the 'school readiness' agenda set out by the revised Early Years Foundation Stage, and supported by Ofsted, it would appear that England seems to be moving in the opposite direction to the pioneers, away from their view of the child as rich in natural resources, resourceful, enquiring, engaged within a nurturing, socialising community that was respectful of the child's individual and human rights.

This book will seek to outline high-quality early years theory and practice for twenty-first-century early years practitioners, with a view to supporting them to become the worthy heirs of Pestalozzi, Owen, Froebel, Steiner, McMillan, Montessori, Isaacs and Malaguzzi, helping them to draw upon the most highly respected theory and practice, both in history and from current early years theory and practice around the world, and making these relevant within their practice and knowledge base.

Case study: current modes of assessment in England and Wales

At the Yarborough Street nursery school (a local authority maintained setting), staff were engaged in a heated debate about the lack of training available for the revised EYFS, and how changes were still being made to it year on year. The nursery school is one of the few remaining nurseries in England built around Margaret McMillan's vision of the open-air nursery; it is very light and airy with easy access to outdoors.

There had been complaints prior to this particular staff meeting about how the 2014 changes to the revised EYFS had been handled. A number of staff recalled how the 2008 version of the EYFS had been rolled out through a series of external detailed training sessions which the local authority early years advisors had provided to key persons in each setting. Some practitioners felt the 2012 consultation period had been hurried, while others felt their views had not been sufficiently listened to. Important changes (some statutory) had been 'drip fed' to settings through the government website, and without any hard copy available. This had led to some confusion about the interpretation of what now officially constituted good-quality practice, particularly with a view to Ofsted requirements. The greatest area of concern for all staff was the increasingly outcomes-based emphasis on assessment.

Linda, the setting's deputy head teacher, was trying hard to counter the negativity that change often brings, by focusing upon the more positive aspects of this revised framework. She pointed out that the developmental milestones, detailed on the Development Matters website (www.early-education.org.uk/development-matters), had still been retained, knowing that many staff relied on its useful guidance when assessing an individual child's progress and 'next steps'. Another important aspect, particularly in relation to daily practice, was the relaxation of the need to make daily observations of each child. A further benefit Linda pointed out was the change from a nine-point assessment scale linked to 69 Early Learning Goals (ELGs) to a more manageable 17 ELGs and the introduction of *emerging*, *expected* and *exceeding* as assessment descriptors.

Connie, an EYGP, who was the nursery's co-ordinator for literacy, immediately reminded staff that the goals might be fewer in number, but the expectancy in achievement levels had increased. In literacy, the goalposts had moved from children using their phonic knowledge to understand 'regular words' to an expectation they would 'write sentences others could understand'. Julie, the numeracy co-ordinator, agreed, saying the expectation for understanding 'number' had seen a 100% increase from numbers 1–10 to 1–20. She also disliked the return to the name 'mathematics'; 'it's problem solving that gets children interested in maths, they should have retained that. Don't the government understand that children need *active* learning? Froebel knew all about that two centuries ago'. Rebecca, the nursery Special Educational Needs Co-ordinator, added: 'It's all to do with "school readiness". They're trying to impose the expected levels for Key Stage 1 on five year olds – they're *not* ready for it, and it's making life really difficult for the summer born children and children with additional needs. "P" scales aren't right, but what's the alternative?'

Linda looked at the nursery's head teacher, Cerys, for support.

'You've been home recently, Cerys, how are they managing at your sister's school with the three to seven year olds?' Cerys hesitated. 'The Welsh Early Years Foundation Phase has also been subject to change. In some ways the EYFS is ahead, like identifying the need for more highly qualified staff for the birth to threes especially, and besides there's talk in Wales, too, about introducing more formal assessment across the birth to seven age range, and the

Foundation Phase does also have a targets and outcomes system. All these reviews seem to want is more standardisation – it's all about measuring outcomes – globalisation and the need for workplace skills. You begin to wonder when children can be children. When the Welsh Early Years Foundation Phase first came out – do you remember – we had that discussion about social pedagogy? Modelled on the good practice in Scandinavian and Reggio schools – I was envious of their ratios and the extended age range to seven years. It seemed to make for a more seamless transition to their Key Stage 2. I hope they still retain that – giving time for children to mature. We wouldn't be having all this discussion about "school readiness" if we could keep them in our Foundation Stage – with all its flaws – until they were seven.'

Connie was not convinced: 'Not if they make it more formal for the four and five year olds. I for one wouldn't be happy – neither would Margaret McMillan!'

Cerys agreed: 'It's interesting to look back at what those early pioneers thought. It wasn't all perfect though. I think we would challenge some of their ideas today, particularly old-fashioned attitudes to class, gender and ethnicity – it's easy to idealise them! We have to deal with different governments having different views – look at how we've had to adapt our practice in just the last five years! What I liked and still like about the Welsh system is how they assess in a holistic way. They look at how a child thinks and their levels of involvement. It starts from what they *can* do, it's not just a deficit model, looking at the 'gaps' and trying to fill them. The Welsh system does at least attempt to start from the ground up, rather than from the top down 'school readiness' approach that seems to be an obsession for English Governments.'

Reflection

From your reading of the above and this chapter consider the similarities and differences in assessment procedures between the English EYFS and the Welsh Early Years Foundation Phase (see recommended reading at the end of the chapter), and compare these with ideas on assessing young children held by the early years pioneers. Then consider how these have translated into modern interpretations of their ideas, for example in contemporary Steiner, Montessori and Reggio Emilia practice.

Conclusion

This chapter has considered some of the origins of modern early years education practice, and briefly outlined the theory and practice of some famous pioneers, considering the origins of their constructions of childhood and of how young children might best be educated. We have also considered how some of these ideas have been carried forward into contemporary practice.

Who were the 'pioneers' and what is their place in the history of early years practice?

We have briefly considered the theories and practice of **Pestalozzi**, **Owen**, **Froebel**, **Steiner**, **McMillan**, **Montessori**, **Isaacs** and **Malaguzzi**. We have found that there were many similarities between these pioneers in terms of their determination to centre education upon the child rather than a fixed programme of learning, a belief that conflicted with the mainstream pedagogies of the cultures in which they lived. All of them delivered their practice as something of an experiment, and all of them generated some amount of evidence from which to claim that their pedagogical experiments had met with some success. All had to cope with opposition, both in terms of censure from the mainstream, and in terms of sometimes rapidly shifting environmental conditions. It is certainly worth remembering that the development of the pioneers' practice was not all plain sailing, when we feel, like the example staff team depicted above, that we are struggling to maintain our own practice ethics within prevailing conditions.

Where did each pioneer stand on the question of curriculum, assessment and the role of the adult in children's learning?

We found that it is sometimes difficult to apply modern concepts such as 'curriculum' and 'assessment' to the type of experimental practice undertaken by the pioneers, as they did not have regional or national structures either to support or to worry them, and they did not have access to the vast body of theoretical and practice knowledge of child development and learning available to contemporary practitioners. However, we can access some clues about the ethos that each pioneer operated from and built upon, drawing on the historical record, particularly with respect to Froebel, Steiner, Malaguzzi and Montessori, whose ideas and practices are still active within specialist areas of contemporary early years practice.

What relevance do the pioneers have to current practice in the early years?

This question may be more effectively considered when you have come to the end of this book. Chapter 10 in particular will help you to reflect more deeply upon issues relating to early childhood first raised by the pioneers, and how early years practice has developed from these roots in different nations from such early origins. It would be useful to keep these ideas in mind as you move through the chapters that follow.

Recommended reading

Cunningham, H. (2006) *The Invention of Childhood*. London: BBC Books.

Giardiello, P. (2013) *Pioneers in Early Childhood Education: The roots and legacies of Rachel and Margaret McMillan, Maria Montessori and Susan Isaacs*. Abingdon: Routledge.

Jarvis, P., Swiniarski, L. and Holland, W. (2016) *Early Years Pioneers in Context: Understanding theories about early childhood education and care*. Abingdon: Routledge.

The Welsh Foundation Phase: http://gov.wales/topics/educationandskills/earlyyearshome/foundation-phase/?lang=en

Thomas, G. (2013) *Education: A very short history*. Oxford: Oxford University Press.

Young-Ihm Kwon (2002) Changing curriculum for early childhood education in England. *Early Childhood Research and Practice*. 16(1–2). Retrieved from: http://ecrp.uiuc.edu/v4n2/kwon.html 29th May 2015.

References

American Montessori Society (2015) *Early History of Montessori*. Retrieved from: https://amshq.org/Montessori-Education/History-of-Montessori-Education/Early-History-of-Montessori 29th May 2015.

Anthroposophical Society (2015) *About Rudolph Steiner*. Retrieved from: www.anthroposophy.org.uk/index.php 4th June 2015.

Beck, R.H. (1961) Kilpatrick's critique of Montessori's method and theory. *Studies in Philosophy and Education*. 1(4–5), 153–62.

British Humanist Association (2014) *BHA Briefing: Concerns about the state funding of Steiner Schools*. London: British Humanist Association.

Bruce, T. (2005) *Early Childhood Education* (3rd Edn). London: Hodder Arnold.

Bruce, T. (2012) *Early Childhood Practice*. London: Sage.

Bruhlmeier, A. (2010) *Head, Heart and Hand: Education in the spirit of Pestalozzi*. Cambridge: Sophia.

Dahlberg, G., Moss, P. and Pence, A. (1999) *Beyond Quality in Early Childhood Education and Care: Post modern perspectives*. London: Falmer Press.

Davis, R. and O'Hagan, F. (2010) *Robert Owen*. London: Bloomsbury.

DfE (2014) *The Early Years Foundation Stage*. Retrieved from: www.gov.uk/government/uploads/system/uploads/attachment_data/file/335504/EYFS_framework_from_1_September_2014__with_clarification_note.pdf 9th June 2014.

Epstein, A. (2015) *All about Highscope*. Retrieved from: www.highscope.org/Content.asp?ContentId=291 29th May 2015

Erikson, E. (1950) *Childhood and Society*. London: Vintage.

Feminist Voices (2015) *Karen Horney*. Retrieved from: www.feministvoices.com/karen-horney

Graham, P. (2009) *Susan Isaacs: A life freeing the minds of children*. London: Karnac.

Hainstock, E.G. (1997) *Teaching Montessori in the Home: The school years*. New York: Plume.

Hendrick, J. (Ed.) (2003) *Next Steps to Teaching the Reggio way: Accepting the challenge to change*. Upper Saddle River, NJ. Prentice Hall.

Isaacs, S. (1968) *The Nursery Years*. New York: Shocken.

Isaacs, S. (1933) *Social Development in Young Children*. London: Routledge and Kegan Paul.

Jarvis, P. (2015) It's against human nature to send two year olds to school. *The Conversation*. Retrieved from: https://theconversation.com/its-against-human-nature-to-send-two-year-olds-to-school-37180 27th May 2015.

Jarvis, P. and Liebovich, B. (2015) British nurseries, head and heart: McMillan, Owen and the genesis of the education/care dichotomy. *Women's History Review*. Retrieved from: www.tandfonline.com/doi/abs/10.1080/09612025.2015.1025662?journalCode=rwhr20#.VUZripPff4U

Jarvis, P., Newman, S. and George, J. (2014) Play, learning for life: In pursuit of well-being through play. pp. 270–99 in A. Brock, P. Jarvis and Y. Olusoga (Eds) *Perspectives on Play: Learning for life* (2nd Edn). Abingdon: Routledge.

Le Blanc, M. (nd) Friedrich Froebel: His life and influence on education. Retrieved from: www.communityplaythings.co.uk/learning-library/articles/friedrich-froebel 7th December 2015

Lillard, A.S. (2008) *Montessori: The science behind the genius*. New York: Oxford University Press.

Malaguzzi, L. (1993) For an education based on relationships. *Young Children*. 49(1). 9–17. Retrieved from: https://reggioalliance.org/downloads/malaguzziyoungchildren.pdf

Malaguzzi, L. (1997) A charter of rights. pp. 214–15 in T. Filippini and V. Vecchi (Eds) *The Hundred Languages of Children: Narrative of the possible*. Washington, DC: Reggio Children.

New Zealand Ministry of Education (1996) *Te Whariki Early Childhood Curriculum*. Retrieved from: www.education.govt.nz/assets/Documents/Early-Childhood/te-whariki.pdf

Pope Edwards, C. (2002) Three approaches from Europe: Waldorf, Montessori and Reggio Emilia. *Early Childhood, Research and Practice.* 4(1).

Rousseau, J. (1762) *Émile, or on Education.* Retrieved from: http://oll.libertyfund.org/titles/2256

Rubi, H. (2014) *Pestalozzi's Biography.* Retrieved from: www.bruehlmeier.info/biography.htm

Stevinson, E. (1954) *Margaret McMillan: Prophet and pioneer.* London: University of London Press.

Stoker Bruenig, E. (2015) What some conservatives call kids now: 'human capital'. *New Republic.* Retrieved from: www.newrepublic.com/article/121112/reformocons-want-invest-children-capital

Woods, P., Ashley, M. and Woods, G. (2005) *Steiner Schools in England.* Bristol: University of the West of England. Retrieved from: http://webarchive.nationalarchives.gov.uk/20130401151715/http://www.education.gov.uk/publications/eOrderingDownload/RR645.pdf 29th May 2015.

Section 1

The children's agenda

Principles in children's development, social policy and inclusion

2 Principles in childcare and education

Pam Jarvis and Jane George

CHAPTER OVERVIEW

This chapter will address the following key questions:

✔ What are the main English Early Years Foundation Stage (EYFS) principles, and how do they relate to mainstream development theory and research?
✔ What are the main theoretical perspectives that describe how children develop and learn, particularly between birth and their sixth birthday?
✔ How can we recognise and meet the needs of individuals?
✔ What influences and experiences in the setting and beyond including transitions can impact on children's well-being, development, learning and behaviour, and how can we connect these to the theoretical perspectives introduced in the earlier section?

Case study: the culture of childcare – 'then' and 'now'

Caroline, an Early Years Graduate Practitioner (EYGP), was very surprised at the level of distress that her mother, Jean, exhibited on being told that her three-year-old granddaughter, Maisie, would have to undergo a series of treatments as a hospital in-patient. Jean had known that Maisie would need treatment since she was born; the situation was not life-threatening, and had a very positive prognosis: Maisie had a slight deformation of her feet, which would respond to a series of routine operations between the ages of three and five. Caroline reassured her mother: 'She will be fine, Mum'.

'That's what my mum thought when I had my tonsils out in 1963', replied Jean, with tears in her eyes. 'I was only three, too – she didn't see how much I cried when she wasn't there. I still remember a nurse who got very cross with me and told me to "pull myself together" – I didn't even know what that meant, so I asked my mum at visiting time. There was also the sister in charge of the ward – she wouldn't let your Auntie Sue come in because, your grandma told me later, she said "10 year olds are crawling with germs". Even your grandma got upset the first time she visited me – I don't remember this, but she told me that I said "I don't live with you any more, mummy, do I?" She tried to explain, but she could only visit for an hour a day … apparently, I was only in for a week, too, but it seemed like a year to me …'

'Oh, mum', said Caroline, now feeling tears welling in her own eyes, 'don't be silly. This isn't the Dark Ages now. One of us will be with Maisie nearly all of the time when she is in hospital. She's also going to get a visit from one of the staff before she goes in, and she is going to visit the ward, so it won't seem so strange to her. There's a nursery nurse and a teacher attached to the ward, so Maisie will be able to do nearly all the activities that she would be doing at nursery. But they will only keep her in for the shortest time that they need to, hopefully only a few days after each operation, and her nursery have already discussed with the hospital how they are going to look after her while her feet are still in plaster.'

'She's going to nursery with her feet in plaster?' said Jean. 'They wouldn't have let you in my day …'

'But an awful lot of things have changed since your day, like treating children as individual human beings with their own set of needs, for a start', replied Caroline. 'Now … we need to discuss when you will be available to stay with Maisie when she is in hospital this time. I'm working out a rota, so all the people she is attached to can take a turn. Don't you remember, attachment theory? I did a project on it at college.'

'No', said Jean more cheerfully, 'I don't. But it sounds like an awful lot of things have changed for the better since I was three years old …'

Introduction

Jean is certainly right about one thing – an awful lot of things *have* changed in the field of early years practice since she was a young child, including our understanding of children's emotional development, and the capacity for practitioners to engage in multi-agency working, including ongoing liaison with parents, who are now seen as the most important 'experts' in the pursuit of defining their child's individual needs.

The underpinning principles of childcare and education require that leading practitioners have a solid, up-to-date working knowledge of the current national guidelines for early years practice, and of a range of theoretical principles that describe how children develop emotionally, socially and intellectually. This chapter will outline a summary of the principles of the current English Early Years Foundation Stage (EYFS) guidance (DfE, 2014), followed by a summary of the core theoretical perspectives that have underpinned the huge changes in early years practice that have occurred over the last 50 years. The Recommended reading list will give you a range of texts to study further on these topics. It is hoped that you will use this chapter as a reference base for the key underpinning theories of child development and the key content and principles of the EYFS, returning when necessary from the later chapters in the book to check (for example) developmental stage information or references to theoretical concepts.

What are the main English EYFS principles, and how do they relate to mainstream developmental theory and research?

The EYFS principles (DfE, 2014) focus around three prime areas and four specific areas of learning. The prime areas are proposed to relate to the underpinning knowledge and skills for 'school readiness' and it is proposed that they should be developed through activities within the specific areas.

The **prime areas** are:

- Communication and language
- Physical development
- Personal, social and emotional development.

The **four specific areas** are:

- Literacy
- Mathematics
- Understanding the world
- Expressive arts and design.

The EYFS also requires that practitioners additionally use **four guiding principles** to inform practice in early years settings. These are:

- That every child is a **unique child**, who is constantly learning and can be resilient, capable, confident and self-assured;
- That children learn to be strong and independent through **positive relationships**;
- That children learn and develop well in **enabling environments**, in which their experiences respond to their individual needs and there is a strong partnership between practitioners and parents and/or carers; and
- That **children develop and learn in different ways and at different rates**, including those children who have special educational needs and disabilities.

The EYFS proposes that to plan and guide children's activities, practitioners should reflect on the different ways that children learn and utilise these in their practice. It is proposed that the characteristics of effective teaching and learning are:

- **Playing and exploring** – children investigating, experiencing and 'having a go';
- **Active learning** – children should be encouraged to continue their concentration and to keep on trying if they encounter difficulties, enjoying the eventual achievement;
- **Creating and thinking critically** – children developing their own ideas, making links between ideas, and working out strategies for getting a specific result.

There is also a requirement for every child under five to be assigned a Key Person, who manages the child's learning to address their individual needs, and who interfaces with the child's parents and family. In order for this to be done effectively, there is a clear need for highly skilled staff in early years settings.

By the time the child arrives at the transition to Key Stage 1, the expectation is that they will be able to do the following.

Communication and language

- Listen attentively, and respond with relevant comments, questions and actions.
- Speak effectively, showing awareness of listeners' needs, using past, present and future forms accurately. They should be able to create their own narratives and explanations, connecting ideas or events.

Physical development

- Show good control and coordination in large and small movements. Move confidently in a range of ways, safely negotiating space. Fine motor skills are in place, allowing them to handle equipment and tools effectively, including pencils for writing.

Health and self-care

- Know the importance for good health of physical exercise, and a healthy diet, and how to basically keep healthy and safe.
- Manage their own basic hygiene and personal needs, including dressing and going to the toilet independently.

Personal, social and emotional development

- Have the confidence to try new activities, and say why they like some activities more than others.
- Have the confidence to speak in a familiar group about their ideas, choosing the resources they need for their chosen activities.
- Have the confidence to say when they do or don't need help.

Managing feelings and behaviour

- Have the ability to talk about how they and others show feelings.
- Be able to discuss their own and others' behaviour, and its consequences with the knowledge that some behaviour is unacceptable.
- Be able to work effectively as part of a group or class, understanding that they must obey certain rules.
- Be able to adjust their behaviour to fit particular situations.
- Be able to cope with changes of routine.

Making relationships

- Play cooperatively, taking turns with others, sharing ideas about how to organise an activity.
- Show sensitivity to others' needs and feelings, and form positive relationships with adults and other children.

Specific area targets

The specific area targets for children leaving the Early Years Foundation Stage (in the school year that they become six) are summarised below.

Literacy: children read and understand simple sentences, using phonic knowledge to decode regular words. There is growing knowledge about decoding common irregular words, and comprehension of what they have read and they can talk to others about it. Children should also be able to use their phonic knowledge to write words in ways which match their spoken sounds. They can write simple sentences, additionally using some irregular common words which can be read by themselves and others.

Mathematics: children count reliably with numbers from one to 20, place them in order and say which number is one more or one less than a given number. They can also add and subtract two single-digit numbers and count on or back to find the answer, and are able to double, halve and understand 'fair shares'. They have the ability to talk about issues relating to size, weight, capacity, position, distance, time and money, comparing quantities and objects to solve problems. There is recognition, creation and description of patterns. They explore characteristics of everyday objects and shapes and use basic mathematical language to describe them.

Understanding the world: children talk about past and present events in their own lives and in the lives of family members. They know about similarities and differences between themselves and others, and among families, communities and traditions, and are sensitive to the fact that people do not always enjoy the same things. They know about similarities and differences in relation to places, objects, materials and living things, talking about their immediate environment, making basic comparisons with other environments. They make observations of animals and plants and try to explain changes. They know that various technologies are used in homes and schools, and are able to select and use technology for particular purposes.

Expressive arts and design: children sing songs, make music and dance, and experiment with these. They safely use and explore a variety of materials, tools and techniques, experimenting with colour, design, texture, form and function, using what they have learnt about media and materials in original ways, thinking about uses and purposes. They are able to represent their own ideas, thoughts and feelings through design and technology, art, music, dance, role-play and stories.

(DfE, 2014)

This will be revisited in many of the following chapters, so do not worry if this all seems rather a lot to take in at first. To keep up with what is required in your work, particularly when you are leading practice, you will need to engage in continuing professional development activities once qualified; see Chapter 9 for further information on this point. Senior practitioners also need to lead and liaise with other professionals in cross-agency practice, based on the guidelines contained in the *Common Core of Skills and Knowledge for the Children's Workforce* (DCSF, 2010). These are as follows:

- Communicating and engaging effectively with a wide range of colleagues, including those from other professional sectors that provide services for young children and their families.
- Understanding how children and young people develop and being clear about one's own professional role to support them in this process.
- Safeguarding and promoting the welfare of the child based on a core knowledge of current legal procedures and frameworks.
- Supporting transitions, being able to skilfully judge when and how to intervene in this process.
- Multi-agency working from the basis of an understanding of one's own role and the complementary roles of other professionals.
- Sharing information from the basis of an understanding of the complexities involved in this, balancing families' rights for confidential services with an understanding of when and how to share information and concerns with colleagues and professionals from other agencies, based on an underpinning knowledge of current policy guidance and legislation.

The EYFS uses six overlapping phases of child development, in which the following features are identified. You can find more details on this in the online resource 'Development Matters' at: www.foundationyears.org.uk/files/2012/03/Development-Matters-FINAL-PRINT-AMENDED.pdf.

Birth to eleven months

The initial stage where babies are focused principally upon physical and social development. They learn to control the basic movements of their bodies, understand in basic terms the information that is being filtered through their senses, and begin to communicate with the other people who inhabit their world.

Pearson Education Ltd/Jules Selmes

Eight months to twenty months

From eight months infants begin to learn about locomotion, rolling, crawling and eventually walking. From the middle of the first year they begin to show attachment to familiar people in their world, and as they move towards the final third of their first year, the first words are uttered; these are often the names of people who represent the infant's closest bonded attachments, e.g. 'mama', 'dada', 'gan'.

Pearson Education Ltd/Jules Selmes

Sixteen months to twenty-six months

Children moving from babyhood to toddlerhood are frequently full of energy, using their new skills of mobility to investigate every inch of their surroundings. Safety considerations within everyday environments now become paramount; children of this age will have little understanding of everyday dangers, so, for example, fireguards, electric socket shields and stair gates will be necessary in order to protect them from potentially harmful results of such investigations. Children will also usually enter the two-word utterance stage of language development during this stage (see below), and, while they will become quite skilled at communicating meaning to familiar adults, there may be misunderstandings with people with whom they do not regularly interact. The will to do or communicate something may not always be matched by the necessary capacity at this stage, meaning that there may be frustration and temper tantrums that need skilful handling by carers.

Pearson Education Ltd/Jules Selmes

Twenty-two to thirty-six months

Language continues to develop to the point that the child becomes more able to interact successfully with a wide range of others, including peers. If children have the opportunity to mix with a range of adults and peers during this stage they will become more socially competent, developing rudimentary skills of peer negotiation, although where difficult situations arise they will turn to bonded adults for help. Children in the later part of this stage will typically begin to deal with simple intellectual challenges such as shape-matching, simple counting, naming colours and learning simple songs and rhymes. Fine motor skills develop rapidly, meaning that children in this stage will typically enjoy mark-making and simple construction activities.

Pearson Education Ltd/Jules Selmes

Thirty to fifty months

Children's abilities to engage in peer interactions increase; in particular they are able to engage in and enjoy increasingly intricate collaborative make-believe scenarios with their peers. Gender preferences in play styles and play companions begin to emerge, as does recognition of cultural differences and curiosity relating to this. There is a growing independence in 'self-care' activities such as toileting and dressing. Children will be happy to leave bonded adults for increasing periods of time, while still needing readily available help from familiar adults when confused, or comfort when distressed. The first literacy skills emerge, usually starting with the child's ability to recognise and then write their own name, moving on to recognise and copy other familiar words and phrases.

Pearson Education Ltd/Jules Selmes

Forty to sixty months

The child is now beginning to build an increasingly independent role in the peer group, typically engaging in literacy and numeracy activities with enjoyment and increasing understanding. Independent problem-solving and reasoning skills are now developing quickly and children of this age are very capable of having a simple (albeit usually quite brief!) reasoned debate. They are also increasingly capable of controlling their own behaviour towards a projected end; this includes a developing ability to delay gratification for short periods of time.

These stages have been drawn from many years of developmental research. We have provided a brief overview of such research below. However, you are advised to read more widely on this point, using the recommended reading list at the end of the chapter as your starting point and ensure that you keep up-to-date with current research and development.

Pearson Education Ltd/Jules Selmes

Reflection: alternative UK frameworks

You were introduced to the Welsh Early Years Foundation Phase at the end of chapter 1. You will find it at http://gov.wales/topics/educationandskills/earlyyearshome/foundation-phase/?lang=en.

Compare it with the English Early Years Foundation Stage, considering similarities and differences. Scotland's Curriculum for Excellence is more recent, and still evolving at the time of writing; it is based upon the Froebelian principles you read about in chapter 1. You can read about its development at www.educationscotland.gov.uk/learningandteaching/earlylearningand childcare/curriculum/index.asp.

Children's physical development may sometimes be overlooked, particularly in a culture that places so much emphasis upon cognitive development and academic skills. Nevertheless, it is important, and as Margaret McMillan realised a century ago (see chapter 1), physical activity can be an important catalyst for what the EYFS currently calls 'understanding the world'. It is, of course, also one of the prime areas of the EYFS framework. Table 2.1 gives some key features of children's physical development from birth to five years.

Children's physical development processes, like all other areas of development, are not set on a completely standard trajectory, and individuals may be 'quick' in some ways and slower in others. Additionally, and it must always be remembered, when a child says s/he 'can't do it' this may mean s/he *won't* do it, particularly if s/he is tired or upset. For example, it is very common for children who have newborn siblings to regress slightly, particularly with respect to toilet training. Patience and gentle encouragement are always the best responses, but if there are a growing number of unexplained delays, seeking the advice of a specialist practitioner is sensible.

Mary Sheridan (1899–1978) wrote a book that was for many years the international standard text on physical development for early years practitioners. This has recently been developed into a more modern format by Ajay Sharma and Helen Cockerill (2014). Versions of the original Sheridan text are still freely available for a few pence on book websites on their 'used books' pages.

Table 2.1 Physical development, birth to five years

Birth to 4 months	Waves arm, moves legs up and down Startle reflex in response to loud noise Turns head in response to a touch on the cheek Blinks/shuts eyes in bright light Begins to lift head when lying on stomach Reaches for dangling objects
4–8 months	Pulls at own feet and toes Begins to pull to sit but still needs support Can raise head and chest and begins to 'swim' when lying on stomach Begins to roll from back to stomach Can reach for and grasp objects Turns towards sound of voices

Table 2.1 (continued overleaf)

Table 2.1 (continued)

8–12 months	Begins to pull to stand and 'walk', holding on to furniture for support Can sit unaided Transfers objects from hand to hand and may inaccurately throw them May begin to crawl (but not all babies do this) May begin to stand alone/take a step or two by the end of this period Can grasp a spoon, but struggles to transfer food to mouth Feeds self 'finger foods' with little difficulty Can roll a ball, and may crawl after it
1–2 years	Walks, begins to try to run, can crawl up stairs May attempt to balance on one foot May 'dance' to music Can climb on furniture Can kick/throw a ball Can feed him/herself with a spoon/fork Can hold a crayon in his/her fist and make marks with it Begins to turn book pages Squats steadily to focus on objects at floor level Can drink from a bottle/training cup unaided
2–3 years	Walks, runs, climbs, kicks and jumps skilfully Walks up stairs, but needs to put both feet on each stair Can catch a ball that is rolled to him/her Can start, stop and avoid objects effectively when walking Holds a crayon in pincer grip Begins to intentionally draw lines and circles Begins to 'help' dress him/herself Can drink from an open cup or beaker, but may still find comfort in a bottle, particularly when tired Clean and dry during the day
4–5 years	Can dress and undress him/herself with a little help (e.g. with small buttons) Begins to stand steadily on one foot, hop and skip Walks up stairs in the adult manner, one foot on each stair Begins to attempt to catch a ball that is thrown to him/her Becomes an increasingly adventurous climber Holds a crayon or pencil between finger and thumb Most children will have a clear preference for either left or right hand Drawing is increasingly under conscious control (e.g. can draw a recognisable circle if shown how to do so) Begins to use scissors, although cutting may not be very accurate Clean and dry night and day; usually manages him/herself in the toilet Can learn simple dances and songs with actions (e.g. 'heads, shoulders, knees and toes')

What are the main theoretical perspectives that describe how children develop and learn, particularly between birth and their sixth birthday?

The first questions to be asked about human psychology were posed by the ancient Greek philosophers. They proposed that human beings expressed individually different temperaments, which they named as sanguine (easy-going), phlegmatic (sluggish), choleric (irritable) and melancholic (depressive) (Galen, second century BC in Thomas, 1990). Modern theorists reject such early conclusions, but the study of personality – in its infant guise, temperament - is still ongoing today (see below), increasingly underpinned by the biological knowledge that is continually being developed by studies in the fields of human genetics and brain biology.

Modern studies of human development have their roots in the 'Enlightenment', the beginnings of scientific study that began in the late seventeenth century in Europe, following the Renaissance. Some of this research was carried out in the field of pedagogy, and you will read about this in chapters 5, 6 and 7, which deal with early years education practice. This chapter will introduce you to the principal theorists and theories in the field of developmental psychology.

Introduction to emotional development: attachment theory

Attachment theory was originated by the British psychologist John Bowlby (1969) over the period directly following World War II (1939-45). It was based on a mixture of Freudian ideas (see chapter 1) and extrapolation of concepts from studies that biologists had carried out on non-human animals and their offspring. Bowlby's central proposal was that human mothers and babies have a natural, evolved instinct to form a strong emotional bond. While this fixed focus on mothers was later found to be highly problematic, Bowlby's concept of the 'Internal Working Model' is still a central facet of modern attachment theory. He proposed that, based on the earliest relationship (nowadays relationships), infants construct an Internal Working Model (IWM) of what to expect from other people, and of their own level of 'lovability'. Bowlby proposed that a positive mother-child relationship creates an 'other people are nice and I am lovable' IWM, whereas a troubled mother-child relationship creates an 'other people are unkind and I am *not* lovable' IWM. This basic belief, he proposed, was the basis of all subsequent interactions and relationships for the child. Robin Dolby (2007) has created a practical advice document on this point, which introduces the concept of 'The Circle of Security'.

Bowlby also carried out studies with James Robertson, a social worker (Robertson and Bowlby, 1952), on the problems that children experienced in the hospitals of the time, where visits by parents were extremely limited (consider Jean's memories of being in hospital earlier in this chapter). This research indicated that children went through a process of initial distress, followed by despair, and, if contact with attachment figures was lost altogether, they finally detached from the adult concerned. If the detachment stage was reached, the relationship became very difficult to rebuild. The younger the child at the time the relationship was put under strain, the more quickly they went through the stages and the greater the negative effect the process had upon their psychological health and subsequent emotional development.

Schaffer and Emerson (1964) found, in a longitudinal study of babies from birth to two years, that *several* bonds with adults were formed in the first months. The babies tended to have one primary attachment and several secondary attachments, being perfectly content to be cared for by any of these 'bonded' adults. Only approximately 50% of these babies had the primary attachment to the mother; the other 50% had formed a primary attachment to another member of the family (most commonly the father or grandmother, and sometimes older siblings). The primary attachment tended to be the person in the family who showed the most sensitive responsiveness to the baby. The studies of Mary Ainsworth (e.g. Ainsworth and Bell, 1970) also indicated that the quality of attachment that a child had to the main carer had a lasting effect on the IWM. However, later studies found her 'strange situation' methodology to be flawed, particularly in its tendency to diagnose problematic attachments in children from non-Western cultures, where, on examination of the child's life outside the laboratory situation that Ainsworth created for her tests, no such problems appeared to exist.

Modern studies of the attachments children build in daycare have produced complex and controversial findings, but the picture that emerges is that children in high-quality daycare do not suffer attachment problems, while those in low-quality daycare suffer a range of problems relating to both emotional and intellectual development. Such findings led directly to the New Labour Government's decision to fund a range of improvements in daycare provision over the first decade of the twenty-first century, although progress has not been sustained under subsequent governments. A summary of findings and the resulting recommendations is presented in Table 2.2.

Table 2.2 Recommendations for daycare drawn from attachment theory

Developmental psychology	Recommendations for daycare
Children under 3 (and preferably under 7) need **regular care** from adults to whom they are **attached**, and can **rely upon**	Daycare settings need to do everything in their power to **avoid high staff turnover**, e.g. good wages and working conditions, employment of well-qualified, dedicated staff
Children need a lot of **individual attention** from adults, including one who takes a particular interest in them and their family; this is intended in the creation of the 'Key Person' who shows **sensitive responsiveness** to the child, showing a genuine interest in their communications, and an understanding of what they want/need at different times and in different situations (**sustained shared thinking**)	Daycare settings must have a **high number of adult staff** so that children can receive a lot of individual attention, much of which should be given by a **Key Person** whose role is to provide care for a small group of children
	Staff in daycare settings need to be **specifically trained to work with children under five**, and to have enough **professionalism, personal maturity and experience** to be able to 'decentre' from their own thoughts and needs to understand and show interest in the sometimes mundane communications of small children
Children need **developmentally appropriate play resources** and **help/ encouragement from adults** to progress in their learning	Daycare settings should be **well-resourced** with toys and large indoor and outdoor play equipment, and **adults should be specifically trained to understand how young children learn**, particularly what levels of understanding to expect in children throughout the birth to five developmental period

Note: Basic hygiene/health and safety practices, etc., are not noted here, but are still obviously important!

Case study: a band of brothers?

Antony James, just five, and three weeks into Year 1 (Y1), called his older brothers, twins Joe and Kieron (Y4), into the Key Stage 1 playground to play with him. First of all the brothers played happily at 'piggy-backs' which involved Antony manoeuvring himself from the back of one twin to the other, then the two older boys picked Anthony up by his ankles and turned him upside down, gently shaking him while he giggled. A line of Y1 boys quickly formed, clamouring to 'have the next go'.

Meanwhile, a little further inside the younger children's playground, Cameron, also in Y1, called to his Y3 brother, Jordan, to demonstrate some of his football skills. Jordan brought along two of his friends, one who took on the role of goalkeeper. Jordan and his other friend lined up some of the younger boys in front of the 'goal' (marked out by two discarded pullovers), showing them how to form a defence, while they took 'free kicks'. All the boys involved in this game were clearly happy and absorbed.

The head teacher, who had recently returned after working in Finland for three months on an exchange programme, had made the decision to allow mixed age play during recreation times, as she felt that the younger children would gain a greater sense of security from being able to interact with their older siblings during the school day, and that the older children could also help to socialise their younger peers in general, as she had observed in Finland. The parents involved in school governance were very positive about the plan, particularly as a lot of money had recently been spent on the Key Stage 1 playground, converting it into a mixture of 'soft surface' matting and grassed areas. The head also made a further decision to explicitly allow the children to engage in consensual 'rough and tumble' play, which she had also observed in Finland; this too was enthusiastically endorsed by the parents.

At their briefing, the staff raised concerns about the potential for injuries, and the requirement for more gradual change, so a compromise was reached to continue with separate designated playgrounds for children in Key Stage 1 and Key Stage 2, but to allow Key Stage 1 children to *invite* the older children into their playground. Key Stage 1 children were subsequently told that they could not venture into the Key Stage 2 playground, and Key Stage 2 children were instructed to keep very boisterous play within their own area.

When Emily, the playground duty teacher, ate her lunch later that day with her friend Rose, the Reception teacher, she complained about the stress that playtime supervision now caused her: 'I don't care if the children are laughing; it is us who will get into trouble if someone is hurt. And those James twins are just a menace, pure and simple. I don't see what it accomplishes to allow them to roll around with Antony in the way that they do. And getting other Year 1 boys to join in ... well, it just shouldn't be allowed.'

Rose hesitated for a moment. Then she said 'you know, Emily, when Antony first came into Reception he was like a lost sheep. He would put his nose up against the gate to the older children's playground and cry for Joe and Kieron when they were out. Between us, I actually let them in for a few minutes from time to time, but told them they had to *sit* and play with Antony with the toy cars or the blocks or we would all get into trouble, and they always did what I asked – I know, because I watched them like a hawk. Now Antony seems a much happier little boy to me. I was in the EYFS outdoor area during playtime and I could hear him giggling from there. Those boys have got such a strong attachment to each other, it seems cruel not to let the youngest one have any contact with his brothers at all during the school day'.

'That is all very well' said Emily grimly, 'and I suppose it would all work out OK if it was just the older *girls*. But those James twins, they really are double trouble – I think it's irresponsible to let them loose in an area with the Key Stage 1 children. You mark my words; someone is going to get hurt.'

Reflection

If you were leading practice with respect to playtime supervision, would you be prepared to facilitate mixed-age play of this nature? Consider the complex factors that are involved here, relating to emotional well-being, gendered play issues, making provision for active play and judgement of 'acceptable risk'. You will meet the 'risk' issue again in chapter 7.

Introduction to individual differences: temperament theory

The underpinning idea for a concept of 'temperament', came from a very famous psychologist Hans Eysenck. He was concerned with adult psychology and is the originator of the modern concepts of an extravert/introvert, neurotic/stable personality. Eysenck (1981) proposed that there were very subtle differences in the brain biology of individuals, rather like the setting of a thermostatic mechanism. This, he proposed, would underlie our outwardly expressed personality. Developmental researchers soon proposed that the origins of adult personality could be discerned within infant styles of interacting with the external environment; this area of individual difference was termed 'temperament' (Figure 2.1).

Based on the New York Longitudinal Study of temperament, which began in the 1950s, Thomas and Chess (1977) proposed that they had discovered nine dimensions of infant temperament:

- Activity level
- Quality of mood
- Approach/withdrawal
- Rhythmicity
- Adaptability
- Threshold of responsiveness
- Intensity of reaction
- Distractibility
- Attention span.

Not surprisingly, these proved difficult to define reliably in more short-term studies. It was subsequently proposed that these dimensions were not all fully independent of each other, and could be collapsed into three basic 'types': the 'Easy', 'Difficult' and 'Slow to Warm Up' child. Other researchers and practitioners did not necessarily find potentially judgemental labels such as 'easy' and 'difficult' particularly helpful, however!

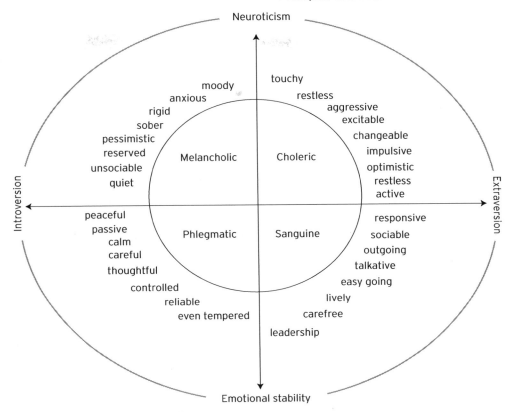

Figure 2.1 Dimensions of personality

Source: Adapted from Gross, R. (1996) *Psychology: The science of mind and behaviour*, p. 888.

Buss and Plomin (1984) proposed that they could simplify Thomas and Chess's temperament dimensions to three, and that these could be related to Eysenck's theory of adult personality:

- Emotionality (relates to neuroticism)
- Activity (relates to extraversion/introversion)
- Sociability (also relates to extraversion/introversion).

Buss and Plomin further proposed that impulsivity and shyness might also be independent dimensions from the three named, although they maintained that their 'EAS' system was an adequate model of temperamental differences between infants. Kagan (1988) suggested that there was a firm physiological basis for differences underlying temperament types, due to regulation of neuronal activity in the limbic system – again, similarly to Eysenck's theory. Kagan's theory was based on strength of emotional reaction, a continuum which he proposed was principally responsible for levels of personality traits such as sociability, shyness, adventurousness and talkativeness. Kagan proposed that people could consciously try to modify their behaviour and reactions, but that they could not change the biological activity that occurred in their bodies, e.g. increased heart rate and pupil dilation; hence, he proposed, the basic temperament 'type' was determined by genetic inheritance. More recent studies (see below) have suggested that stress response is not only determined by individual inheritance, but also by external events occurring during gestation and early childhood.

Dunn and Kendrick (1982) suggested that events that the child was exposed to in infancy and early childhood (particularly the birth of a sibling) could have a considerable effect on their behavioural style, and that, as time went on, transactions in the relationships between the carers and the siblings would have an important impact on all the children's temperaments and eventual adult personalities. Chess and Thomas (1984) suggested that 'goodness of fit' between a child's temperament and that of their regular carers has a huge effect on the child's self-confidence and resilience. These ideas have been picked up by more modern researchers such as Suzanne Zeedyk, who seek to explore the complex interactions between biology and environment, whose website you will find in the Recommended reading list. This leads back to the concept of 'sensitive responsiveness' evoked in attachment theory, and how important this can be for a child during unsettling 'transition' phases in their life.

Case study: Kayleigh and Sarah – 'sensitive responsiveness' to children and their parents during times of transition

Kayleigh was a premature baby who spent three weeks in an incubator before coming home for the first time. Her mother Sarah had always been rather anxious about her, and as she has grown older Kayleigh has shown many of the signs of being what Chess and Thomas might call a 'difficult' child. She shows high emotion and great sensitivity to environment; she does not like to mix with strangers, either adults or children. Sarah has identified that Kayleigh seems very sensitive to her emotional responses, and realises that this can create a 'vicious circle', in the sense that Sarah will worry that Kayleigh will respond poorly to a situation, and her concerns will seem to communicate themselves to Kayleigh, so Kayleigh's emotional responses are heightened. Kayleigh is now just three, and in good health, and Sarah is five months pregnant. She wants to settle Kayleigh into a private nursery class for four mornings a week before the baby arrives. She has taken Kayleigh for an introductory session, during which Kayleigh cried and clung to her mother most of the time, apart from a short period of interest at the painting table. Kayleigh is to return next week, and Sarah is already dreading the experience. Jenny, the EYGP in the setting, who manages the transitions, is aware of the situation.

Jenny talks to Barbara, the nursery teacher, and Jill, the nursery practitioner who is to be Kayleigh's Key Person, about how to proceed. They decide the following:

- Jill will undertake another home visit, and talk to Sarah about Kayleigh's normal activities and routines, and how these might be a little more closely aligned with the activities and routines of the nursery class, so that Kayleigh feels some familiarity within the nursery environment.
- Jill will also try to ensure that Sarah feels as much at ease with her, and with the situation, as possible, so that Kayleigh is not picking up so many negative emotions from her mother about the situation.
- Amber, who lives next door to Sarah and Kayleigh, is attending the nursery for one more term before moving on to the Reception class in the school in September. Kayleigh knows Amber a little, and they have sometimes 'visited' to play. Jill is going to suggest that, if possible, the parents take turns in bringing Kayleigh and Amber to nursery together (Sarah for the first week if she prefers), so that Kayleigh does not come in alone.

- Jill will also find out if Kayleigh has a favourite toy that she would like to bring to nursery, one that can act as what attachment theorist Winnicott (1951) called a 'transitional object', providing some comfort when people to whom she has bonded attachments are not physically present.
- Sarah and Jill will agree a schedule via which Sarah will leave Kayleigh for longer and longer periods over the first few weeks of her attendance until she is attending the whole session without Sarah. Jenny explains to Jill that this will not only involve providing reassurance for Kayleigh, but also for Sarah.

Reflection

Such conversations with parents cannot be wholly planned, as the practitioner undertaking them needs to be able to respond to the situation as it unfolds, sometimes involving other staff on a 'need to know' basis. By this time Sarah will be nearly six months pregnant, and perhaps helping her to focus on how she will maintain Kayleigh's routine when the new baby arrives (which should include the three-hour session at nursery) might help Sarah to move on in the previously agreed schedule, leaving Kayleigh for progressively longer periods in the nursery. Jenny will try to help Sarah to consider that, if Kayleigh is used to spending the full session at nursery without her mother present by the time the baby arrives, the resulting changes will not unbalance Kayleigh's routine so dramatically, and thus minimise the unsettling events arising for her from the new arrival. If Jill (who is currently completing her Foundation Degree in Early Years) is informed and involved in this process, Jenny will also be able to model good practice in working with parents for her.

Introduction to social development

Uri Bronfenbrenner (1979) did not deny that genetics was very important in determining what children become in later life. However, he proposed that crucial interactions with the child's 'nature' were created by the 'nurturing' environment. Many highly influential childhood intervention and enrichment projects eventually grew from the basis of Bronfenbrenner's ideas. He proposed that children inhabited a series of systems that were nested one within the other like a set of Russian dolls (Figure 2.2).

- The innermost system is the **Microsystem**, which describes the child's everyday environments (e.g. home, school).
- The **Mesosystem** provides the contacts between the structures of the microsystem (e.g. a parent–teacher association or a local parent and toddler group).
- The middle system is the **Exosystem**, which describes aspects that have a direct influence on the microsystem environment (e.g. parents' jobs, relationships with extended family and friends).
- The outer system is the **Macrosystem**, which describes the cultural surroundings of these environments (e.g. language, culture, wealth and poverty, ethnicity and religion).

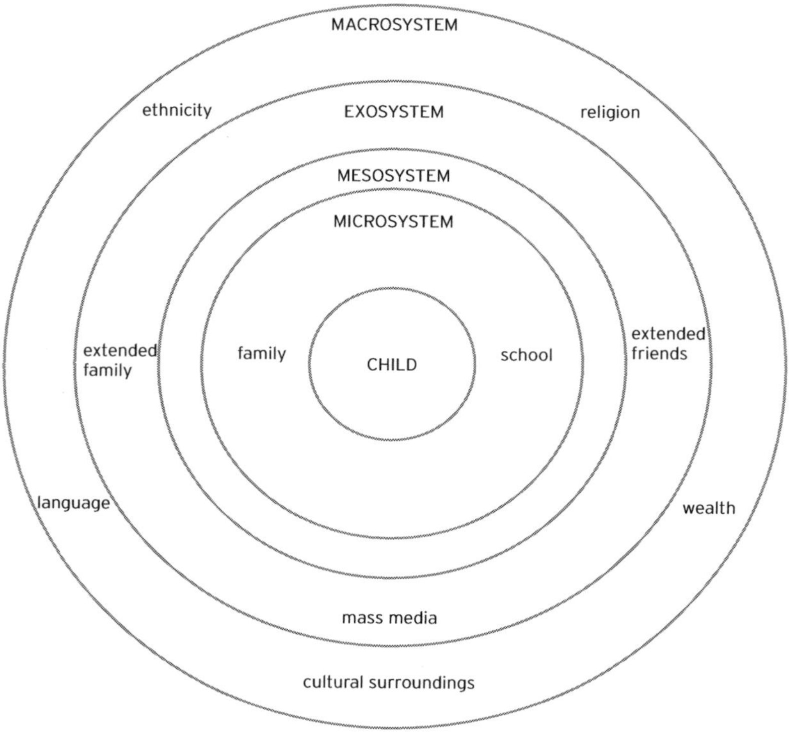

Figure 2.2 Bronfenbrenner's concept of 'systems'

Source: Adapted from Dockrell, J. and Messer, D. (1999) *Children's Language and Communication Difficulties: Understanding, identification and intervention*, p. 139.

At a time when many scientific discoveries were beginning to indicate that what we 'are' is determined to a great extent by genetics, Bronfenbrenner emphasised the still crucial influence of the environment. He made it clear that, while nature determined how 'long' individual human potential was, nurture determined how far it was going to be 'pulled' (see Figure 2.3). His theories have subsequently been the launching pad for two very high-profile childhood enrichment programmes on both sides of the Atlantic, Head Start in the US (National Head Start Association, 2015) and Sure Start in the UK (Eisenstadt, 2011). These projects are further explored in chapter 4.

Dunn and Kendrick (1982) considered children's development in family environments during the period when they were aged between three and seven years. The following important environmental influences upon children's early social development were indicated by the findings of this study:

- Children's interactions with friends and family strongly impacted on their ability to understand emotions and 'other minds' ('theory of mind').
- Frequent discussion about why people do/feel what they do especially seemed to develop 'theory of mind' skills in young children; in other words, the ability to accurately predict what other people are feeling and thinking.

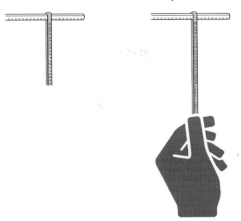

Figure 2.3 Extending children's development. 'The elastic band theory': Nature determines how long it is, but nurture determines how far it is extended.

- Young children very quickly learned to use different types of discussion and argument with different family members.
- Children who develop early skills of emotional understanding build on this and are more advanced at later stages.
- Child–child relationships were very important in their development of these skills, both with siblings and with friends.

Case study: five-year-old football play and resulting peer relationship learning

(Author's observations)

Pearson Education Ltd/Jules Selmes

Quite a few years ago now, I carried out an ongoing series of observations in primary school, of which one of the aims was to study the relationships developed by the children through their outdoor free play. Some of the observations undertaken were of the five- and six-year-old boys in the group when they engaged in football play.

Extract 1

Noted at the beginning of the observation: Adam had just had the plaster removed from a recently broken arm, and was not really supposed to engage in football play at all.

'Adam gets the ball. The other boys are very careful not to tackle Adam and they let him have his turn with the ball ... He kicks it, and all the other boys run after it. I hear Leo's voice: "Tom, it's my turn". Tom kicks at goal, and Adam saves it in front of Benji. We seem to have three goalkeepers now, Aiden also standing by the goal post. Benji takes the ball from Adam and kicks it out. It hits Ashley on the hand and a cry goes up: "hand ball". Adam picks up the ball and takes it out of play. He says "I'm taking it, hand ball". (Chanting: "score, score, score".) He puts it down, takes a kick at goal and scores. He says "like Beckham".'

Extract 2

'The ball rolls out of play down to the tarmac. Tom brings it back up. He is standing on the hill looking like he is going to throw in, but he kicks it instead. It goes behind the goal. Adam takes the next throw in. They seem very sure about the boundaries of their football pitch, but it is not clear to an adult observer ... He puts the ball down and kicks it through the goal sideways and then jumps up and down (children cheer). Benji says "no goal" as he was not in the goal at the time ... But they are not counting the goals anyway. Benji is saying "no, no" and holding on to the ball. They all chant at him: "time waster". So he kicks the ball back out into play again.'

There are many aspects of social learning through peer relationships that can be identified in these short extracts. Though only five, these children realised that Adam could not play unless they gave him some special consideration, and it is clear that they effectively managed to do this. This indicates some amount of ability to decentre from their own situations to understand the situation of another, currently recovering from injury. The children show some rudimentary knowledge of the rules underlying football in their invocation of 'hand ball', 'time wasting' and 'goal scoring', and their understanding that there is a designated area outside which the ball is no longer in play, but it is clear that this is still at a very basic level, which I noted was additionally demonstrated by the presence of three goalkeepers and a complete lack of team-based play. Benji indicates that, while he can evoke the rules as he understands them, he is also willing to acquiesce to majority opinion and send the ball back into play – a highly flexible response to social pressure, which also indicates some underlying 'Theory of Mind'. As these children play, they co-create rules and practices.

My analysis, after several observations of this nature, was that their learning about the rules of the game was very much secondary to their learning about the social interactions that they had with each other, all underpinned by the impetus to achieve the continuation of a play situation that they were all enjoying. There is little that is required from adults in such a situation, apart from a discreet vigilance to ensure that physically dangerous or 'bullying' situations do not develop.

During my time on this piece of research, I occasionally saw adults intervening in the children's play in attempts to completely change the meanings that the children had created between themselves, with the inevitable result that such play broke down. For example, when a group of boys were playing a chasing game which involved Benji dragging a skipping rope while the other boys chased him, the female teacher on playground duty stopped their game, and gathered the group together to talk to them. She showed them how to turn the rope, with one child at each end. All the boys tried to skip, but none seemed to have any idea of when to jump as the rope swung around. The teacher then called to Miranda to demonstrate ... she was very good at skipping, but the boys lost interest and wandered off. The chasing game soon began again, with Benji at the front, this time with a 'push wheel'. When the bell went, I asked him what they were playing. 'Fire engines', he replied. I wondered if that was also the game ongoing with the skipping rope. If so, the play narratives used by the boys and the adult were not at all compatible. It could also be theorised that some of these differences were underpinned by a cross-gender misunderstanding, something that all female Early Years Practitioners (who massively outnumber men within the profession) need to consciously consider. You have met this issue before, in the 'Band of Brothers' case study above.

Reflection

The only real 'rule' here is that each situation must be approached on its own merits, underpinned by an adult's aim to build on and extend the children's ideas, rather than attempting to impose their own agenda on top of them. There are many instances where building shared understandings with other children is the most important aspect of a play event, whether or not those understandings are judged as 'correct' by an adult. The key point here is to focus on the activity's processes rather than its outcomes. You need to consider this point deeply during the observations that you undertake in the early part of your training (see below). Such a focus will develop your knowledge and sensitivity in this area, which will in turn help you to support other staff towards a greater understanding of the benefits of child-led play, a very important element within children's developmental processes.

Introduction to cognitive developmental theory

Jean Piaget was the first theorist to produce a comprehensive theory of human intellectual development. In *The Psychology of the Child* (Piaget and Inhelder, 1969) he outlined his theory that children learn in interaction with the *concrete* world (i.e. world of objects), with experiential learning underpinning the child's construction of a cognitive network of schemas, assimilating and accommodating new knowledge. A schema is, in Piaget's context, a set of mental connections. At the time of Piaget's research there was little evidence of how the living brain worked, but now we know that infants and children do indeed rapidly build up connections between brain cells (called neurons) over the developmental period. Piaget proposed that the child either assimilates a new experience (taking it into thought without creating a new concept, e.g. you lick an ice cream and you also lick an ice lolly) or accommodates it (creating a new concept in thought, e.g. you can't pick up spaghetti with just a spoon, or a knife and fork; you have to learn a new action with a spoon and a fork). The child moves towards accommodation by a process of 'equilibration', which means needing to balance all related schemas against one's current picture of reality.

Piaget proposed that building thought processes to adult competence continued until the child was 12. Nowadays, we know it takes much longer than this, and that there is a wealth of individual and cultural difference in such construction. However, Piaget's concept of stages is still useful as a rough guide to children's intellectual competence in the early years of life. He carried out an extensive series of experiments that indicated babies under about six months do not even realise that objects that they cannot immediately see still exist within the world; hence he proposed that such young infants have no concept of 'object permanence'. This, he proposed, relates to lack of mental connections within such an immature mind. Babies do not yet have the available symbols within their mind to 'hang' such concepts and memories upon. Achieving the concept of object permanence is one of the major goals of the sensorimotor stage (birth to 18 months), alongside organising information coming from the senses, and the achievement of basic motor skills (walking, holding objects, etc.). Children aged approximately 18 months move on to the 'pre-operational' stage, where they will spend approximately four and a half years building schemas relating to developing linguistic and social competence and reducing egocentricity (a focus solely on the self and one's own point of view). Children in the earlier periods of this stage are unable to hypothesise logically with respect to social or intellectual situations, frequently showing 'centration' (a focus on only one simple, surface-based aspect of a situation). Margaret Donaldson (1978) outlined a series of experiments undertaken by her research team that indicated that, once a child understood the social situation in which a problem was embedded, they were much more likely to be able to work towards a successful solution. It is therefore common, but not inevitable, that children will show more sophistication in dealing with social situations than intellectual situations as they move through this stage. A Piagetian concept that can be used to describe this inconsistency is 'décalage' (literally 'gap' or 'interval'). Once children reach the next stage, that of 'Concrete Operations' (7–12 years), their ability to think logically about both social and intellectual situations becomes more flexible and mature.

The Russian developmental psychologist, Lev Vygotsky, was also a theorist in the constructivist tradition, like Piaget, proposing that children built their understanding of the world on the basis of their interactions within it. However, Vygotsky (1978) placed more emphasis upon the role of interaction with other people, proposing that language was crucially important in learning, in that it was the principal medium through which a child would begin to 'internalise the external'. While Piaget proposed that cognition precedes language, Vygotsky proposed that language precedes cognition. While Piaget proposed that a child had to be 'ready' to grasp a particular skill or idea, Vygotsky proposed that interaction, particularly with an adult or a more able peer, could take a child one step further in their learning than they were able to move alone. He referred to the area into which a child could be 'coached' as a 'Zone of Proximal Development' (ZPD). Jerome Bruner, who brought Vygotsky's work to the attention of the West, proposed that the adult's ongoing role in a teaching and learning process is to progressively *scaffold* the child's learning at an appropriate level, i.e. within the ever-progressing ZPD (Wood *et al.*, 1976). Building on this concept, Wood and Middleton (1975) proposed that the best way adults can help children learn is by creating a contingency, by consciously and carefully tailoring adult input on a minute-to-minute basis so it is always contingent to the child's learning (i.e. supporting the child into the constantly moving zone of proximal development). This leads us back to the concept of 'sustained shared thinking' that is advocated in the EYFS.

Case study: on a bear hunt with Pinky – developing sustained shared thinking

Three-year-old Anastasia is constructing a picture based on a story that her teacher has read the group called *Bear Hunt* (Brown, 2010). There is a box of pre-cut card bear shapes on the table, and a basket of brown furry material. Anastasia has spread glue on her bear shape, but she is looking around for some pink furry material, because she wants the bear to look like Pinky, her favourite teddy who sits on her bed at home. She goes to the trainee nursery practitioner, Vanessa, who has designed the activity and is working with the children at the table. Anastasia holds out a piece of brown material to Vanessa and says 'Where's the pink?'. 'Can't you stick it on, Anastasia?' says Vanessa, 'Here you are.' She sticks the material on to the middle of Anastasia's bear shape and says, 'There. Can you do the next one?'. Anastasia shakes her head, and wanders off to the painting table, where she finds some pink paint. She is soon in conversation with Brenda, the centre EYGP, about the picture she is painting of Pinky, her teddy bear. Vanessa finds the abandoned bear shape on the table at the end of the session when the children have gone home. She shrugs, and then puts it into the waste paper bin.

Brenda sees Vanessa put the unfinished bear picture into the bin. She has picked up from her conversation with Anastasia that the child had abandoned the activity; she also knows that Anastasia was not the only child in the setting to do so during that session. She has allowed Vanessa to design and run the activity in this way so that she can learn from the experience, but Vanessa's response to this indicates that she has not intuited that there is anything wrong with the activity; in fact, Brenda heard her telling another member of staff during the session that the children 'are not very good at sticking activities'.

Reflection

In order to access Anastasia's zone of proximal development, Vanessa needed to listen to what Anastasia was saying to her and respond appropriately, i.e. to consider what the child was thinking rather than seeing the situation from her own adult point of view. Anastasia was presenting Vanessa with a problem-solving situation, but Vanessa provided a solution that Anastasia had already considered and rejected. In doing so, Vanessa has missed the opportunity to help the child to solve the problem in a way that she would comprehend as useful and effective.

It can sometimes help with very young trainees to give them a very limited set of paints and ask them to paint a picture of themselves – they will very quickly comment that they haven't got the right colour for their hair/eyes, etc., and from that personal, practical experience they can more easily move on to consider how every craft activity should offer children a choice and a chance to personalise their work. From there they can then move on to understand why the perennial early years prompt to 'tell me about your picture' is such a crucial interaction between young children and their carers, and why forcing children of this age into the 'Blue Peter' situation (where they are required to make a copy of something an adult has made earlier!) is not particularly helpful at this stage of their development. Indeed, it can lead adults to the erroneous conclusion that the task is 'too difficult' for the child rather than considering the situation from the child's point of view. If Vanessa had responded to the situation with more insight, she might have also moved on to consider that the activity itself was very limited, given the materials available to the children, and then towards some ideas on how to improve the activity next time by providing a wider range of materials.

Introduction to language development

Words are *symbols*. Each word that we utter 'stands for' something, in our own minds, and (hopefully!) in the minds of the person we are talking to. Usually these meanings match – if they do not, there can be misunderstandings, which may be quite amusing. For example, in a very old joke:

> 'I say, I say, I say – my dog has no nose.'
> 'Your dog has no nose? How does he smell?'
> 'Terrible!'

Some words will stand for simple concrete objects, e.g. 'dog', 'cat', 'table'. Other words stand for complex abstract ideas, e.g. 'love', 'peace', 'justice'. However, the average 10-year-old child will have a working (if not exact) idea of what all these words mean.

When we converse with someone we match the symbols in our heads with the symbols in theirs. This is usually possible when we use the same sounds (and squiggles, if we include written language) to stand for the same ideas and objects, although we may not always communicate exactly what we intend. If people use different sounds and squiggles from us to stand for the same ideas and objects (i.e. they speak a different language), translation is often possible, but this inserts an extra 'step' which makes communication even more imperfect.

The basic stages of language development proceed as follows.

Proto-conversation

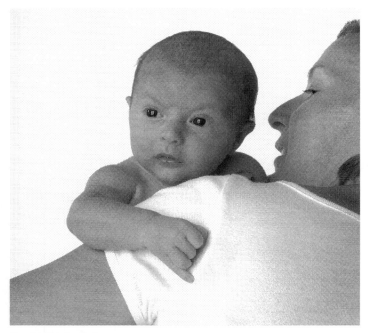

Pearson Education Ltd/Jules Selmes

'Proto-conversation' was first described by Mary Bateson in the 1970s. She described 7-15-week-old infants responding to their mothers' talk with appropriately timed smiles and coos in a give-and-take, dialogue-like pattern, hence 'proto' (stands for) conversation (Bateson, 1975). The adult will often act as though the baby's 'responses' are intentional. In this way, Bateson proposed, the baby learns the turn-taking conventions of adult conversation.

Stage 1

This is the one-word stage; the child develops a small repertoire of single words, usually the names of familiar people and objects, e.g. 'mum', 'dad', 'cup' (around 1 year to 18 months).

Stage 2

Two-word sentences which tend to be simple descriptions of actions and possessions now emerge, e.g. 'my ball', 'throw ball'. This stage was referred to as **telegraphic speech** (Oates and Grayson, 2004) – nowadays we might be more likely to call it 'text speech'. The point is that the child usually manages to convey a surprising amount of information in very few words (alongside gestures and facial expressions) (around 18 months to 2½ years).

Stage 3

Simple grammatical sentences are now beginning to be uttered, and towards the middle of this phase their content begins to encompass past tenses, reflecting a growing understanding of past and future. Children start to use grammatical constructions, e.g. 'I walked', but in doing this they sometimes inadvertently 'regularise' irregular verbs, e.g. 'that tree growed' instead of the grammatically correct 'that tree grew'. This indicates that they are not just simply repeating adult speech but learning (and sometimes stumbling on) grammatical rules to underpin their own original utterances. They also begin to learn to play with language in songs and rhymes (around 2½–3½ years).

Stage 4

The 'where, what, why' stage. The child becomes a competent language user, and begins to use this new skill to ask adults everything the child wants to know about the world. As any parent knows, some of these questions will be impossible to answer; for example, at this age my son once asked his father 'Why elephants?'. On further investigation this did not refer to *what* elephants were, or what they *did*, but simply *why* they 'were'. Children of this age sometimes appear to use their new linguistic competence to engage in a developmental stage of what could be termed basic philosophical enquiry (around 3½–4½ years).

Stage 5

Children may now use more complex sentences involving more than one clause. For example, they will begin to use the more grammatical 'Who is playing with that ball?' structure, rather than the more babyish 'Who play ball?' (around 4–5 years).

Stage 6

Children now join sentences smoothly together with conjunctions like 'and' and 'but', e.g. 'John and Asif came with me' and 'I used to like Samantha, but I don't like her now'. They can also turn the meanings of sentences around, e.g. 'Is that your coat?' and 'That is your coat', and enjoy playing with language in this way; for example, see the joke at the beginning of this section (around 4$\frac{1}{2}$–5$\frac{1}{2}$ years).

Children who have had other developmental problems also tend to have delayed development of linguistic competence. This may be particularly in evidence if hearing loss has been a problem. Children who have been diagnosed with, or are in the process of being investigated for, conditions within the autism spectrum disorder category also typically have a range of difficulties with language development.

The day-to-day adult role in assisting children with their language development is very important. As outlined above, carers and small babies show turn-taking behaviour in interactions that psychologists have labelled 'proto-conversation' (Dougherty, 1999). Later on, when children begin to speak, adults and older children automatically simplify their speech when talking to small children, emphasising key words and often repeating key phrases. This has been referred to as 'parentese' or the 'baby talk register', but adults who are not parents, and even older children will usually instinctively do this when conversing with children under two. Another instinctive adult technique is to introduce a 'frame', e.g. 'What is this? It's a frog. What is this? It's a fish'. A lot of toddler books are constructed in this fashion; a favourite with my children was *Where's Spot?* (Hill, 1980), which repeats 'Where's Spot? He's not in the ...' over a few pages until Spot is found.

Traditional songs and rhymes that small children are taught to sing are also frequently constructed in this fashion as well, e.g. 'The Wheels on the Bus' and 'Ten Green Bottles'. This format presents a nugget of information in a familiar 'frame', so the child pays attention to and learns the new information without the pressure and confusion of a continually changing 'frame'. Such games can be very useful in extending children's language competency.

Introduction to biological perspectives of child development

The human central nervous system begins developing at two weeks' gestation. The human brain weighs around 350 grams at birth; by the end of the first year it weighs 1,000 grams. An adult brain weighs between 1,200 and 1,400 grams. This illustrates the huge importance of the first year of life for brain development. When we are born we have many more neurons (brain cells) than we actually need. Over the first few years of life, the human brain undergoes a huge neuronal connection programme. Those neurons that are not connected to others shrivel and eventually die. Most children have a 'good enough' environment, but if they experience extreme neglect their brains do not develop as they should; in particular, there is a fixed 'window' for some skills to be triggered (e.g. language). If this window is missed, the child may not be able to make up the lost ground at a later point in their life. A well-documented case of this type is that of 'Genie', a 13-year-old American girl who was found locked in her bedroom in the early 1970s (Rymer, 1994). The evidence that could be put together suggested that she had been locked away from other people since she was a very small child. Although she was unable to speak when she was discovered, she initially made good progress in learning individual words; however, she never progressed to putting these words together to form grammatical sentences. The researchers concluded that the developmental window for learning grammar and syntax had passed for 'Genie', that the neurons that should have been dedicated to this task had died away, and were not able to be reactivated. Modern research increasingly indicates that much early brain development, while underpinned by genetic programmes, is shaped by a child's early environments. A good example of this is how easily small children learn to be bi- or even multi-lingual, developing native competence in all languages learned in infanthood, while adults struggle to learn subsequent languages and seldom become accomplished enough to speak them without a foreign accent.

Recent biological research also suggests that the amount of stress that children are placed under in infancy has a crucial 'thermostat setting' effect on the biological mechanisms relating to the stress response, commonly known as 'fight or flight'. Children who have a lot of stress in infancy, in particular that created by experiences of being passed from carer to carer with little or no attention paid to the time to form bonded relationships, are vulnerable to developing abnormalities in the levels of the hormone cortisol, which mobilises the 'fight or flight' mechanisms in all mammals. Children experiencing ongoing stress typically have abnormally high resting levels of cortisol and these take longer to return to baseline after individual stressful experiences.

Initial studies of children in Western daycare suggested that, across the board, they appeared to show cortisol levels that rose steadily throughout the day, a very worrying finding. However, antipodean researchers Sims, Guilfoyle and Parry (2006) compared the cortisol levels of children in daycare settings judged as 'high-quality' against the cortisol levels of children in daycare settings judged as 'satisfactory'. They found that, while the children's cortisol levels rose throughout the day in the satisfactory settings, they fell throughout the day in the high-quality settings. These researchers went on to outline what features defined a 'high-quality setting':

- **Staff relationships:** happy engaging atmosphere, with staff guiding children's behaviour positively.
- **Respect:** staff initiate and maintain communication with children, accommodating their individual needs, including the recognition of social and cultural differences.
- **Partnership:** staff and families exchange effectively both verbal and written information about the children, and about the centre's routines and expectations.
- **Staff interaction:** staff communicate effectively and function as a team.

- **Planning and evaluation:** the centre programmes reflect a clear centre philosophy and shared goals, which cater for the needs, interests and abilities of all the children, and all the children are helped towards successful learning.
- **Learning and evaluation:** the centre programmes encourage children to make confident choices and take on new challenges.
- **Protective care:** staff supervise children at all times, and individual needs for safety, rest and comfort are met. Children are appropriately dressed for indoor and outdoor play. Toileting and nappy procedures are positive experiences.
- **Managing to support quality:** staffing policies and practices facilitate continuity of care for each child.

(Sims *et al.*, 2006)

These features lead us back to the beginning of the chapter, where similar aspirations can be found in the content of the EYFS.

Focus on practice

Providing a calm environment in a stressful world

It is a Monday morning, 9.20 a.m. Four-year-olds Jenna, Shaun and Olivia are hanging up their coats at the day nursery that they regularly attend. Jenna's father has just been made redundant, and her mother has just finished her nursing degree. Jenna's mother is currently working on a series of part-time temporary contracts, still looking for a permanent job. This morning, Jenna heard her parents arguing because her mother wanted her father to take Jenna to the setting, but he was still in bed. Both of Shaun's parents work long hours, and his father, who brought him to the centre, was running late today. He made a business call on his mobile phone as soon as he got out of the car outside the centre, and forgot to kiss Shaun, or to say goodbye. Shaun looks out of the window, watching his father pull quickly out of the car park. Olivia lives with her single mother and her 11-year-old sister Amy. Amy has some important tests at school today and, when Olivia started to sing at the breakfast table this morning, Amy (who can be quite nice sometimes) screamed at her to 'shut up'.

The children all have their own pegs in the cloakroom, and they recognise the pictures that have been there since they started at the centre over a year ago. Although all their families were running a little late this morning, there is no pressure for the children to be exactly 'on time'; the morning starts with the children's self-registration, which is accomplished by their removing a name tag that hangs on their coat pegs so they can hang their coats up, and then putting the tag in a basket by the playroom door. The children are not called together as a group until 9.30 a.m., although it is standard practice for their Key People to greet them on arrival, and speak briefly to their parents.

As they hang up their coats and put their tags in the basket, the children can see their Key People interacting with other children playing with the activities on the tables in the playroom. The children know that they can ask any of the adults in the setting for help at any point, and that their request will meet with a calm and helpful response. A snack will be available shortly, and the children will be able to have this any time between 9.30 and 11.00 a.m. Lunch, afternoon snack and tea will also be served at regular intervals in the day, and there will be regular activities that punctuate the day, for example a story before lunch and a song with actions just before the afternoon snack is available.

The setting is light and roomy, and the staff try to ensure that no one pushes or shouts, although the children are allowed to be a little noisy when they are running around and laughing outside. The equipment is well maintained and the centre policy is to maintain a slightly higher adult–child ratio than the minimum required by law.

The adults work well as a team; all of them are fully aware of the centre practices and policies, and the children's parents are encouraged to engage with the children's activities in the centre; this is more often successful at the end of the day rather than at the beginning, when the parents' schedules may be very tight.

Shaun runs in and joins in a game with the toy cars that has already begun between his friends Jon and Andrew. Olivia makes her way to the painting table, dips a brush into the red paint and begins spreading the paint across the paper. 'That's very bright, Olivia', says Rob, the setting's nursery teacher, and Olivia's Key Person. 'It's Amy, she's cross about her SATs', says Olivia. 'Oh dear', says Rob, 'I was cross when I had SATs, too. What other colours are sort of "cross" do you think?' Olivia thinks for a moment, and then dips her brush into the yellow paint. She applies it to the paper so that it drips into the red, creating a bright orange. 'That's great, Olivia', says Rob, 'all really sort of "cross" colours, look at that orange you've made with the red and the yellow.' Jenna goes into the Home Corner and picks up a doll. When Dominic follows her in she says, 'why can't you take her to school, Daddy? I'm busy'. 'OK', says Dominic. They begin to put the doll into the little buggy, which Jenna then takes outside.

A new placement student in the setting runs after Jenna, intending to tell her not to take the doll and the pushchair outside. Rob intercepts her to explain that it is important for the child to move through her narrative with the doll and the pushchair, and that if it ends with the toys abandoned in the corner of the playground, they can easily be brought inside again by an adult, once s/he is sure that the child has finished with them.

Reflection

In common with many other examples outlined in the activity boxes above, the key issues here focus around the adult decentring to the child's position, and sometimes offering the type of 'sustained shared thinking' response that Rob demonstrates, 'tapping in' to the art activity in which Olivia has engaged. In doing so, he manages to extend Olivia's understanding of colour mixing, while validating her feelings and those of her sister, and not interfering in a self-defined activity which appears to be offering Olivia some amount of emotional catharsis, a concept that can be traced back to the practice of Susan Isaacs (see chapter 1). Consider the stresses that the children have been exposed to in their home lives, and how the practice in the setting has helped them to settle down more calmly to their day after a rather fraught start at home. Go through the description above, producing your own bullet points relating to the relevant practices.

How can we recognise and meet the needs of individuals?

If you have little or no previous experience in childcare/education, it is crucial that you develop good observational skills and effective recording while you are on your training pathway, as not only will you need to carry out professional observations of children in your day-to-day practice, but one of your key roles will also be to support the development of observational skills in more junior staff. There are many good texts about child observation, some of which are listed in the Recommended reading below. You will also need to develop a good understanding of attachment relationships between children and their caregivers so you can assess the quality of their attachment relationships with each other. Strong attachment relationships act as a protective factor in preventing child abuse and neglect (Howe, 2011).

The ever-increasing demands for 'official' data on each child in all settings have led to the rise of what is termed 'Post-it' observations; that is, practitioners are asked to write a brief record of a momentary achievement that they have seen, with the various Post-it notes then being collected together in a child's profile and written up into a more co-ordinated record. This has in turn led to some settings relying principally upon such record keeping, but the data generated are highly fragmented. Best practice requires that more detailed observations are carried out both on individual children and within the setting as a whole. The case studies below will give you some summarised examples of observation and data analysis techniques, to underpin your further learning, which you can begin by drawing from the resources in the Recommended reading list. You can also consider the emphasis place on focused observation by the early years pioneers, particularly Isaacs and Montessori, by reviewing chapter 1.

Case study: learning how to observe effectively

Basic observation techniques include:

- *Diagrammatic:* including tracking and sociogram, and that you are able to present your results on simple charts (e.g. bar chart, pie chart).
- *Sampling:* including target child, focal child, time sampling, snapshot, event sampling.
- *Observations using checklists:* Many settings will use the EYFS documentation as their only checklist; we offer you an alternative – the Leuven Involvement Scale for Young Children in the Focus on practice box below.
- *Observations using photograph and video records:* this must crucially include an understanding of conventional ethical practice when handling data generated in this way.
- *Participant observation:* where you observe children while taking part in their activities (useful for understanding the event from the perspective of your own engagement).
- *Non-participant observation:* where you observe children without participating in their activities (useful when you want to adopt a more objective orientation to the information gathered).

Collecting objective data

It is important to ensure that an acceptable level of objectivity is present in the observation records of the setting, relating to both individual children and specific areas. This is ensured by:

- Carrying out regular non-participant observations;
- Making sure that the child/area is observed by two or more members of staff within a two- to three-week period;
- Carrying out 'paired' observations where two people observe the same area or child simultaneously;

- Discussing any concerns that may arise from your observations with other practitioners on a 'need to know' basis (e.g. with the leading practitioner or Key Person).

Enacting more than one measure of the same person or area is called **triangulation** and ensures some level of **validity** (if observation notes/evaluations agree, you can be more confident that you are observing what you initially thought you were observing, for example that a particular child really is clumsy, or a particular outside area always becomes very slippery after even a light fall of rain) and **reliability** (if more than one person observes the same individual/area and arrives at the same conclusion, this increases the possibility that the points raised are going to arise again in subsequent observations).

Having grasped the basic techniques you must ensure that you can select and enact a suitable observation method to gather information relating to:

- Children's individual personalities and 'styles';
- Children's individual and collective needs;
- How children learn;
- How children interact with peers and adults;
- Behaviour changes that might indicate illness and/or, other underlying problems; this will be further discussed in chapter 3;
- How to plan future practice and activities;
- How children use resources.

And to gather information about individual children's:

- Physical and sensory development;
- Intellectual/cognitive development;
- Language development;
- Emotional development;
- Social development;
- Aesthetic/spiritual development.

Focus on practice: The Leuven Involvement Scale for Young Children

In 2007, UNICEF produced the report *An Overview of Child Well-Being in Rich Countries.*

> The true measure of a nation's standing is how well it attends to its children – their health and safety, their material security, their education and socialization, and their sense of being loved, valued, and included in the families and societies into which they are born.
>
> (2007, p. 13)

A report published by UNICEF in 2013 ranked rich countries for child well-being. Many European countries (particularly the Netherlands and those on the Scandinavian peninsulas) were high in the rankings, whereas the UK was sixteenth (UNICEF, 2013, p. 4). You will find this point further discussed in chapter 10. One way to go about assessing children's level of well-being is to analyse your observations using the Leuven Involvement Scale for Young Children (Laevers, 2005).

Case study: example of an observation evaluation method – The Leuven Involvement Scale for Young Children

A summarised description of Laevers' (2005) method is outlined below.

The child involvement scale consists of two components:

- a list of 'involvement signals'; and
- the levels of involvement on a five-point scale.

The child involvement signals

Concentration: the level of attention the child directs towards the activity.

Energy: the effort the child invests in the activity.

Complexity and creativity: the level of competence the child shows in the activity, as measured against their previous best efforts; consideration of whether the child is moving into their 'zone of proximal development' in engagement with this activity.

Facial expression and posture: the intensity of the child's posture and facial expression. Do they appear to be completely absorbed in the activity?

Persistence: the duration of concentration that the child gives to the activity, and the ease/difficulty of distraction.

Precision: the attention to detail within the activity.

Reaction time: how quickly a child reacts to further stimuli within the activity, showing motivation and keenness.

Language: how does a child talk about a particular activity, e.g. do they ask to do it again, or state that they enjoyed it?

Satisfaction: how proud is a child of their achievements within the activity? (NB: this does not have to relate to satisfaction with a specific product – it could be satisfaction with an experience).

The child involvement scale

The child involvement scale is to be used with reference to the involvement signals.

Level 1 – low activity: stereotypic, repetitive and passive, with little effort or indication that the child feels that much is demanded. They are easily distracted, after which the activity is forgotten. In extreme cases the child may actively reject the activity, and show signs of distress or anger if an adult insists that they must continue.

Level 2 – a frequently interrupted activity: the child is engaged in an activity for part of the time, but spends approximately half of the observed period not paying direct attention. They are relatively easily distracted, after which the activity is forgotten.

Level 3 – mainly continuous activity: the child seems busy at an activity but there is the feeling that 'something' is lacking and that the task is routine. They are relatively easily distracted, and may not return to the activity.

Level 4 – continuous activity with intense moments: there are some signs of intensity in the child's engagement. They can be interrupted, but not wholly distracted, seeking out and resuming the activity again following the interruption. They may resist interruption in some cases. Attention may fluctuate a little but, in general, there is high concentration and focus.

Level 5 – sustained intense activity: the child shows concentration, creativity, energy and persistence for almost all the observation period. They show little response to interruptions, and have clear motivation to continue the activity. They may also smile, show clear confidence in their actions, and if very absorbed may hum or even talk quietly to themselves about what they are doing/plan to do next.

Reflection

Student practitioners learning to use this scale often struggle with observing and writing detailed notes at the same time; however, they improve with practice and they can soon develop sufficient familiarity with the scale to competently assess a child's involvement and well-being, finding it a useful means of sharing information. The only way to learn how to observe and how to analyse your observations is frequent practice, and constructive but critical feedback on your observations and evaluations from more experienced practitioners. Clearly, using this scale and any other scale would come with all the warnings you would expect to be attached to the process of observing children and allocating a score to the observed behaviour, because it can create the illusion of objectivity with respect to a scoring system that will always remain inherently subjective.

What influences and experiences in the setting and beyond can impact on children's well-being, development, learning and behaviour, and how can we connect these to the theoretical perspectives introduced in the earlier section?

We have seen from the information above that the underpinning theory and the current early years guidelines indicate that young children need to gradually develop their knowledge and understanding of the world principally through self-selected play-based experiences. These should involve active learning in calm, well-resourced environments where they are supported cognitively and emotionally by adults who have a sound underpinning knowledge of child development, and an understanding of each child's unique individual needs. While no setting is perfect, this chapter has led us to the consideration of what 'good practice' may actually entail, and how to define this against practice which is not so enlightened.

Case study: developing the independent learners of the future

We are going to provide you with an example of two different (fictional and highly stereotyped) settings to consider:

Brilliant Babies	Jolly Jumpers
Has a fixed start time	Has a flexible start time
Has very fixed routines which serve the convenience of the adults	Has flexible routines which serve the needs of the children

Brilliant Babies	Jolly Jumpers
Has set tasks that the children must complete	Has a range of activities from which the children can choose freely
Has a set routine that the adult staff must follow, whether or not this fits in with the needs of the children in their care	Expects adults to self-regulate their duties in partnership with others (including parents) and encourages them to be as flexible as possible
Has a set regime for recording that the adults must follow, even where the procedures do not 'fit' with the information they wish to record	Allows the adults to record how and what they judge to be useful, as long as enough information on every child is collected via the processes undertaken
Adults tell the children what to do	Adults are emotionally and cognitively available to the children
Adults feel that their role is to direct and instruct	Adults feel that their role is to support the children's development and learning
The practice is driven by targets and 'box-ticking'	The practice views the current Early Years Framework as a set of useful guidelines
The leaders in the setting 'direct practice' and 'manage learning'	The leaders in the setting 'lead practice' and 'support learning'
The child is dependent upon the adults and learns to blindly obey	The child becomes an independent learner, building their knowledge and understanding of the world principally through a range of self-selected, play-based activities with sensitive adult support
The child enters later years of schooling unable to evaluate a situation in order to make judgements and choices	The child enters later years of schooling able to evaluate and make choices on the basis of their own judgements

Of course, you are unlikely to find a 'pure' example of 'Brilliant Babies' or 'Jolly Jumpers'; most settings have features of both, although they may have more features of one than the other! By this point in the chapter, you should be very clear about which setting is exhibiting the best practice; however, the challenge remains as to how to achieve this in a 'real world' environment, where highly directive regimes may be imposed by misguided practices formulated by policy-makers with no significant knowledge of child development.

Reflection

Even experienced professionals are likely to experience some qualms when considering how to defend child-centred, play-based learning, even if it does not generate the 'correct' mechanical responses to fixed assessment measures that more structured practice may produce in very young children. One way to deal with this is to evoke the principles of the pioneers you read about in chapter 1. You will also find good practice examples in both the Scottish and Welsh Early

Years Frameworks, and in some of the practice advice websites that draw from the EYFS, for example Development Matters (see the recommended reading list).

Early years practitioners must remain firm in their core understanding that an emotionally secure, reflective, independent learner is not quickly produced within the process of development and learning. We can look for inspiration to the Scandinavian countries and their measured 'educare' approach to early years education for support in this respect, particularly with regard to the excellent outcomes their children achieve in the later years of development (see chapter 10).

Developmentally appropriate practice

We have been discussing 'developmentally appropriate practice' all through this chapter, but as we come to the end we would just like you to take a moment to focus upon this as a discrete concept. It may seem obvious that one would not expect to teach and care for 16-year-olds in the same way as one would teach and care for six-year-olds. However, development is so rapid over the first five years it can be difficult to keep up with ongoing changes, sometimes over a period of weeks rather than months and years.

The American National Association for the Education of Young Children proposes that developmentally appropriate practice can be achieved if practitioners focus on the following aspects:

1 What is known about child development and learning – referring to knowledge of age-related characteristics that permits general predictions about what experiences are likely to best promote children's learning and development.
2 What is known about each child as an individual – referring to what practitioners learn about each child that has implications for how best to adapt and be responsive to that individual variation.
3 What is known about the social and cultural contexts in which children live – referring to the values, expectations, and behavioral and linguistic conventions that shape children's lives at home and in their communities that practitioners must strive to understand in order to ensure that learning experiences in the programme or school are meaningful, relevant, and respectful for each child and family.

(National Association for the Education of Young Children, 2009, pp. 9–10)

You will see a lot here that you can relate to the theories above, particularly Bronfenbrenner, Piaget and Vygotsky. However, it is easy to be lulled into a false sense of security in collective settings, in the sense that just because you have a comprehensive approach to continuous provision, you must be engaging in developmentally appropriate practice. This was at the heart of a debate that raged for over 20 years in primary education, as a response to the Plowden report (Department of Education and Science, 1967). Eventually, it was suggested that some teachers had misunderstood Piagetian theory and its representation in the Plowden report to the extent they had the idea that children could be almost entirely left alone to structure their own learning within an environment of developmentally appropriate resources (e.g. Gillard, 2004).

Leading developmentally appropriate practice within a collective care and education environment is by contrast a much more difficult prospect than 'teaching from the front'. The adult has to educate the child from the basis of the child's own agenda, being fully aware of the zones of proximal development of all the children under their care, and carefully working within these to scaffold learning, which requires much 'decentring' from the adult position in order to engage in authentic sustained shared thinking with each individual child.

Case study: Zac's trains

Three-year-old Zac is clearly deeply involved in solitary play with a train set, to the extent that a practitioner carrying out a Leuven-based observation might score his attention level at five. A volunteer parent–helper, Clive, asks him what he is doing, and he responds that the train track 'has broken so the trains can't go any further'. Clive sits down next to him and says 'well then, you need to put in a signal'. Zac does not respond, so Clive continues with a barrage of questions to find out what Zac knows about signals ('What does red mean? What does green mean? ...'). Zac does not reply; then as the adult questioning continues, he puts the train down and wanders off to the painting table.

Reflection

Olusoga (2014, p. 47) shares her experience of a classroom practitioner who fired questions at children 'one after another, with virtually no gap in between ... the children ... tried to deal with what increasingly resembled an interrogation! Within minutes some of the group began to drift off ... One of the children who had left the activity came up to me and said 'my head hurts, miss'.

Think back to Anastasia's pink teddy above, and then consider how Clive might have more sensitively interacted with Zac to find out why he proposes the track is broken, and what he thinks should be done about it. Again, this is a matter of sustained shared thinking, and extending the child's learning by following his/her train of thought rather than relentlessly imposing your own, which may introduce so many new ideas that they completely overwhelm the child.

Coping with transitions

Children undergo a range of transitions in their first five years, some more than others. While some may be a feature of simply 'growing up' (e.g. from nursery to school), others may be unplanned and less easy to control (e.g. from living with mother and father to living with mother and grandmother if parents separate). It is the role of the Key Person to help children cope with transitions in their lives and to work through these with the least amount of upset possible.

Allingham (2011) suggests that adults need to promote the following aspects:

- Positive attitudes
- Diversity and difference
- Safety
- Valuing individuals
- Listening

- Respect
- Cultural identity
- Physical and emotional well-being
- Building relationships
- Confidence
- Feeling safe to take risks
- Positive sense of self and others
- Secure relationships
- Autonomy
- Independence
- Positively affirming environments.

Reflection

Think about how you felt when you made a recent transition in your life – for example, moving house, moving to a new job or starting your current training programme. Apply the above bullet points to this, reflecting in your journal what may have gone well and what may not have gone quite so well. Once you have undertaken such a process for yourself, you should find it easier to apply to the children with whom you work. It is important to have this level of insight, particularly when working with key children.

Conclusion

What are the main EYFS principles, and how do they relate to mainstream developmental theory and research?

Summaries of the EYFS principles and the mainstream developmental theories/research are detailed above, and we hope you will view this chapter as a key source of reference as you move through the following chapters, returning to its pages where authors raise related points. You are also directed to the DfE website, where you will find regular updates on the EYFS. You should also find that the child development content of your training programme/ degree will give you a range of opportunities to relate theory and research to the EYFS and your day-to-day practice. If you want to supplement your reading, you will find some ideas for recommended texts and websites at the end of this chapter.

What are the main theoretical perspectives that describe how children develop and learn, particularly between birth and their sixth birthday?

While it was impossible to cover all theoretical perspectives that might be useful in this respect, this chapter has been designed to get you off to a good start, by introducing central theories and theorists in the areas of emotional, cognitive, social, language and biological development, and theories of individual difference underpinned by temperament. We hope that you will use the directions to Recommended reading below to increase your knowledge in these areas, and engage in discussions with your fellow students and colleagues relating

Pearson Education Ltd/Jules Selmes

to the more controversial aspects of each area of theory. The more widely you read, the more confident you will become in such debates. You should also become a regular reader of at least one of the journals listed below, so you can keep up with theoretical, policy and practice developments in your chosen professional field. Leaders in any field must be, by definition, independent learners.

How can we recognise and meet the needs of individuals?

You have been introduced to the basic process of child observation above, and an example method of analysis. You can extend your knowledge of observation with the texts in the recommended reading below, and as we have said above, the way to build your skills in this area is by practice and feedback. In observation, the early years practitioner becomes a detective, seeking clues to the child's current modes of thinking and levels of well-being. It is a hugely important process, as young children often lack the language skills and/or depth of self-reflection to tell us what they know and how they feel; as such they rely on the sensitivity of practitioners to intuit their needs, both in terms of the next steps in their learning and in terms of care that might be needed to deal with social and emotional issues arising, which may relate to routine developmental issues, or to specific issues arising in the home or setting environment.

What influences and experiences in the setting and beyond can impact on children's well-being, development, learning and behaviour, and how can we connect these to the theoretical perspectives introduced in the earlier section?

You should now be beginning to make such connections, for example:

- Attachment theory with the Key Person system
- Zone of Proximal Development, scaffolding and contingency with sustained shared thinking
- Biological theory relating to the initial calibration of the arousal mechanisms within the infant brain with calm, flexible routines within childcare and education settings.

The wide range of concepts introduced within this chapter should serve as a platform from which to access the following chapters within this book, so please feel free to return to this base as many times as you wish to reflect upon the later ideas with which you are presented. You have now launched your journey towards becoming an expert and leader in child development, and hence the hub around which the practice of a childcare and education setting will revolve.

Recommended reading

Bee, H. and Boyd, D. (2013) *The Developing Child*. Harlow: Pearson.

Bruce. T., Louis, S. and McCall, G. (2014) *Observing Young Children*. London: Sage.

Doherty, J. and Hughes, M. (2009) *Child Development: Theory and practice*. Harlow: Longman.

Gerhardt, S. (2014) *Why Love Matters: How affection shapes a baby's brain* (2nd Edn). Abingdon: Routledge.

Lindon, J. (2012) *Understanding Child Development: Linking theory and practice* (3rd Edn). London: Hodder Arnold.

Nutbrown, C. (2011) *Threads of Thinking: Young children learning and the role of early education* (4th Edn). London: Sage.

Palaiologou, I. (2012) *Child Observation for the Early Years* (2nd Edn). London: Learning Matters.

Sharma, A. and Cockerill, H. (2014) *Mary Sheridan's From Birth to Five Years*. Abingdon, Routledge.

Smith, P.K., Cowie, H. and Blades, M. (2011) *Understanding Children's Development* (5th Edn). Oxford: Blackwell.

Whitebread, D. (Ed.) (2008) *Teaching and Learning in the Early Years*. Abingdon: Routledge.

Some useful websites

Development Matters: www.foundationyears.org.uk/files/2012/03/Development-Matters-FINAL-PRINT-AMENDED.pdf

HighScope Approaches to Learning: www.highscope.org/Content.asp?ContentId=719

Reggio Children: www.reggiochildren.it/?lang=en
Suzanne Zeedyk's Science of Human Connection: http://suzannezeedyk.com
The Circle of Security International: http://circleofsecurity.net
The Open University: www.open.edu/openlearn (follow the link to 'Childhood and Youth').

Journals

Child Development
Children Now
Early Years – an International Journal of Research and Development
Early Years Educator
Educational Researcher
Nursery World
Psychological Review

References

Ainsworth, M.D.S. and Bell, S.M. (1970) Attachment, exploration, and separation: illustrated by the behavior of one-year-olds in a strange situation. *Child Development*. 41, 49–67.

Allingham, S. (2011) *Transitions in the Early Years*. London: MA Education.

Bateson, M.C. (1975) Mother–infant exchanges: the epigenesis of conversational interaction, in D. Aaronson and R.W. Rieber (Eds) *Developmental Psycholinguistics and Communication Disorders: Annals of the New York Academy of Sciences, Volume 263*. New York: New York Academy of Sciences.

Bowlby, J. (1969) *Attachment and Loss: Volume I. Attachment*. New York: Basic Books.

Bronfenbrenner, U. (1979) *The Ecology of Human Development: Experiments by nature and design*. Cambridge, MA: Harvard University Press.

Buss, A. and Plomin, R. (1984) *Temperament and Early Developing Personality Traits*. Hillside, NJ: Lawrence Erlbaum.

Chess, S. and Thomas, A. (1984) *Origins and Evolution of Behaviour Disorders*. New York: Brunner Mazel.

DCSF (2010) *The Common Core of Skills and Knowledge for the Children's Workforce*. Leeds: CWDC. Retrieved from: http://webarchive.nationalarchives.gov.uk/20120119192332/http:/cwdcouncil.org.uk/assets/0000/9297/CWDC_CommonCore7.pdf 11th June 2015.

DfE (2014) *The Early Years Foundation Stage*. Retrieved from: www.gov.uk/government/uploads/system/uploads/attachment_data/file/335504/EYFS_framework_from_1_September_2014__with_clarification_note.pdf 11th June 2015.

Department of Education and Science (1967) *Children and their Schools*. Retrieved from: www.educationengland.org.uk/documents/plowden/plowden1967-1.html 7th December 2015.

Dockrell, J. and Messer, D. (1999) *Children's Language and Communication Difficulties: Understanding, identification and intervention*. London: Continuum.

Dolby, R. (2007) *The Circle of Security*. Retrieved from: http://apollo.hutchins.tas.edu.au/community/asc/Resources%20for%20Parents/Promoting%20Positive%20Behaviour/The%20Circle%20of%20Security%20-%20building%20relationships%20with%20children.pdf 10th June 2015.

Donaldson, M. (1978) *Children's Minds*. London: Fontana.

Dougherty, D. (1999) *How to Talk to Your Baby*. New York: Perigree.

Dunn, J. and Kendrick, C. (1982) *Siblings: Love, envy and understanding*. London: Grant McIntyre Ltd.

Eisenstadt, N. (2011) *Providing a Sure Start: How government discovered early childhood*. London: Policy Press.

Eysenck, H. (1981) *A Model for Personality*. Berlin: Springer Verlag.

Gillard, D. (2004) *The Plowden Report*. Retrieved from: www.infed.org/schooling/plowden_report.htm

Gross, R. (1996) *Psychology: The science of mind and behaviour*. London: Hodder Arnold.

Hill, E. (1980) *Where's Spot?* London: Heinemann Young Books.

Howe, D. (2011) *Attachment across the Life Course*. London: Palgrave Macmillan.

Kagan, J. (1988) Temperamental contributions to social behaviour. *American Psychologist*. 44, 668–74.

Laevers, H. (2005) *Sics (Ziko)*. Leuven: Research Centre for Experiential Education. Retrieved from: www.kindengezin.be/img/sics-ziko-manual.pdf 11th June 2015.

National Association for the Education of Young Children (2009) *Developmentally Appropriate Practice in Early Childhood Programs Serving Children from Birth through Age 8*. Retrieved from: www.naeyc. org/fileposihais/psdap.pdf 5th April 2012.

National Head Start Association (US) (2015) *About the National Head Start Association*. Retrieved from: www.nhsa.org/about-us/mission-vision-history 3rd May 2015.

Oates, J. and Grayson, A. (2004) *Cognitive and Language Development in Children*. Oxford: Blackwell.

Olusoga, Y. (2014) 'We don't play like that here': social, cultural and gender perspectives on play, in A. Brock, P. Jarvis and Y. Olusoga (Eds) *Perspectives on Play*, pp. 39–58. Abingdon: Routledge.

Piaget, J. and Inhelder, B. (1969) *The Psychology of the Child*. New York: Basic Books.

Robertson, J. and Bowlby, J. (1952) Responses of young children to separation from their mothers. *Courrier of the International Children's Centre, Paris*. II, 131–40.

Rymer, R. (1994) *Genie: A scientific tragedy*. London: HarperPerennial.

Schaffer, H.R. and Emerson, P.F. (1964) The development of social attachments in infancy. *Monographs of the Society for Research in Child Development*. 29 (Serial No. 94).

Sharma, A. and Cockerill, H. (2014) *Mary Sheridan's From Birth to Five Years*. Abingdon: Routledge.

Sims, M., Guilfoyle, A. and Parry, T. (2006) Child care for infants and toddlers: where in the world are we going? The First Years – Nga Tau Tuatahi. *New Zealand Journal of Infant and Toddler Education*. 8(1), 12–19.

Thomas, A. and Chess, S. (1977) *Temperament and Development*. New York: Brunner Mazel.

Thomas, K. (1990) Dimensions of personality, in I. Roth (Ed.) *Introduction to Psychology*, pp. 373–416. Hove: Lawrence Erlbaum.

UNICEF (2007) *An Overview of Child Well-being in Rich Countries*. Florence: UNICEF. Retrieved from: www.unicef.org/media/files/ChildPovertyReport.pdf 10th June 2015.

UNICEF (2013) *Child Well-being in Rich Countries: A comparative overview*. Florence: UNICEF. Retrieved from: www.unicef-irc.org/publications/pdf/rc11_eng.pdf 10th June 2015.

Vygotsky, L. (1978) *Mind in Society*. Cambridge, MA: Harvard University Press.

Winnicott, D.W. (1951) Transitional objects and transitional phenomena: a study of the first not-me possession. *International Journal of Psychoanalysis*. 34, 89–97.

Wood, D.J. and Middleton, D.J. (1975) A study of assisted problem solving. *British Journal of Psychology*. 66, 181–91.

Wood, D., Bruner, J. and Ross, G. (1976) The role of tutoring in problem solving. *Journal of Child Psychology and Psychiatry*. 17, 89–100.

3 Safeguarding, child protection and children in need in the early years

Sue Elmer

CHAPTER OVERVIEW

This chapter will help Early Years Graduate Practitioners (EYGPs) and Early Years Teachers (EYTs) to develop and reflect upon practice and leadership skills in safeguarding, and promoting the welfare of children at risk or in need. It will consider the practice and leadership skills necessary to promote children's safety, protection and well-being, and is based on the English legal and policy framework, particularly The Children Act 1989 (CA) Sections 17 and 47.

CA 1989 Section 47 sets out in detail what local authorities and the courts should do to protect the welfare of children. It charges local authorities with the 'duty to investigate' if they have reasonable cause to suspect that a child is 'likely to suffer significant harm' (Legislation.gov.uk, 1989, online).

CA 1989 Section 17 proposes that a child shall be taken to be in need if s/he is unlikely to achieve or maintain, or to have the opportunity of achieving or maintaining, a reasonable standard of health or development without the provision for him/her of services by a local authority, or if his/her health or development is likely to be significantly impaired, or further impaired, without the provision for him/her of such services or if s/he is disabled (Legislation.gov.uk, 1989).

The chapter will particularly reflect on Standards 12, 13 and 14 of the National Standards for Under 8s Daycare and Child Minding and also on *Working Together to Safeguard Children* (HM Government, 2015). The United Nations Convention on the Rights of the Child, Article 3: The Best Interests of the Child will also be considered (United Nations, 2015). The chapter explores differences between a child at risk of harm (CA Section 47) and a child in need (CA Section 17), and how EYGPs and EYTs can both assist and lead integrated working with other professionals, who may become involved, to ensure a child-centred response to concerns.

The text will address the following key questions:

✔ What are the legal requirements and guidance on safeguarding and promoting the welfare of children, and where can I find help and advice on these?
✔ How do I recognise children who are at risk of significant harm?
✔ How do I ensure my colleagues communicate their child protection concerns effectively and ensure cooperation from parents and carers, colleagues in my setting, and professionals in other agencies?
✔ If a child in my setting is a child in need, what should I consider in acting as a lead practitioner or Key Person in my setting?
✔ If I have to lead in my setting with respect to safeguarding, or a child in need, how should I go about it, in terms of policies and procedures, in particular the development and implementation of a safeguarding policy?
✔ How do I establish a safe environment and instil practices that promote children's safety and well-being on an everyday basis?

Introduction: What are the legal requirements and guidance on safeguarding and promoting the welfare of children, and where can I find help and advice on these?

Legal frameworks and policy guidance

Early years workers have to comply with local safeguarding procedures. Given the role of EYGPs and EYTs in leading practice, they must apply considerations of child safety and protection to colleagues, stakeholders and visitors (Reid and Burton, 2013). Alongside being aware of the basic contents of the Children Acts 1989, 2004 and 2014, and the Childcare Act 2006, which are outlined in chapter 4, EYGPs and EYTs also need to be aware of the legal requirements introduced in the Protection of Children Act 1999 (Legislation.gov.uk, 1989) and the guidance provided by *Working Together to Safeguard Children* (HM Government, 2015). These outline appropriate professional safeguarding policies for childcare and education settings. Comprehensive information on all legislation that is currently relevant can be viewed by using the search facility on www.legislation.gov.uk

Case study: the National Standards for Daycare (2012)

In 2003 the DfES published a set of National Standards for Daycare. These standards are still valid, and concepts within them have informed the past and current iterations of the Early Years Foundation Stage (DfE, 2014). Standards 12, 13 and 14 are reflected on in a case study below as they are key to child protection and safeguarding in early years settings and underpin current practice.

The National Standards for Daycare (DfES, 2003) are as follows:

Standard 1 - Suitable Person: Adults providing daycare, looking after children or having unsupervised access to them should be suitable to do so.

Standard 2 - Organisation: The setting meets required adult:child ratios, ensures that training and qualifications requirements are met and organises space and resources to meet the children's needs effectively.

Standard 3 - Care, Learning and Play: The setting meets children's individual needs and promotes their welfare. Activities and play opportunities are planned and provided to develop children's emotional, physical, social and intellectual capabilities.

Standard 4 - Physical Environment: The premises are safe, secure and suitable for their purpose. They provide adequate space in an appropriate location, are welcoming to children and offer access to the necessary facilities for a range of activities which promote their development.

Standard 5 - Equipment: Furniture, equipment and toys are provided which are appropriate for their purpose and help to create an accessible and stimulating environment. They are of suitable design and condition, well maintained and conform to safety standards.

Standard 6 - Safety: The setting takes positive steps to promote safety within their premises and on outings, and ensures proper precautions are taken to prevent accidents.

Standard 7 - Health: The setting promotes the good health of children and takes positive steps to prevent the spread of infection, and appropriate measures when they are ill.

Standard 8 - Food and Drink: Children are provided with regular drinks and food in adequate quantities for their needs. Food and drink is properly prepared, nutritious and complies with dietary and religious requirements.

Standard 9 - Equal Opportunities: The setting and its staff actively promote equality of opportunity and anti-discriminatory practice for all children.

Standard 10 - Special Needs (including special education needs and disabilities): The setting staff are aware that some children may have special needs and are proactive in ensuring that appropriate action can be taken when such a child is identified or admitted to the provision. Steps are taken to promote the welfare and development of the child within the setting in partnership with the parents and other relevant parties.

Standard 11 - Behaviour: Adults caring for children in the provision are able to manage a wide range of children's behaviour in a way which promotes their welfare and development.

Standard 12 - Working in Partnership with Parents and Carers: The setting and its staff work in partnership with parents to meet the needs of the children, both individually and as a group. Information is shared.

Standard 13 - Child Protection: The setting complies with local child protection procedures approved by the Area Child Protection Committee (now Safeguarding Boards) and ensures that all adults working and looking after children in the provision are able to put the procedures into practice.

Standard 14 - Documentation: Records, policies and procedures which are required for the efficient and safe management of the provision and to promote the welfare, care and learning of children are maintained. Records about individual children are shared with the child's parent.

Reflection

It would be helpful for readers with extensive work experience to reflect on your own responses to the changes in child protection policies and procedures that the early years workforce has experienced during your working life, particularly safeguarding training and any Early Help Assessment/Common Assessment Framework training you have attended. For less experienced readers, the Recommended reading at the end of this chapter and chapter 8, added to guidance from and discussion with more experienced practitioners either within your workplace or in other settings, can be beneficial.

Case study: the Common Assessment Framework and the Early Help Assessment

The idea of a Common Assessment Framework or CAF was introduced in England and Wales by the New Labour Government in 2004. At that time the intention was that CAF documents would be the same across the whole nation, that they would be used by all professionals working with children and families, and that information would be electronically shared across Local Safeguarding Boards. The national electronic sharing proved logistically difficult and was not enacted; however, all Local Safeguarding Boards in England now use their own version of a CAF within their local areas. For further information on this in your local area, a Google search for the Common Assessment Framework should bring up the relevant information. Here is a comprehensive example from Cornwall:

http://cornwall.childrensservicedirectory.org.uk/kb5/cornwall/fsd/site.page?id=FWDzyOLUcMw

Many Local Safeguarding Board areas are now moving towards a more streamlined approach to the CAF, called an Early Help Assessment, or EHA. For example, Northumbria provide a comprehensive advice website for practitioners in their area on the topic of the EHA (Figure 3.1).

www.northumberland.gov.uk/default.aspx?page=16984

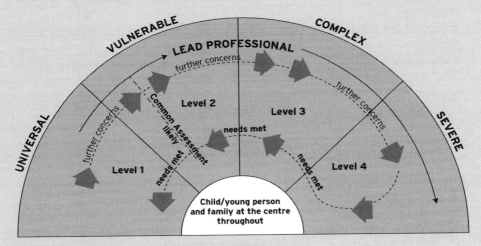

Figure 3.1 The Common Assessment Framework process
Source: www.nelincs.gov.uk

Reflection

Have you ever filled in a CAF or an EHA? If not, download one of the Local Safeguarding Boards' CAF or EHA documents (preferably the one used by the Local Safeguarding Board (LSB) in your area) and fill it in using an example of a 'child in need' with whom you have previously worked.

The introduction of the Early Years Foundation Stage (EYFS) in September 2008 prompted a review of all setting policies related to health, safety and child welfare to ensure that they were compliant with the most recent guidelines. The updated EYFS (DfE, 2014) should have prompted a further review; however, in settings with high standards of practice, reviews of policies and procedures are in any case carried out at least yearly, and also following incidents to evaluate their effectiveness. Dates of completed policy reviews and planned future reviews should be noted in the policy itself. These documents give us clear guidance on minimum acceptable standards for welfare and protection, including detail on staffing and suitable persons, following the Bichard Report (HMSO, 2004). The case of Vanessa George, a childcare worker who exploited her position to indecently assault very young children, and to take and subsequently distribute photographs of these incidents on her mobile phone (Savill and Bunyan, 2009), has brought practitioner conduct into sharp relief. For example, the EYFS (DfE, 2014, online) states: 'The safeguarding policy and procedures must include an explanation of the action to be taken in the event of an allegation being made against a member of staff, and covers the use of mobile phones and cameras in the setting'. This serves to remind leaders of practice that they must extend safeguarding vigilance with respect to the conduct of individuals working within the setting, even if they have presented with clear enhanced Disclosure and Barring Service (DBS) criminal record checks (for further guidance see: www.gov.uk/disclosure-barring-service-check/overview).

Legislation, guidance and related policies will go some way towards safeguarding children. The key legislation in protecting children from abuse or neglect is the Children Act 1989 (see the discussion of CA Sections 47 and 17 above).

The subsequent Children Act 2004 introduced the requirement that all agencies must work together to protect children. This enacted the introduction of local Children Safeguarding Boards (see for example: www.leedslscb.org.uk). Safeguarding Boards have the role of monitoring all safeguarding activities in each local authority area.

The Munro Review (DfE, 2011) examined the effectiveness of safeguarding, emphasising the monitoring role that local Safeguarding Children Boards play. Safeguarding guidance was consequently updated for early years and other professionals in the 2015 policy document *Working Together to Safeguard Children*. This refers to significant harm as:

> The threshold that justifies compulsory intervention in family life in the best interests of children, and gives Local Authorities a duty to make enquiries to decide whether they should take action to safeguard or promote the welfare of a child who is suffering or likely to suffer significant harm.
>
> (HM Government, 2015, p. 6)

Under this guidance early years providers have specific responsibilities as follows:

> Early years providers have a duty under Section 40 of the Childcare Act 2006 to comply with the welfare requirements of the Early Years Foundation Stage. Early years providers should ensure that:

- staff complete safeguarding training that enables them to recognise signs of potential abuse and neglect; and
- they have a practitioner who is designated to take lead responsibility for safeguarding children within each early years setting and who should liaise with local statutory children's services agencies as appropriate. This lead should also complete child protection training.

(HM Government, 2015, p. 56)

Social workers have a duty to investigate child protection concerns where these are raised; however, it is often the case that early years practitioners are the first to identify such concerns, because babies and toddlers are at particularly high risk of abuse and neglect. The World Health Organization (WHO) reports that:

> The highest rates of fatal child abuse are found among children aged 0-4 years. The most common cause of death is head injury, followed by abdominal injuries and intentional suffocation.

(World Health Organization, 2002, online)

As the EYGP/EYT in the setting you will need to consider:

- How to support and protect children who may be experiencing neglect, physical, sexual or emotional abuse and, in some cases, a combination of these.
- How to develop and review a child protection policy for the setting, and how you will ensure that staff understand and comply with this, particularly in terms of recording and reporting concerns that a child may be at risk, within the staff team and involving other agencies where this is necessary.
- How to designate a safeguarding/child protection lead for your setting who can effectively liaise with parents, staff and other agencies where specific concerns are identified.

People who work with children and young people across the children's workforce in England have responsibilities to safeguard and promote their welfare. This is an important responsibility and requires careful attention. It means being able to recognise when a child or young person is not achieving their developmental milestones or when their physical or mental health is impaired. It means recognising when a child is displaying risky or harmful behaviour, or is being neglected or abused. It also means being able to identify appropriate sources of help for them and their families (CAHMS Review, 2008). Sometimes more than one risk factor may be affecting a child or young person and it may be necessary to work with others to address them.

Child protection involves making difficult judgements, as *The Munro Review* argues:

> There are particular challenges involved in assessing whether children are suffering, or are likely to suffer, significant harm. Statutory guidance tells those working with

families to refer such children to social care, but making this decision is not straightforward.

(DfE, 2011, p. 79)

You will need to reflect on these points yourself, as an EYGP/EYT and in partnership with the staff team in your setting.

The ideal characteristics of happy families are as follows:

- Parents are strongly bonded to each other, and communicate their feelings openly and honestly.
- They have and express a high level of warmth towards each other.
- They use criticism sparingly and constructively.
- They set clear boundaries and avoid the three-step dance (parent instructs, child objects, parent relents).
- Children feel strongly bonded and can be intimate with parents, siblings, extended family and peers.
- All members can communicate outwardly with their own friends and have strong support.

While not all families will fit all these criteria all of the time, where none of these characteristics apply, risk inevitably arises. The issue for all who work with children is to be aware when the family environment is a place in which children are at risk of significant harm (CA Section 47).

How do I recognise children who are at risk of significant harm?

Case study: Adam and his family

Adam is three years old and the middle child of three siblings, all under five years. He lives with his mother, Joan, aged 24 years and her new partner, Steven, aged 35 years. Joan and the children recently moved to the area to live with Steven, shortly after they met online.

Steven works as a security guard and tends to be controlling towards Joan and the children.

Adam has recently started attending a day nursery, and so far he appears to have settled well. He is rather quiet but can socialise with other children. Steven brings Adam to the early years centre for his morning session.

Rachel, Adam's Key Worker, notices that Adam does not seem to be using his left arm when playing in the sand tray. She also notices that Adam seems pale and tired. Rachel asks Adam if he is OK, he tells Rachel that his arm is hurting and he has a headache. When they look at Adam's arm together, Rachel notices bruising to his arm in the shape of fingers and a thumb print ('petechial' bruising) and the pattern of bruises appears to her to be a non-accidental injury. She cannot see bruises under Adam's hairline but he is complaining that his head hurts to the touch. When Rachel asks Adam what happened, Adam tells her that Steven was cross because he wasn't dressed in time and that 'he picked me up by my arm and squeezed it'. Rachel is aware that Joan has recently started a new job and may be unaware of this event. However,

Rachel is not making assumptions about this. She is the designated child protection lead for the centre and needs to consider what actions she should take, in consideration of the advice in *Working Together to Safeguard Children* (HM Government, 2015).

Rachel has previously attended multi-agency safeguarding training and is aware of the need to follow the early years centre safeguarding policy and procedures. She will need to record what she observed, including Adam's explanation, and report her concerns effectively to other agencies responsible for safeguarding children; she will also need to reflect on whether she or other members of staff have seen and recorded any other bruises or other injuries Adam has had, or any other concerns that have been recorded in the period he has attended the centre.

It is important that Adam is not repeatedly asked to describe what happened by professionals who come into contact with him. In particular Adam needs to feel that he is not in trouble and needs to be reassured on this point.

Adam's mother needs to be informed about these concerns and encouraged to express her views. She may not be aware of Adam's injury and may also need to be supported to work with Rachel and other professionals responsible for ensuring Adam's safety and well-being and that of his siblings. All three siblings will need to be assessed. To ensure Rachel maintains an effective working relationship with Joan, she will need to work respectfully and sensitively with her, whilst at the same time ensuring that she fully understands what Joan knows about Adam's injury.

Rachel will need to listen carefully to any explanation she is given and to record this, remaining aware that parents who cause or are complicit in non-accidental injuries to their children tend to give inconsistent accounts about how these injuries have happened.

Rachel will need to meet with the setting manager and record a joint decision to contact the duty social work team responsible for child protection investigations. It is good practice to speak directly to parents to let them know that the setting has concerns and that a decision has been made to refer their child to a social work team, explaining the decision and being clear about the concerns. This can be a difficult conversation but one in which parents can be helped to focus on the needs of their child (Horwath, 2009; Ferguson, 2011).

Rachel will need to phone the duty team and also email the team on the same day, to ensure the concern is recorded in writing. In her email, Rachel will need to be explicit about the bruising she has seen, the other observations she and possibly others have made, and the explanation given by Adam together with any explanation given by his mother. Rachel will also need to be explicit about any previous concerns she or other staff may have had.

The social worker will want to know whether this is the first bruising Adam has had or whether there have been other less serious injuries which appeared concerning at the time, and where explanations were given which reassured the setting that Adam was not at risk of significant harm.

The social worker will want to speak to Adam's mother and is likely to make arrangements to have Adam examined by a specialist medical practitioner who can diagnose non-accidental injury. After speaking to Adam's mother and gaining her permission to see his personal file, the social worker may also want to see any records the setting has of previous concerns and explanations given. The social worker is also likely to contact other professionals who may have current or previous involvement with Adam and his siblings to establish a chronology of events. S/he will also want to know whether the centre has any specific knowledge of Adam's siblings.

On completing an initial assessment, the social worker will co-ordinate a multi-agency strategy meeting to agree what actions need to be taken. It is essential that parents are actively involved in such meetings (DfES, 2003, National Standards for Daycare S12; Ferguson, 2011; Adams, 2012). The setting staff will have an important role in this process and it is good practice for the safeguarding lead/setting manager to keep the staff fully informed of agreed actions, particularly where these involve subsequent observation and monitoring of children who may be at further risk of significant harm.

Following the strategy meeting the social worker will be in a position to establish whether there is evidence that Adam and his siblings may be at risk of significant harm. If this is the case, the social worker and her/his manager will make the decision to convene an initial child protection conference, and the multi-agency conference may conclude that an outline child protection plan is necessary to protect the children from further risk of significant harm. It is the role of the social worker to:

> Convene, attend and present information about the reason for the conference, their understanding of the child's needs, parental capacity and family and environmental context and evidence of how the child has been abused or neglected and its impact on their health and development.
>
> (HM Government, 2015, p. 43)

Reflection

If you were in Rachel's position, consider how you would expect the setting staff to respond and what training they might need to ensure that, as a staff team, they are all aware of the safeguarding policy for the setting and of subsequent actions they would need to take (DfES, 2003, National Standards for Daycare S13).

In cases such as Adam's, it is also worth considering any potential exposure to domestic abuse (Elmer, 2013). The Serious Case Review concerning Daniel Pelka's death noted that:

> Domestic abuse was clearly a major pattern of this family's lifestyle and occurred in relation to three consecutive different male partners … There were two key components to an effective professional response to the domestic abuse lifestyle; firstly to acknowledge that this was a pattern of family life rather than an unconnected set of isolated events, and the second was to recognise and respond to the child protection needs of the children who were living within such a violent and chaotic household.
>
> (Coventry Local Safeguarding Children Board, 2014, pp. 37–8)

Professionals need to follow the safeguarding procedures agreed by all agencies represented at the local Safeguarding Children Board. The role of referral and multi-agency working is also crucially important within safeguarding procedures (Cheminais, 2009; Beckett, 2010; Adams, 2012). It is important to note that unless you are employed within a local authority or NSPCC team with specific responsibility to deal with child protection issues, you will not be called upon to *diagnose* safeguarding issues relating to individual children, but to *communicate* any concerns to the agencies responsible for investigating them, under Section 47 of the Children Act 1989.

Good practice skills were described in Lord Laming's review as 'doing the basics well' (Laming, 2009, p. 39). Again for the EYGP/EYT, this aspect of practice is also about reflecting on your own actions and your role in leading best practice in others (Action for Children, 2013; Evangelou *et al.*, 2014).

Safeguarding procedures are based on the legal and policy framework. The development of these is also influenced by the United Nations Convention on the Rights of the Child (UNCRC), in particular 'Article 3: best interests of the child':

> The best interests of children must be the primary concern in making decisions that may affect them. All adults should do what is best for children. When adults make decisions, they should think about how their decisions will affect children. This particularly applies to budget, policy and law makers.
>
> (United Nations, 2015, online)

How do I ensure my colleagues communicate their child protection concerns effectively and ensure cooperation from parents and carers, and colleagues in my setting and professionals in other agencies?

It is important to be able to make a distinction between a child in need and a child at risk of significant harm. All of the professionals involved and hopefully a child's parents will collaborate to assess her/his needs on the basis of the principles and parameters of a good assessment outlined in *Working Together to Safeguard Children* (HM Government, 2015).

High-quality assessments:

- are child centred. Where there is a conflict of interest, decisions should be made in the child's best interests;
- are rooted in child development and informed by evidence;
- are focused on action and outcomes for children;
- are holistic in approach, addressing the child's needs within their family and wider community;
- ensure equality of opportunity;
- involve children and families;
- build on strengths as well as identifying difficulties;
- are integrated in approach;
- are a continuing process not an event;
- lead to action, including the provision and review of services.
- are transparent and open to challenge.

(HM Government, 2015, p. 21)

These principles of good assessment practice may seem self-evident and part of your everyday good practice; however, successive serious case reviews have found that these are inconsistently applied. For example, the recent serious case review into the death of

Peter Connelly found that each injury was treated as a first event and not seen by the professionals trying to work with his family as a series of related and increasingly harmful events, which posed a significant level of risk of serious harm to Peter and his siblings (Haringey Local Safeguarding Board, 2009). While cases subject to serious case reviews make harrowing reading, they have all critically informed the child protection frameworks that we work with now (Batty, 2003; Brandon *et al.*, 2010). When such cases occur, they inevitably create waves of concern in the media, which ripple through the entire population and impact upon national concepts of the children's workforce. *The Munro Review* states:

> An analysis of press reporting of social work in national daily and Sunday newspapers in England between 1 July 1997 and 30 June 1998, showed that nearly two thousand articles were devoted exclusively to discussions of social work and social services. The 15 most common messages, accounting for 80 per cent of the total, were negative with regard to social work and included: 'incompetent', 'negligent', 'failed', 'ineffective', 'misguided' and 'bungling'.
>
> (DfE, 2011, p. 122)

Reflection

Think about what specific evidence you would need to identify whether a child is in need or at risk of significant harm. Write some 'prompt' questions to help you consider the evidence you might be able to gather, and what additional information you may need to consider the level of risk a child may face (DfES, 2003, National Standards for Daycare S13).

If a child in my setting is a child in need (Children Act 1989, Section 17), what do I need to consider in acting as a lead practitioner or Key Person in my setting?

Case study: instigating an Early Help Assessment

Sara, aged three years, is one of four siblings who live with their mother, Anne, and Anne's partner, Kyle, who is the father of the youngest child, a boy aged two months. Sara has an older brother and sister, both in primary school.

Sara attends a daycare setting. She has poor concentration. She is often disruptive and is having difficulty learning to play socially with other children, although her intellectual ability appears to be within the average range. Sara sometimes seems hungry on arrival at the setting, and she is sometimes dressed in clothes she has worn on successive days.

Sara's GP has known the family since they moved to her locality three years ago. She has treated Anne for post-natal depression. Anne has previously had drinking problems, and developed diabetes during her recent pregnancy. Belinda, an EYGP and Sara's Key Person, asked the family's recently qualified health visitor, Grace, to monitor the family because she was concerned for the well-being of the children *and* their mother.

At the health centre, Grace eventually 'got to grips' with her new job and realised that the new baby had missed his six-week check. She contacted Sara's mother to make an urgent appointment to see her and the new baby. She also contacted Belinda to discuss the setting's concerns about Sara.

Belinda has in the meantime discussed a referral of Sara and her siblings to children's social care with the setting manager because she has concerns about their care. She is concerned about possible neglect and this formed quite a large element of the discussions. It was agreed that Belinda would discuss an Early Help Assessment with Sara's mother. During this conversation, Sara's mother admitted that she was not coping well and that she might need help to avoid any neglect of the children, and of her own health. She also agreed that Belinda could act as lead professional to co-ordinate and chair a multi-agency meeting with a view to developing an Early Help Plan (EHP) for the family, and fully understood that there would be sharing of information with other professionals who might need to be involved.

Grace and Belinda later discussed the situation and agreed that their collective initial view was that Sara is a child in need (Children Act 1989, Section 17) and that a multi-agency Early Help Assessment was expedient. In the meantime, Belinda would continue her observations of Sara and subsequent record keeping, and both Grace and Belinda would continue working positively with Sara and her family.

Pearson Education Ltd/Jules Selmes

Reflection

An EHP will need to provide multi-agency support for each of the children and possibly Sara's mother. Consider the following questions:

- Will this need to focus on support of the baby as well as Sara?
- What about the older children? What issues might their teachers raise in a multi-agency meeting?
- How might Belinda and Grace's perspective change as a result of information shared in a multi-agency meeting?
- If you were Belinda, how would you recommend that the needs of Sara and her siblings are balanced with those of her mother and step-father?
- Do you agree that Belinda and Grace were right to call a multi-agency meeting at this point?
- What would need to happen in the meeting to effectively put together a support package for the family?

The Early Help Assessment is based on the *Framework for the Assessment of Children in Need and their Families* (Department of Health, 2000).

Early Help is based on assessment in the three domains of the child's developmental need:

- Parenting capacity
- Family factors
- Environmental factors.

In leading a subsequent 'Team Around the Family' (TAF), a leading practitioner's task would be to co-ordinate responses to the assessed needs of the children of the family, agreeing achievable goals and ensuring everyone concerned acts to meet these, including the parents/other adults in the household (Institute of Public Care, 2012).

A further consideration highlighted in *Working Together to Safeguard Children* (HM Government, 2015) in making assessments of children is that

> The Children Act 1989 promotes the view that all children and their parents should be considered as individuals and that family structures, culture, religion, ethnic origins and other characteristics should be respected.
>
> (HM Government, 2015, p. 40)

Under the heading 'multi-agency and integrated working' the *Common Core of Skills and Knowledge for the Children's Workforce* states that:

> To work successfully on a multi-agency basis you need to be clear about your role and aware of and respectful of the roles of other workers and agencies. You should actively seek and respect other people's knowledge and input to deliver the best outcomes for children and young people. These behaviours should apply across the public, private and voluntary sectors.
>
> (CWDC, 2010, p. 18)

Case study: safeguarding and observation

Effective safeguarding of children can be achieved through consistent observations, good written records and practice in articulating what is seen in the pattern of observable behaviour. Where practitioners become aware of any injuries, no matter how minor, these must be accurately recorded, including the date on which they were noticed. Observations allow practitioners to build a chronology of key events in the child's life, and ensure that they are able to see the complete picture and consequently able to contribute to an accurate assessment of risk of significant harm to the child.

As noted earlier, it is essential that observational documentation (DfES, 2013, National Standards for Daycare S14) is sufficient to support the detection of a pattern of non-accidental injuries that come to your attention, so practitioners are able to recognise that there is an ongoing pattern of abuse taking place, rather than construing each injury as separate and unconnected incidents. Many serious case reviews, such as that concerning Daniel Pelka and Peter Connolly and more recently Oliver Sargent, have identified that practitioners have missed vital opportunities to intervene to protect these children because observations made by a range of professionals were not communicated to other agencies, and the chronology that existed was not recorded or communicated effectively. Other agencies including healthcare, children's social care and the police also failed to communicate their assessment of risk effectively and failed to safeguard these children.

Those of you who have studied childcare and education on previous training programmes may already be accomplished at child observation. For those who are less experienced, chapter 2 has introduced you to the basic skills of observation required in an EYGP/EYT. However, these are principally concerned with observation for the assessment of learning (social and intellectual/cognitive), and you may therefore be less familiar with observing from the point of view of looking for indicators of risk, where you are contributing to the development of a multi-agency risk assessment.

Reflection

Make several written observations of the same child, who fits one or several criteria of a child 'in need', over a two-week period, using the Leuven scale which you met in chapter 2.

When the written observations are complete, reflect on what the overall themes are from the set of observations:

- consider how well the observed child engages with other children and the adults caring for her/him;
- consider the child's social and emotional well-being, and how it might be improved;
- consider any impacts that social and emotional issues may have on her/his learning.

If I have to lead in my setting with respect to safeguarding, or a child in need, how should I go about it, in terms of policies and procedures, in particular the development and implementation of a safeguarding policy?

Working with your colleagues, the next step in the process is to review/create your setting's policies with regard to safety, inclusion and protection. We all have a duty to the children and families that we work with to be up to date in our practice. There is so much information available to us via the internet as well as more traditional sources. Subscriptions to online information services are a simple way of getting the 'headlines' which should leave you time to read in more detail articles of specific interest to you and your setting; for example, *Nursery World*, and other publications, as well as government departments offer this service and it is free. If there are a number of you in your setting you could share out the reading and have weekly discussion groups to cascade ideas through your team (Aubrey, 2011). This would be a really good way of engaging all staff in planning and decision-making.

As an EYGP/EYT you will need to develop a critical stance in relation to the guidance provided by *Working Together to Safeguard Children* (HM Government, 2015). The legislative and policy framework continues to evolve and is regularly updated. Consequently, it is vital to remember that the safeguarding policies you develop (DfES, 2013, National Standards for Daycare S14) are working documents; they are plans for action which all colleagues should follow under specific circumstances, and they ensure a minimum quality of experience and consistency in practice. To be effective, all staff must feel ownership of the policies; they need to be consulted when policies are being written, they need to be committed to act within the policy and they need to be involved in the review. Each setting should have a plan for regular review of all policies, but should be flexible and prepared to amend policies which are no longer effective, as and when the need arises.

The cycle of policy amendment should proceed as shown in Figure 3.2.

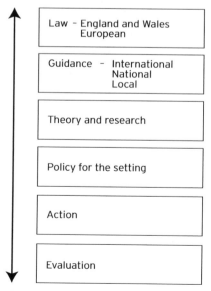

Figure 3.2 Cycle of policy amendment

Extended task: developing a setting safeguarding policy (DfES 2013, National Standards for Daycare S14)

First, make an inventory of the policies in your setting and reflect on the following:

- What policies does the setting have?
- Are there other policies that you think you should have?
- How are staff, children and families and the wider community informed about these policies and how effective is this communication?
- When were the policies last reviewed and are they up to date?
- How are staff inducted into working with these policies?
- What do the staff think about the policies, for example, do they work in practice?

Now consider your role as an EYGP/EYT in leading your setting to ensure that the safeguarding policies serve the needs of all involved with the setting and that they are carried out effectively and consistently.

Writing a policy can be a very challenging task and writing the safeguarding policy with the welfare of vulnerable children at stake can be a particular challenge. Remember that one person should never be *solely* responsible for the protection of all children, but that EYGPs, EYTs and other senior practitioners must be key members of this particular team.

The checklist below may help you to frame your thoughts.

A safeguarding policy should:

- Outline clearly what the policy is for.
- Ensure the vetting of staff required by law, and incorporate any changes to procedures that come along 'as and when'; for example in the Protection of Freedoms Act 2012 (Legislation. gov.uk, 2012).
- Confirm understanding of types of abuse and signs and symptoms of abuse or neglect.
- Give clear guidance on recording and reporting, and detail the reporting procedure and how to respond to disclosure by a child, his or her parent or other family member.
- Give clear guidance on procedures concerning contact with parents/carers where abuse is suspected.
- State who the designated person is and name a deputy.
- Give clear guidance on staff supervision.
- Give contact details for relevant local agencies such as police, Local Safeguarding Board, and social care duty team.
- Include guidance on staff conduct.
- Identify potential barriers to disclosure.
- Identify potential barriers to reporting.
- Outline 'whistleblowing' procedures.
- Outline what processes should be followed if there are allegations against a member of staff.
- State the review date of the policy.

Now that you have some ideas on what you should include, try to create a first draft of a safeguarding policy and ask other team members to review and evaluate your draft; then possibly work on a further draft together. It is vital that the policy is 'fit for purpose' and the key point here is writing a policy which is robust but is written in language that all staff can understand and commit to.

How do I establish a safe environment and instil practices that promote children's safety and well-being on an *everyday* basis?

Two key areas of practice can help you to identify how safe your practices are on an everyday basis. The first concerns information sharing. External agencies may have different policies and protocols to your early years centre. Protocols concerning information sharing throw differences into sharp relief.

A second issue is that of thresholds of risk at which referrals are made by one agency to another. For example, at what point will a Key Stage 1 leader in a primary school setting make a written referral concerning a child such as Adam's older sibling, and when and how will the setting attended by a younger sibling find out about this?

It is worth remembering that the vast majority of safeguarding activities that EYGPs and EYTs undertake on a day-to-day basis are quite mundane, and involve supporting children from troubled families in which parents lack understanding of children and childhood, rather than life-threatening abuse. However, there must always be an *awareness* that, in some cases, life-threatening abuse is a real possibility. Commenting on the case of eleven-month-old Oliver Sargent, a serious case review (in which Oliver is referred to as Child B) found that:

> 'Although there is no guarantee, there is a probability that had health professionals been clearer in recognising that there was no plausible explanation for the injuries, Child B would have been subjected to child protection procedures and consideration given to protecting Child B by removing them from the home ... Health professionals were in a position to raise concerns when Child B was observed to have bruising and occipital swelling ... The parents either gave no explanation for the bruising or the explanation was questionable. ...' Oliver died in hospital on 27 July 2012, five days after sustaining a skull fracture during an assault. His injuries were consistent with shaking. He was not previously known to social care services or police, the report said. The review noted poor quality in recording of injuries at Princess Royal Hospital and a lack of consideration of previous admission and/or injuries.
>
> (BBC News, 2015, online)

As an EYGP/EYT, you will need to approach your day-to-day practice with an up-to-date knowledge of legislation, guidelines, policy and practice, a knowledge of children gained from close working relationships with parents and carers and highly developed observation skills. These skills will put you in the best possible position to notice, observe and record changes in behaviour and demeanour which may indicate a child at risk, and/or a child/family experiencing difficulty. In carrying out your role effectively, you are in a position to produce a vital piece of the safeguarding jigsaw relating to an individual child, or support one of your colleagues to do this; remember, if this had occurred within each of the cases cited in the frame of 'child protection tragedy', the escalation of factors leading up to the ultimate outcome might have been neutralised *before* the child came to serious harm.

One thing is certain – you, like any other professional working with children and families, will need to work in partnership with colleagues both within and outside your own profession. Serious case reviews have consistently found that it is only when a number of pieces are put together through multi-agency working that a coherent picture is produced (see www.nspcc. org.uk/preventing-abuse/child-protection-system/england/serious-case-reviews). As an EYGP/EYT, you are a part of a multi-agency team which may include many different professionals, including social workers and health and education professionals. Within the role of setting lead professional, you may also act as co-ordinator in Early Help Assessments (Frost *et al.*, 2009). Your most important role is to record concerns and, when necessary, to ensure that these are expediently communicated to professionals outside the immediate setting, to ensure the safety and well-being of the child.

Conclusion

This chapter has sought to answer the following questions.

What are the legal requirements and guidance on safeguarding and promoting the welfare of children, and where can I find help and advice on these?

The complex issues of safeguarding and risk and what constitutes 'well-being' have been discussed above. If you have to cover a work-based learning module in the course of your training, it might be worth considering a project in this area of policy, which is currently high on the early years reform agenda, and a subject of discussion in many different arenas, both academic and practitioner oriented (see for example: Ferguson, 2011; Adams, 2012).

Your key resource for practice at the time of writing, if you are located in England, is *Working Together to Safeguard Children* (HM Government, 2015). For practitioners in Wales, www.childreninwales.org.uk/our-work/safeguarding should point you towards some useful resources. The National Guidance Document for Child Protection in Scotland can be found at www.gov.scot/Resource/0045/00450733.pdf, while the Safeguarding Board for Northern Ireland is at www.safeguardingni.org. Other nations will have their own approaches; if in doubt, always consult the local children's department (or equivalent) in your local area.

How do I recognise children who are at risk of significant harm?

The case example of Adam and his family is illustrative of a significant level of risk of harm a child may face in your setting. In Adam's case he looked and behaved differently on the day he suffered an injury, and his Key Worker noticed this and acted promptly to intervene and ensured that he was safeguarded. However as *The Munro Review* (DfE, 2011) points out, it can be difficult to recognise when a child is exposed to neglect or abuse; the indicators are not always as obvious as Adam's injury. Recognising indicators of risk is a matter of training and practice in observation; noticing even small changes in appearance and behaviour is important in monitoring a child who is vulnerable. Such changes need to be systematically recorded (DfES 2013, National Standards for Daycare S14) as a means of establishing a pattern of risk. Effective communication is also really important so that, as colleagues, you have a shared assessment of the level of risk to which a child may be exposed, and from this shared assessment you can agree a joint plan of action.

How do I ensure my colleagues communicate their child protection concerns effectively and ensure cooperation from parents and carers, colleagues in my setting and professionals in other agencies?

Serious case reviews into the deaths of vulnerable children highlighted that poor communication contributed to the failure to act on the part of professionals who were involved with each of them (see www.nspcc.org.uk/preventing-abuse/child-protection-system/england/serious-case-reviews). Your communications as an EYGP/EYT have to be consistently clear and effective. You also need to ensure that each of your colleagues can communicate effectively, both verbally and in writing. Perhaps most important of all is the need to articulate any significant concerns you may have when you attend the multi-agency meetings described earlier in this chapter. Your concerns need to reflect the concrete *evidence* you have of abuse or neglect and must be based on direct observations and on the records you have of any explanations given by the child and by parents or carers. The issue of vigilance concerning staff was also discussed, and again the same effective communication is essential where you have evidence that a colleague's behaviour constitutes a risk of significant harm to the children in your care.

If a child in my setting is a child in need, what do I need to consider in acting as a leading practitioner or Key Person in my setting?

In addition to reading about the legal and policy framework discussed earlier in this chapter, you should also read the case example of Sara and her family and about the role of practitioners in instigating and leading an Early Help Assessment. Again it is useful to think about how you would involve other agencies working with a child and her/his family in your setting and how you would present information to them in a manner which is clear and accessible to the child's parents and other professionals.

Reflection

To rehearse your own responses to a child in need, try to think of a similar case to Sara and her family of which you have knowledge, so you can more easily apply theory to practice.

Write a brief description of the family you have in mind for your Early Help Assessment exercise. In this you can use a charting system called a 'Genogram' which is explained at http://genograms.org

Once you have done this, make a list of key areas that you think might be important in carrying out an Early Help Assessment on this family. You will then need to discuss your analyses with fellow students or colleagues, as of course all Early Help Assessments are in reality carried out as team exercises. You could then go on to specifically consider whether the key areas you have identified accurately represent all areas that would need to be considered in a multi-agency meeting.

You will find that different practitioners, parents and other caring adults will have different viewpoints on the needs of children and families. As long as you have considered your duties under the law, and you have taken a 'common sense' approach, you will find your own way on this as your experience of leadership grows. Again, I would urge you to engage in all available simulation tasks during training/professional development in order to gain experience prior to being asked to undertake this process in earnest on being appointed to a setting as a leader or manager. In particular, take opportunities to shadow a more experienced practitioner who is attending a multi-agency meeting, where information is shared between agencies and decisions concerning either level of need or level of risk are made.

If I have to lead in my setting with respect to safeguarding, or a child in need, how should I go about it, in terms of policies and procedures, in particular the development and implementation of a safeguarding policy?

Your leadership in respect of safeguarding practice is essential to the overall effectiveness of the team you will be leading. You will need to ensure that your colleagues understand and work to the policy guidelines discussed in this chapter. If you undertake the tasks in the chapter relating to constructing a draft safeguarding policy, you will begin to see that this can be a relatively straightforward task, particularly if you involve your peers in this exercise. You can carry these processes out for the first time as an exercise rather than in earnest; again, the 'real thing' will then seem less daunting when it arises for the first time in the future – as it inevitably will for a leading practitioner within a childcare setting. You should also find chapter 4 of use in terms of reviewing the legal/policy background, and chapter 8 in terms of dealing with leadership issues. You will need to ensure that the policy you develop reflects the requirements for early years practice that are set out within your practice location. In England, at the time of writing, the key documents in this respect are *Working Together to Safeguard Children* (HM Government, 2015) and the current EYFS guidance, the document issued in 2014 (DfE, 2014). If you are reading this book some years after publication, however, as is always the case for leading practitioners in the caring professions, you will need to research further to ensure that you are *fully* up to date with policy and practice.

Recommended reading

Beckett, C. (2010) *Assessment and Intervention in Social Work*. London: Sage.

Cheminais, R. (2009) *Effective Multi-Agency Partnerships: Putting* Every Child Matters *into practice*. London: Sage.

CSIP (2008) *A Practical Guide to Integrated Working*. Available at: www.wales.nhs.uk/sitesplus/documents/829/ICN%20Practical%20Guide%20to%20Integrated%20Working.pdf

Evangelou, M., Goff, J., Hall, J., Sylva, K., Eisenstadt, N., Paget, C., Davis, S., Sammons, P., Smith, T., Tracz, R. and Parkin, T. (2014) *Evaluation of Children's Centres in England: Parenting services*. DfE Report No. DfE-RR368. London: DfE. Available at: www.gov.uk/government/publications/evaluation-of-childrens-centres-in-england-parenting-services

Horwath, J. (Ed.) (2009) *The Child's World: The comprehensive guide to assessing children in need* (2nd Edn). London: Jessica Kingsley.

Vincent, S. (2015) *Early Intervention: Supporting and strengthening families (protecting children and young people)*. London: Dunedin Academic.

Websites

Children England. *Positively Safe – a practical guide to safeguarding:* www.childrenengland.org.uk/upload/Positively%20safe%20Final.pdf

Dudley Metropolitan Borough Council. *Safeguarding and Child Protection* – contains a link to an audit tool: www.dudley.gov.uk/resident/early-years/for-providers/safeguarding-and-child-protection

Herefordshire Council. *Safeguarding for Early Years Practitioners:* www.herefordshire.gov.uk/education-and-learning/early-years-and-childcare/support-for-early-years-practitioners/safeguarding-for-early-years-practitioners

Pre-School Learning Alliance. *Safeguarding:* www.pre-school.org.uk/providers/support-and-advice/430/safeguarding

Schools Online Swindon. *Safeguarding Guidance Documents:* http://schoolsonline.swindon.gov.uk/sc/cp/Pages/safeguarding.aspx

References

Action for Children (2013) *Early Intervention: Where now for local authorities?* Retrieved from: www.actionforchildren.org.uk/media/5740124/afc_early_intervention_-_final.pdf 10th February 2015.

Adams, R. (Ed.) (2012) *Working with Children and Families*. London. Palgrave Macmillan.

Aubrey, C. (2011) *Leading and Managing in the Early Years* (2nd Edn). London: Sage.

Batty, D. (2003) *Catalogue of Cruelty*. Retrieved from: www.guardian.co.uk/uk/2001/jan/13/childprotection.society4 23rd June 2015.

BBC News (2015) *Oliver Sargent Death: Safeguarding opportunities missed*. Retrieved from: www.news.live.bbc.co.uk/news/uk-england-shropshire-32963741 22nd June 2015.

Beckett, C. (2010) *Assessment and Intervention in Social Work*. London: Sage.

Brandon, M. *et al.* (2010) *Building on the Learning from Serious Case Reviews: A two year analysis of child protection database notifications 2007-2009.* London: Department for Education. Retrieved from: www.education.gov.uk/publications/standard/publicationdetail/page1/DFE-RR040 21st February 2015.

CAMHS Review (2008) *Improving the Mental Health and Psychological Well-being of Children and Young People.* Retrieved from: http://webarchive.nationalarchives.gov.uk/20130107105354/http://www.dh.gov.uk/prod_consum_dh/groups/dh_digitalassets/@dh/@en/documents/digitalasset/dh_090398.pdf 22nd June 2015.

Cheminais, R. (2009) *Effective Multi-Agency Partnerships: Putting* Every Child Matters *into practice.* London: Sage.

Coventry Local Safeguarding Board (2014) *Serious Case Review: Daniel Pelka.* Retrieved from: www.coventrylscb.org.uk/dpelka.html 22nd June 2015.

CWDC (2010) *The Common Core of Skills and Knowledge for the Children's Workforce.* Retrieved from: http://webarchive.nationalarchives.gov.uk/20120119192332/http:/cwdcouncil.org.uk/assets/0000/9297/CWDC_CommonCore7.pdf 22nd June 2015

DfE (2011) *The Munro Review.* Retrieved from: www.gov.uk/government/uploads/system/uploads/attachment_data/file/175391/Munro-Review.pdf 22nd June 2015.

DfE (2014) *The Early Years Foundation Stage.* Retrieved from: www.gov.uk/government/uploads/system/uploads/attachment_data/file/335504/EYFS_framework_from_1_September_2014__with_clarification_note.pdf 22nd June 2015.

DfES (2003) *National Standards for Daycare.* Retrieved from: www3.imperial.ac.uk/pls/portallive/docs/1/46973696.PDF 20th February 2015.

Department of Health (2000) *Framework for the Assessment of Children in Need and their Families.* Retrieved from: http://webarchive.nationalarchives.gov.uk/20130401151715/https:/www.education.gov.uk/publications/eOrderingDownload/Framework%20for%20the%20assessment%20of%20children%20in%20need%20and%20their%20families.pdf 22nd June 2015.

Elmer, S. (2013) Marginalised children in marginalised communities: the challenges for early years and parenting support services where there is domestic violence. *North East Branch Newsletter.* Winter 2013. London: British Psychological Society.

Evangelou, M., Goff, J., Hall, J., Sylva, K., Eisenstadt, N., Paget, C., Davis, S., Sammons, P., Smith, T., Tracz, R. and Parkin, T. (2014) *Evaluation of Children's Centres in England: Parenting services.* DfE Report No. DfE-RR368. London: DfE.

Ferguson, H. (2011) *Child Protection Practice.* London: Palgrave Macmillan.

Frost, N., Elmer, S. and Eley, S. (2009) *'The Budget Holding Lead Professional' – a study of process and outcomes.* Unpublished Report: Children Leeds.

Haringey Local Safeguarding Children Board (2009) *Serious Case Review: Baby Peter.* Retrieved from: www.haringeylscb.org/sites/haringeylscb/files/executive_summary_peter_final.pdf 26th January 2015.

HM Government (2015) *Working Together to Safeguard Children.* Retrieved from: www.gov.uk/government/uploads/system/uploads/attachment_data/file/419595/Working_Together_to_Safeguard_Children.pdf 22nd June 2015.

HMSO (2004) *The Bichard Report.* Retrieved from: http://dera.ioe.ac.uk/6394/1/report.pdf 22nd June 2015

Horwath, J. (Ed.) (2009) *The Child's World: The comprehensive guide to assessing children in need* (2nd Edn). London: Jessica Kingsley.

Institute of Public Care (2012) *Early Intervention and Prevention with Children and Families*. Retrieved from: http://ipc.brookes.ac.uk/publications/pdf/Early_Intervention_and_Prevention_with_Children_and_Families_June_2012.pdf 22nd June 2015.

Laming, H. (2009) *The Protection of Children in England: A progress report*. Retrieved from: http://dera.ioe.ac.uk/8646/1/12_03_09_children.pdf 23rd June 2015.

Legislation.gov.uk (1989) *The Children Act 1989*. Retrieved from: www.legislation.gov.uk/ukpga/1989/41/contents 22nd June 2015.

Legislation.gov.uk (2012) *The Protection of Freedoms Act 2012*. Retrieved from: www.legislation.gov.uk/ukpga/2012/9/contents 22nd June 2015.

Reid, J. and Burton, S. (2013) *Safeguarding and Protecting Children in the Early Years*. Abingdon: Routledge.

Savill, R. and Bunyan, N. (2009) *Nursery Worker Child Sex Abuse Case: Vanessa George profile*. Retrieved from: http://www.telegraph.co.uk/news/uknews/crime/6249672/Nursery-worker-child-sexabuse-case-Vanessa-George-profile.html 23rd June 2015.

United Nations (2015) *Fact Sheet: A summary of the rights under the Convention on the Rights of the Child*. Retrieved from: www.unicef.org/crc/files/Rights_overview.pdf 22nd June 2015.

Vincent, S. (2015) *Early Intervention: Supporting and strengthening families (protecting children and young people)*. London: Dunedin Academic.

World Health Organization (2002) *Child Abuse and Neglect Facts*. Retrieved from www.who.int/violence_injury_prevention/violence/world_report/factsheets/en/childabusefacts.pdf 22nd June 2015.

4 Families and the state

The ongoing development of social policy

Pam Jarvis

CHAPTER OVERVIEW

This chapter will outline a brief history of social policy for children and families in England, and then turn to the rise of the rights, inclusion and equality agendas, both nationally and internationally. It will address the following questions:

✔ How and why did legislation for children and families develop in England?
✔ What are the key aspects of social policy and legislation that underpin the work of contemporary Early Years Graduate Practitioners (EYGPs) and Early Years Teachers (EYTs) in England, and how can they keep up with ongoing changes?
✔ What are 'human rights' and 'children's rights'; how are these protected through international policy?

The recommended reading list at the end of this chapter will introduce readers to a range of texts and online resources in which to read further on these topics.

Case study: listening to children

Making policy for children should involve taking into account what *they* have to say about their lives. Childhood, after all, is not just a journey into adulthood, it is an integral human life stage that people should be able to live 'within the moment' and enjoy.

Unfortunately, being defined as a child frequently leads to an assumption that one cannot speak for oneself, and that adults who 'know what is best' will make all the decisions. The western discourse of childhood contains a strong presumption that children cannot be trusted to make decisions about their own lives, and the younger the child, the less s/he is presumed able to make choices, or express preferences. This often leads to adults deciding why children do things without asking them, not allowing them to explain their own actions and viewpoints, and talking down to, patronising or simply ignoring children who attempt to communicate independent thoughts and opinions. The youngest children within society are frequently the least listened to, particularly on the national stage, when policies are created that have powerful effects upon their lives.

Peter Moss (2006) reflects:

> The problem is that listening to young children requires adults to learn, or relearn, and revalue other languages [see 'The One Hundred Languages of Children': www.youtube. com/watch?v=mQtLOu99BfE], and I think a lot of the issues in listening to children become much more interesting once we get beyond the idea that listening involves one person talking and the other person hearing them at different points in time.
>
> (Moss, 2006, pp. 17–18)

Reflection

How do you listen to the voices of the children within your setting? What input do they have to the day-to-day planning and policy? You can find some resources to help you to develop your setting's 'listening' here: www.ncb.org.uk/areas-of-activity/early-childhood/resources/publications/listening-and-participation

As you read through the policies in the first part of this chapter, consider whether children's opinions on the aspects that affect them were considered by the people in charge of English policy development and legislation.

Introduction

The underpinning principles of childcare and education require that EYGPs/EYTs not only have a grasp of contemporary social policy and legislation relating to children's issues, but also the sociological grounding and personal flexibility to understand the reasoning behind policy-making, particularly that relating to equality and inclusion policy. It is also a requirement that individuals invested with the responsibility for leading practice continually keep up to date with new legislation, and become able to engage in debate relating to ongoing changes. In doing so, as their career unfolds, they build the potential to become one of those leading practice development both locally and nationally.

How and why did legislation for children and families develop in England?

The first formal Poor Law in England was established in 1598 by Queen Elizabeth I, who decreed that 'parish relief' would be distributed to the 'destitute'. A medieval parish covered an area served by a specific church, and it was proposed that parish relief should be collected, managed and distributed by the church in every district. Sunday schools subsequently arose (particularly under the Cromwells' Puritan rule, between 1653 and 1660) and took a role in the education of the poor, teaching children 'moral' behaviour and, increasingly, basic reading and counting skills. Elizabeth initially created the parish relief legislation to deal with aggressive roving beggars who were causing concern, as illustrated by the following rhyme:

> Hark, hark the dogs do bark
> The Beggars are coming to town
> Some in rags and some in jags
> And one in a velvet gown.
> (Traditional)

(The Tudor meaning of 'jag' was a fashionable slit in a garment exposing a material of a different colour underneath.) The underlying reason for the law was to encourage each parish to 'look after its own' and avoid the violence that ensued when people in a particular town or village (with no formal law enforcement mechanisms beyond the village squire and priest) decided to run potentially undeserving strangers out of their territory! This mixture of compassion and practical governance can still be discerned in today's social legislation, as we will see later in this chapter.

The parish system operated for over three centuries, until industrialisation changed the ways that people were employed, creating a huge expansion in city-based living as people moved into the rapidly expanding towns to work in the new factories and mills. Parish relief was no longer practical in such large and impersonal communities, and in 1834 it was replaced by the unpopular workhouse system. 'Pauper' families were split up and sent to segregated male, female and children's sections in large institutions where they lived like prisoners, carrying out menial work for a place to stay and basic sustenance. Most families did everything they could to remain out of the workhouse system, even if it meant living in extreme poverty. An additional cause for concern for such families was the hidden agenda for workhouse children, that of a processing system which transferred them from the workhouse to factories, as cheap labour for industry: 'parish apprenticeship was an important aspect of the labour market' (Schwarz and Boulton, 2007).

Reflection: the remnants of the workhouse

There are a lot of old Victorian workhouse buildings still in existence in Britain, many of which have been converted to a wide variety of purposes. Why not see if you can find an old workhouse building in the city nearest to where you live, and learn something about its history?

Trade unions, created by working men, subsequently started 'friendly societies' where members donated a small percentage of their income to a collective insurance fund so that their families would be able to continue to receive an income (and hence avoid the workhouse) for some length of time if they became unemployed, ill or died prematurely.

The impersonal nature of life in the new cities underpinned many fundamental societal changes, including the creation of a statutory policing system, which began with the London 'Bow Street Runners' in 1829, who were the original Metropolitan Police force. Over the mid-nineteenth century, successive Victorian governments became increasingly concerned about the poverty and squalor in the new cities; for example, in 1870 a Public Health Act (DoH, 1970) made it compulsory for local authorities to provide clean water and sewerage systems paid for by a new local tax on householders called 'the rates' which we now know as the 'community charge'. Under the first Education Act, also passed by Parliament in 1870, publicly funded school boards were set up to ensure that all children aged five to 12 were allocated a free school place and maintained their attendance to ensure that they received a basic primary education, principally inculcating basic literacy, numeracy, practical skills and moral understanding. Mid-Victorian Britain was fast developing a cultural understanding of children as special, vulnerable human beings who needed care, education and protection under the law.

As children from very poor backgrounds began to come into regular contact with middle-class professionals such as teachers and charity workers, concerns began to be raised with respect to their health and physical condition, and were publicly aired in discussions relating to the prevention of neglect and physical ill-treatment. In 1884, the London Society for the Prevention of Cruelty to Children was created (h2g2, 2009). In 1889, the government passed the first Children Act to instigate legal procedures to protect children from physically abusive adults, and the London Society for the Prevention of Cruelty to Children became a national charitable institution, the NSPCC, which, alongside Barnardo's (2008) still continues to provide help for children and their families today.

Case study: the Children Act 1889

This act was the first to impose criminal penalties on those who mistreated children. It enabled the state to intervene, for the first time, in relations between parents and children. Police could arrest anyone found ill-treating a child, and enter a home if a child was thought to be in danger. The act included guidelines on the employment of children and outlawed begging, which frequently involved children (DoH, 1889).

Throughout the nineteenth century, the British government gradually extended the right to vote to working-class men (women had to wait until 1928 to get the vote on the same terms), which changed the political landscape, as politicians scrambled for working-class votes. This eventually resulted in the birth of the Labour Party (emerging from the Trade Unions Congress as the political party for working men) in 1900, although it had to wait until 1924 for its first very short term of government. For most of the twentieth century, the Labour movement would espouse a *collectivist* approach to government, raising taxation to fund services that acted to equalise the population, while the Conservative movement would bring an opposing *individualistic* orientation, cutting taxation on the basis that individuals and families had the right to decide upon the services that they required, and pay for them on a private basis.

Case study: the Children's Charter 1908

- Established juvenile courts.
- Introduced the registration of foster parents, which had the effect of regulating 'baby-farming' and wet-nursing, which in turn had the emergent effect of reducing infanticide (people secretly 'doing away' with unwanted children!).
- Prevented children working in dangerous trades and prevented them from purchasing cigarettes and alcohol.
- Local authorities were granted powers to keep poor children out of the workhouse and protect them from abuse; this led to many councils setting up social services departments and county orphanages.
- Raised the minimum age for execution to 16, later raised to 18 in the Children and Young Persons Act 1933 (see below).

(DoH, 1908)

Over the early years of the twentieth century, the Liberal Party's popularity began to fall behind that of the new Labour Party. This revolution in the political landscape gathered pace in Britain once World War I ended (1918), as all men over 21 and all women over 30 were given the right to vote. However, one of the last Liberal administrations set up the very first national insurance system in 1906, based upon the model created over the previous century by the Trade Unions. At this time, national insurance was only for men, who paid a compulsory small amount that was taken at source from their wages. The resulting fund was used to pay old age pensions, and to insure those who paid into the fund against sickness, unemployment and disability. Some money was also put aside to fund school health checks, free school meals for poor children and the setting up of 'labour exchanges' (early job centres).

Case study: social justice and early years practice

You have read about the Christian Socialist McMillan sisters and their pioneering nursery in chapter 1. The sisters' lobbying was instrumental in the inception of the Education (Administrative Procedures) Bill of 1907, and once the Act was passed, they subsequently innovated and managed a range of highly successful experiments in child health promotion and liberal primary/early years pedagogy for disadvantaged children, focused intently upon children's holistic individual needs.

Margaret McMillan was elected as the first president of the Nursery Schools Association in 1923. In 1927, reflecting on her pedagogy in a BBC radio broadcast, she said:

> You may ask, why should we give all this to the children? Because this is nurture, and without it they can never really have education. The educational system should grow out of the nursery schools system, not out of a neglected infancy ... If Great Britain will go forward with nursery schools she will sweep away the cause of untold suffering, ignorance, waste and failure.

Reflection: individual or society?

The political backdrop to the Education (Administrative Procedures) Bill of 1907 was a concern amongst the British establishment that had been raised relating to the state of unfitness that had been detected in many city-reared men in the UK during the army recruitment process associated with the Boer War 1899–1902 (Roebuck, 1973).

Do you think the politicians of this time were most concerned with the health of the children as individuals, or do you think they were most concerned with the fate of a nation that, in times of war, would rely on the future health and strength of these children? You will find examples throughout the history of public service development that can be very effectively analysed from this perspective. You have met a similar theory before in chapter 1, that of children as human capital.

When you have read the section below on the United Nations Convention on the Rights of the Child, undertake some further consideration of the complexities that underlie the relationship between the focus on the individual and the focus on the value of the individual to society that exists at the root of social policy creation for children and families, both currently and in history.

Unfortunately, an international economic slump during the early 1930s exposed the inadequacy of the Liberal social reforms. Men were laid off work for long periods of time, and as their unemployment pay ran out, several child deaths due to starvation occurred in families who refused to endure the misery, separation and degradation of the workhouse. Full employment was only finally achieved in the late 1930s, principally due to the armament production and military service opportunities that directly preceded and endured throughout World War II.

Case study: the Children and Young Person's Act 1932/1933

- The Children and Young Persons Act 1932 broadened the powers of juvenile courts and introduced supervision orders for children at risk.
- In 1933, a further Children and Young Persons Act collated all existing child protection legislation into one act.

(DoH, 1932/1933)

As the Blitz raged over London in the early 1940s, the war government, a coalition of all political parties, asked William Beveridge (1879–1963), an economist and social reformer, to create a plan for rebuilding British society after the war. Beveridge (1942) proposed that there were 'five giants' of deprivation to slay:

- Want
- Ignorance
- Disease
- Squalor
- Idleness.

When the war ended in 1945, the Labour party was voted into government by a landslide. The franchise now extended to all Britons, male and female, aged over 21. Over their first three years in office, the 1945 Labour government set up the **British welfare state**, based on the recommendations of the Beveridge Report (1942). This comprised:

- The **National Health Service** to tackle **disease**
- A comprehensive, nationally funded **benefits and pensions** system to tackle **want**
- Free high-quality **education** from five to 15 to tackle **ignorance**
- A national **housing** initiative to tackle **squalor**
- A national **employment** initiative to tackle **idleness**.

Case study: 1940s social legislation

The Education Act 1944 was passed by the World War II Coalition government, a year before the post-war Labour government was voted into power. This Act set up a system of state schooling for age 5–11 (primary) and 11–18 (secondary). The minimum school-leaving age rose to 15 (DfES, 1944). This basic structure remains, although the leaving age became 16 in 1972, 17 in 2015, and will be 18 in 2016. There is a longstanding discussion that has continued from the 1970s to the present as to whether apprenticeships and vocational training should be available for 14- to 18-year-olds who have decided, in consultation with their teachers and parents, that they would benefit more from such a pathway than they would from academic study.

Main legislative measures of the post-war Labour government

- 1945 Family Allowances Act
- 1946 National Insurance Act
- 1946 National Insurance (Industrial Injuries) Act
- 1946 National Health Service Act (implemented July 1948)
- 1947 Town and Country Planning Act
- 1947 New Towns Act
- 1948 National Assistance Act
- 1948 Children Act
- 1949 Housing Act.

(The Open University, 2015)

- The Children Act 1948 established a children's committee and a children's officer in each local authority. It followed the creation of the parliamentary Care of Children Committee in 1945 following the death of 13-year-old Dennis O'Neill at the hands of his abusive foster parents.

(DoH, 1948)

These health, benefits and education systems, although much 'worked upon' by subsequent administrations, still form the bedrock of British social policy today. They remained pretty much unsullied throughout the 1950s and 1960s, but by the early 1970s, western economies began to destabilise as rising international oil prices sent the whole western world into economic recession. In Britain, throughout the 1970s, a succession of Conservative and Labour administrations battled with the Trade Unions, as inflation rapidly raised the cost of living and the unions called strike after strike in an attempt to force employers to raise wages to keep pace with prices. In 1978, Britain entered what was to be known as 'the winter of discontent' where nearly all workers in the public and nationalised industries went on strike. Dead bodies remained unburied and piles of rubbish lay uncollected in the streets, attracting swarms of rats (Marr, 2007).

In 1979, Britons voted in the Conservative administration led by Margaret Thatcher, who became Britain's first woman Prime Minister. Under this government, although the welfare state remained materially intact, the value of benefits was slashed, and there were cuts and economies applied to nationally funded services including education and health. In The Housing Act of 1980 (DoE, 1980), the Thatcher government gave tenants the 'right to buy' public housing stock that had largely been built in the period directly after World War II; in areas where this venture did not succeed, the management of public housing was subsequently largely removed from local authorities and sold on to private housing trusts. This government also denied subsidies to unprofitable manufacturing industries, allowing them to close down altogether. By the early 1980s Britain experienced a 10% unemployment level, which disproportionately hit manufacturing industries, raising the unemployment levels in areas which housed factories, mines and mills proportionally well beyond those that had been experienced in the 1930s, particularly among male workers (Marr, 2007). Subsequent urban regeneration projects undertaken over the late 1980s and early 1990s eventually achieved some amount of re-employment by encouraging 'service' and financial industries to set up their offices within the old industrial areas. The resulting new jobs were frequently temporary, part time and low paid, and disproportionately filled by women.

Meanwhile, despite the government's efforts to cut public spending in education and health, the advance of medical science hugely increased the costs of the NHS, as the range of treatments available increased. Technological advances began to create a requirement for a more educated, technically competent workforce, and hence a longer mass education for young people became necessary. The government increasingly began to contemplate how they could create a public education and social welfare support system that inculcated the 'correct' skills and attitudes within the child population to create a steady supply of technologically competent 'useful citizens'. This eventually resulted in the Education Reform Act 1988 (DfES, 1988), which introduced the National Curriculum, swiftly followed by the Children Act 1989 (DoH, 1989) as the government's response to a string of high-profile, controversial national and international debates about children's rights and holistic protection, including the recognition of more insidious areas of child maltreatment including neglect, and emotional and sexual abuse (see chapter 3).

While the age for voting was dropped to 18 in 1970, the school-leaving age was raised to 16 in 1972, and, as the 1970s drew to a close, increasing numbers of young people remained in education until they were 18. Numbers attending university also increased over the 1970s and 1980s; such individuals remained in education until they were 21. However, at the other end of education provision, pre-school opportunities remained largely within the private sector. The Conservative administration remained in office until 1997.

Reflection: recent changes

Was anyone in your family a child in Britain during the 1980s? What do they remember of the culture and society that formed the background to their childhood? For example, what do they remember about adult employment roles and experiences of unemployment, and their effects upon the family? Did they attend pre-school education? I remember that my young twins were only able to attend pre-school for two days a week before they entered primary school in 1991, because the private fees were so high, and pre-school children had no guaranteed right to a nursery place, whether or not they were 'multiples'! Use the resources at the end of the chapter to consider how you think life may have been different (and/or similar) in the late twentieth century to life today for young children and their families.

Case study: the Children Act 1989

Part One: outlines the Paramountcy Principle (the child's welfare is paramount) and the concept of Significant Harm.

Part Two: sets out measures which may be used by social services departments who are in dispute with parents of children within their designated area.

Part Three: sets out the principal responsibilities of local authorities regarding children in their area.

Part Four: sets out the grounds under which courts may make an order, which, in simplified form, relates to evidence that a child has been suffering significant harm, or that a court feels that there is a strong possibility that s/he may be likely to do so in the future in his/her current situation.

Part Five: outlines the introduction of a new Emergency Protection Order to replace the old Place of Safety Order, and stipulates how the new Order may be used, and by whom.

Parts Six to Twelve cover:

- Guidelines regarding residential care
- Guidelines regarding fostering
- Standards concerning nursery and childcare arrangements for under fives
- Court arrangements for dealing with children's issues.

(See chapter 3 for an account of the Children Act 'in action'.)

(DoH, 1989)

What are the key aspects of social policy and legislation that underpin the work of contemporary Early Years Graduate Practitioners (EYGPs) and Early Years Teachers (EYTs) in England, and how can they keep up with ongoing changes?

The New Labour years

In 1997, the British population elected a Labour government, which remained in power for the next 13 years. Labour politics had moved on considerably during their nearly two decades in opposition, and while the new 'New Labour' Government had promised to re-energise the welfare state, it did very little to reverse the cutbacks instigated by the previous Conservative administration. This heralded a more sophisticated orientation to collectivism, ideologically separating 'New' Labour from the more simplistically collectivist Labour policies of the past. New Labour instead frequently sought 'deals' between the government and private sources of funding to manage health and education. Public funding was, however, steadily pumped into education initiatives, still driven by the focus upon producing an educated workforce to make Britain more internationally competitive: the 'children as human capital' agenda. However, New Labour had an additional impetus to try and create a level playing field for all British children, embodied in an ambitious attempt to dramatically reduce the numbers of children living in poverty. To this end, they created the Sure Start initiative (Eisenstadt, 2011), initially based upon the Head Start initiative (National Head Start Association, 2015) in the US. Sure Start centres were initially set up across disadvantaged urban areas in England. Many of these became children's centres, which aimed to provide a 'one-stop shop' for health, education and care services for young children and their families. The initial focus was upon supporting low-income families (including single parents) to find their own way out of poverty through paid work.

Over the final years of the New Labour administration, the number of children's centres grew rapidly. Many provided daycare for the young children of working parents, and the government's plans for the future of children's centres began to expand towards a universal offer of daycare and services to families across the country. This was therefore now moving away from the Head Start model towards the universal eligibility for early years care and education that is found within the Scandinavian nations (see chapter 10).

Case study: Sure Start children's centres expansion 1998–2010

- Sure Start was introduced in the 1998 comprehensive spending review, with the New Labour Government's announcement that it would set up 250 Sure Start local programmes in disadvantaged areas around the country.
- In 2000, the number of Sure Start projects expanded to 524.
- In what was designated 'Phase One' of the children's centres programme (2004–06), 800 existing settings were given the status of 'children's centres'.
- In 'Phase Two' (2006–08), funding was made available to open many more children's centres, taking the overall numbers to 2,500. Most of these additional settings were newly created.
- By late 2008, there were 2,916 children's centres in operation throughout the UK.
- By 2010, at the end of 'Phase Three', the target was for 3,500 centres nationwide (Children, Schools and Families Committee, 2010). This was achieved by May 2010, the month that the New Labour government left office, due to a general election that gave the Conservatives a very small majority.

A government green paper, *Every Child Matters*, was introduced in 2003, signalling a cross-sector approach to policy for children and young people. It proposed: an electronic recording system to track the developmental and educational progress of England's 11 million children; 150 children's trusts; a Children's Director to oversee local children's services; statutory Local Safeguarding Children Boards; and an independent Children's Commissioner for England, to protect young people's welfare and rights. An amalgamation of social services, education and child health was scheduled to be accomplished by 2006.

Case study: *Every Child Matters* – the key outcomes

The *Every Child Matters* (ECM) Green Paper of 2003 identified five key outcomes for children and young people that were to be met both through changes in individual public and independent agencies working with children and through improved inter-agency working:

- **Being healthy:** enjoying good physical and mental health and enjoying a healthy lifestyle
- **Staying safe:** being protected from harm and neglect
- **Enjoying and achieving:** getting the most out of life and developing the skills for adulthood
- **Making a positive contribution:** being involved with the community and society and not engaging in anti-social or offending behaviour
- **Economic well-being:** not being prevented by economic disadvantage from achieving their full potential in life.

(DfES, 2003)

Every Child Matters became the basis for a huge number of policy developments relating to education, health and social care and workforce development across the remaining period of New Labour Government, 2003–10. In 2004, the government passed a new Children Act to implement the main proposals of the Green Paper: electronic children's files, children's directors, local safeguarding boards, Ofsted inspections for the Early Years sector and the Children's Commissioner.

Case study: the Children Act 2004

Parts One and **Two** of the Act provide new structures and duties for England:

- To create a Children's Commissioner for England (already in existence in Wales and Northern Ireland)
- To establish more effective information sharing through electronic means between public authorities for children at risk of abuse or who have been abused
- To establish a new structure for inter-agency cooperation in child protection – Local Safeguarding Children Boards (LSCBs)
- To establish local authority Directors of Children's Services and a lead member for children within councils
- To establish a new inspection framework for children's services
- To establish Joint Area Reviews of services for children.

Parts Three and **Four** deal with the Welsh aspects of this legislation.
Part Five contains miscellaneous provisions that include some updating of elements of the Children Act 1989, the main points of which remain very much 'live', and work in partnership with all new legislation.
Part Six deals with some necessary administrative details.

(DfES, 2004)

In the Childcare Act 2006 (DfES, 2006), the government unveiled the next stage of their plan for children and families. This Act can be construed as the first major legislative extension of the welfare state, nearly 60 years after its instigation; no post World War II government had previously legislated on care for pre-school children, or after-school care for older children. However, just as, with hindsight, it seems clear that the politicians of the 1940s were very naïve about the problems that would emerge with respect to funding the welfare state, and the health service in particular, we now see, a decade later, that this same analysis may be made with regard to New Labour's optimism that, within a British taxation system, the modern welfare state would ever be able to support free-at-source, quality childcare for all.

Case study: the Childcare Act 2006

The Act enshrines in law parents' 'legitimate expectation of accessible high-quality childcare and services for children under 5 and their families':

- Local authorities to improve *outcomes* for all children under the age of five
- Local authorities to *facilitate* the childcare market
- Emphasis on provision for working parents – particularly those on low income and those with disabled children
- Local authorities to ensure a full range of information to parents
- Introduction of the statutory guidance document, *The Early Years Foundation Stage* (2007)
- Reformed and standardised childcare and early years regulation across England.

(DfES, 2006)

Reflection: the childcare transition

Is a mass movement to publicly funded, collective pre-school/after-school childcare a wholly positive development, or might there be potential underlying problems? A source that will help you reflect upon this is the UNICEF report *The Child Care Transition* (2008), which reflects 'the stakes are simply too high for the mass movement towards out-of-home child care to be seen as just another shake of the kaleidoscope in the rapidly changing lifestyles of advanced industrial economies' (p. 13). This issue is also discussed in chapter 10.

The Coalition years

A financial crisis created by worldwide failures in the international banking system cast a shadow over the last two years of the New Labour government, 2008–10. A small fall in the numbers of children officially living in poverty that had been achieved over the first few years of the twenty-first century was reversed, unemployment figures began to rise, and the resulting public disillusionment fed into a narrow victory for the Conservatives in the May 2010 general election. As the Conservatives did not have a decisive majority, they made a pact with the Liberal Democratic party that allowed for the formation of a Conservative/ Liberal Democratic Coalition government. The Coalition did not formally repeal any of the New Labour legislation relating to children and families, and much of their policy-making acknowledged the modern neurobiology research indications (see chapter 2) that the early years is the most important stage of development (see Field, 2010; Allen, 2011). However, this has led to an impetus towards detailed individual testing to identify children whose achievements are giving 'cause for concern'. This has in turn caused some consternation within the early years arena (see chapter 5). This policy orientation is rooted within the stated Coalition intention to 'take Sure Start back to its original purpose' (Coalition government, 2010, p. 10); in the view of the Coalition government this is defined as aiming the project at helping 'troubled' families solve the range of problems underlying their situation, moving back to the Head Start model that was more in evidence in the origins of Sure Start. Prime Minister David Cameron proposed there were approximately 120,000 'troubled families' in the UK (see www.communities.gov.uk/communities/troubledfamilies) living in 'areas of disadvantage', and that their problems needed to be proactively dealt with in order to break a cycle that would be likely to result in the children themselves subsequently creating similarly 'troubled families' in the next generation; what Field (2010, pp. 16–17) refers to as 'the intergenerational cycle of poverty'. The Coalition's initial overview of policy for children and families was summarised in *Supporting Families in the Foundation Years* (DfE, 2011), some of which was formalised in the Children and Families Act 2014 (see chapter 3). An emergent result of this policy direction has been the radical curtailment of the New Labour government's plans for children's centres in every locality which provide state-funded, universal daycare within their range of services for children and families.

Case Study: policy for children and families under the Coalition government 2010–15

The major piece of legislation introduced by the Coalition was the Children and Families Act 2014. It reflects the Coalition's impetus to focus on 'troubled' families, offering a range of measures to improve practice and policy relating to 'looked after' children (those in the care systems of local authorities) and children with special needs, and improving the family justice system, which deals with legal disputes relating to the custody of children. The Gov.uk website (2014) proposes that the Act has been designed 'to improve services for vulnerable children and support strong families'.

With regard to Early Years Practice, Coalition policy focused on the following initiatives:

- Producing a new, more streamlined version of the Early Years Foundation Stage (EYFS) – this was introduced following the Tickell review of 2011 (see www.gov.uk/government/collections/tickell-review-reports and chapter 5).
- Developing a portfolio of formal reports on the attainments of children under five. The current iteration of the EYFS has 17 early learning goals against which a progress report must be made at two, and a summative assessment must be made at five.
- A statutory phonics screening check was introduced for children in Year 1 in 2013. Although this does not strictly fall into the early years sector, some emergent effects have been reported in terms of children being prepared and rehearsed for these tests while still in the EYFS.
- In 2015, the Coalition government announced an intention to begin formally 'baseline testing' all children on their entry to the Reception class. Concerns about 'labelling' children at such an early stage have been raised (see chapters 5 and 10).

Reflection: saving childhood?

On 11 September 2013, a letter from the 'Save Childhood' campaign (www.savechildhood.net) was published in the *Daily Telegraph*. It proposed:

> We are deeply concerned about the impact of the Government's early years policies on the health and wellbeing of our youngest children … current policy suggestions would mean that the tests and targets which dominate primary education will soon be foisted upon four-year-olds … Research does not support an early start to testing and quasi-formal teaching, but provides considerable evidence to challenge it. Very few countries have a school starting age as young as four, as we do in England. Children who enter school at six or seven – after several years of high quality nursery education – consistently achieve better educational results as well as higher levels of wellbeing.
>
> (*Daily Telegraph*, 2013a, online)

In an article published in the same edition of the paper, the following government response was reported:

> A spokesman for Michael Gove, the Education Secretary at that time, said the signatories were 'misguided', suggesting they advocated dumbing down [early years education]. 'These people represent the powerful and badly misguided lobby who are responsible for the devaluation of exams and the culture of low expectations in state schools,' the spokesman said. 'We need a system that aims to prepare pupils to solve hard problems in calculus or be a poet or engineer – a system freed from the grip of those who bleat bogus pop-psychology about "self image", which is an excuse for not teaching poor children how to add up.'
>
> (*Daily Telegraph*, 2013b, online)

On the basis of your practice experience with young children and your theoretical knowledge, which side of the argument would you support, and why?

1   Do you think the response that the government made indicated that it was 'listening'?
2   Do you think that childhood needs 'saving'?

The result of the 2015 election has returned a small Conservative majority in England, and an overwhelming Scottish Nationalist majority in Scotland. This makes for an uneasy relationship between the two nations, given that these two contingents are politically opposed to each other, with Conservatives favouring individualistic policies and Scottish Nationalists favouring collectivism. It is therefore likely that early years policies in England and Scotland will sharply diverge over 2015–20. The drive towards baseline testing in England continues, while children's centres are to remain a resource principally for dealing with 'troubled families'. The Queen's Speech at the opening of the new Parliament contained a pledge for the provision of 30 hours of free childcare for 38 weeks a year for all children under three (BBC, 2015), to be provided within private daycare businesses or primary schools rather than within purpose-designed state-funded facilities. These issues are further considered in chapter 10.

Having covered over 500 years of social policy at some speed above, readers may now be asking what relevance this has to their work within the contemporary early years sector. The answer initially relates to the place of history in everyday life – it allows us to find our own position on an unfolding timeline where continually changing social and political perspectives can otherwise appear as a random, constantly fluctuating morass. It also allows us to reflect upon the fact that governments and populations frequently have to respond in the best way they can to situations that have not been thoroughly planned and may not be entirely of their own making.

Those who work in the early years sector should be very aware that children are particularly vulnerable to the problems and uncertainties created by the constantly shifting social and economic forces that underpin human lives within modern societies. Physical deprivation, family problems and performance-assessment-based stress can have more devastating results upon developing bodies and minds than upon those of adults, and the individualistic mantra to 'fend for oneself' cannot be sensibly applied to those who are not yet old enough to do so. Governments of all political persuasions are often particularly interested in the fate of their nation's children, and not always for the most charitable reasons, being inclined to view them as 'projects' for a collective national future rather than as individuals: the 'children as human capital' agenda. You have read about the role of the drive for strong healthy soldiers in the development of publicly funded health services for children above. Alderson (2008, p. 53) similarly proposed that *Every Child Matters* (DfES, 2003, see above) 'appears to be more concerned with the national economy than with the welfare and protection of young children'. Both of these examples echo the mixture of apparent compassion underpinned by national and societal concerns that was initially raised at the beginning of the chapter as an underlying factor of the Elizabethan Poor Law.

The role of senior childcare and education practitioners in any society in time or geography is inevitably to work within the systems that operate at the time, with a view to doing the best they can for the children under their care. This crucially involves a large amount of independent, analytical thought, reconciling what the practitioner knows to be good practice rooted within their own experience and knowledge of child development and family dynamics. In this way, ongoing changes can routinely be optimistically but cautiously viewed where at all possible as opportunities, and planned for at an early stage. However, the informed, reflective practitioner also needs to heed the ongoing warnings of dissenting voices such as those of Alderson and the 'Save Childhood' movement which perform the essential task of alerting us to what may happen when policy is slavishly instigated by practitioners who think 'two-dimensionally', taking little account of individual children's emotional, social and intellectual needs. EYGPs/EYTs must always be aware that policy created on the basis of national expediency by politicians who are not child development or education professionals, and who have many, often conflicting agendas to address, may not always be simplistically focused on the best interests of children and families.

The section below will briefly explore some important international guidelines that seek to protect the world's children against policy based only within transient and sometimes erroneous concepts of national expediency, forming an over-arching model of good practice for social policy. The emphasis is upon a framework designed to support the human rights of children, young people and families.

What are 'human rights' and 'children's rights' and how are these protected through international policy?

Rights and responsibilities: a complex relationship

In 1942, as Beveridge was drawing up the plans for a post-war British welfare state, the US president Franklin D. Roosevelt wrote of his intention to lead the allies in the creation of a body of 'United Nations' (UN). In 1945, the final year of the war, representatives of 50 countries met in San Francisco to draw up the United Nations Charter, which was signed on 26 June 1945 (United Nations, 2012). The UN's first action was to produce the Universal Declaration of Human Rights (1948) (United Nations, 2012) which set out what are now internationally agreed as the basic human rights that should be extended to all people by all nations, regardless of nationality, ethnicity, race or religion. This reflected international recognition of the additional suffering imposed upon minority ethnic groups by the highly xenophobic Nazi regime. Throughout its history, the UN has consistently demonstrated that it will only sanction international military action against a nation if it is obvious that the basic human rights of some or all of its citizens are being transgressed or ignored by the ruling regime. In 1998, following many years of discussion between the European Union governments, the New Labour government passed a comprehensive Act of Parliament detailing the Human Rights of every person resident within and/or visiting England, including those who do not hold British nationality.

During the late 1940s and early 1950s, a great deal of psychological, sociological and health-oriented research was carried out to study the children and young people of Europe, many of whom had been killed or injured in World War II, and many who, through the extensive displacement influences of the conflict, had lost contact with one or both parents either permanently or for a long period of time. John Bowlby, about whom you read in chapter 2, developed his theory of maternal deprivation from his psychoanalytic work with children who had experienced such separations in very early childhood, many of these due to displacement or evacuation. He gave evidence for the development of the Declaration of the Rights of the Child (UN, 1959), where, for the first time, children were recognised on the world policy stage as 'special' human beings, in need of more care and protection from the state than adults.

The United Nations International Children's Emergency Fund, or 'UNICEF', grew out of the International Children's Fund, created in 1946 to collect money and resources to provide aid for children whose lives had been blighted in various ways by World War II. Since its adoption by the UN in 1947, UNICEF's mission has been to 'mount urgent relief programmes for children and adolescents in war-ravaged countries and for child health purposes generally, with such aid being distributed without discrimination due to race, creed, nationality, status or political belief' (UNICEF, 2015, online). Its work over the years increasingly demonstrated that while the Declaration of the Rights of the Child had been a recognition of children's basic needs, a more comprehensive rights document for children and young people was needed. Many years were spent on its construction, and it was finally published 30 years after the Declaration of the Rights of the Child, being swiftly endorsed by all member nations of the UN apart from the US and Somalia. For England, the discussions undertaken internationally also fed into national legislation, the Children Act 1989, which is outlined above and in chapter 3. As you can see, both the United Nations Convention on the Rights of the Child (UNCRC) and the Children Act 1989 came into being in the same year.

Case Study: the United Nations Convention on the Rights of the Child (UNCRC) 1989

The Convention lists 54 articles in all which outline a comprehensive set of international rights for children. Some of the most important ones that impact upon the work of early years practitioners are as follows:

Article 2: The Convention applies to everyone, whatever their race, religion, abilities, whatever they think or say, and whatever type of family they come from.

Article 3: All organisations concerned with children should work towards what is best for each individual child.

Article 9: Children should not be separated from their parents unless it is for their own good. Even if they are separated for a good reason, e.g. if the child is being neglected or badly treated, in most circumstances, children have the right to stay in contact with both parents.

Article 10: Families who live in different countries should be allowed to move between those countries so that parents and children can stay in contact, or get back together as a family.

Article 12: Children have the right to say what they think should happen, when adults are making decisions that affect them, and to have their opinions taken into account.

Article 14: Children have the right to think and believe what they want, and to practise their religion, as long as they are not stopping other people from enjoying their rights.

Article 15: Children have a right to privacy. The law should protect them from attacks against their way of life, their good name, their families and their homes.

Article 19: Governments should ensure that children are properly cared for, and protect them from violence, abuse and neglect by their parents, and anyone else who looks after them.

Article 20: Children who cannot be looked after by their own family must be looked after properly, by people who respect their religion, culture and language.

Article 22: Children who come into a country as refugees should have the same rights as children born in that country.

Article 23: Children who have any kind of disability should have special care and support, so that they can lead full and independent lives.

Article 25: Children who are looked after by their local authority, rather than their parents, should have their situation reviewed regularly.

Article 27: Children have a right to a standard of living that is good enough to meet their physical and mental needs. The government should help families who cannot afford to provide this.

Article 28: Children have a right to an education, and primary education within signatory nations should be compulsory, and provided free of charge.

Article 29: Education should develop each child's personality and talents to the full. It should encourage children to respect their parents, and their own and other cultures.

Article 30: Children have a right to learn and use the language and customs of their families, whether these are shared by the majority of people in the country or not.

Article 31: All children have a right to relax and play, and to join in a wide range of activities.

(UNICEF, 2012, online)

It was also recommended that every signatory nation should introduce the public post of a Children's Commissioner whose role it would be to oversee the instigation of national laws to comply with the UNCRC, and ongoing compliance with its articles within the relevant country. There was much debate about this in England, which was not finally settled until the Children Act of 2004 brought the post into being.

UNICEF further proposed:

> Many of the rights laid down in the Convention on the Rights of the Child have to be provided by adults or the state. However, the Convention also refers to the responsibilities of children, in particular to respect the rights of others ... If children have a right to be protected from conflict, cruelty, exploitation and neglect, then they also have a responsibility not to bully or harm each other.
>
> (UNICEF, nd, online)

Interestingly, the later African Charter on the Rights and Welfare of the Child (1999, online) contains a section on the child's responsibilities in which the following duties are specified:

a) to work for the cohesion of the family, to respect parents, superiors and elders at all times and to assist them in case of need;

b) to serve the national community by placing their physical and intellectual abilities at its service;

c) to preserve and strengthen social and national solidarity;

d) to preserve and strengthen African cultural values in relations with other members of the society, in the spirit of tolerance, dialogue and consultation and to contribute to the moral well-being of society;

e) to preserve and strengthen the independence and the integrity of the nation of citizenship;

f) to contribute to the best of their abilities, at all times and at all levels, to the promotion and achievement of African Unity.

Reflection

Consider this concept of a balance between rights and responsibilities, making a table or chart that maps the principal rights and responsibilities of practitioners, parents and children within early years settings, considering how these intermesh with each other. Introducing children to this balance of rights and responsibilities (for example, 'if you don't want him to call you names, then you should not call him names') is an extremely important part of children's early socialisation. Most children will be capable of this level of understanding early in the third year of life, quite a while before they begin to understand the more complex concept of showing contrition and asking for forgiveness.

As you can see from the above, besides the balancing of rights and responsibilities, the UNCRC introduced the world to another relatively new concept: children's opportunities for developmentally appropriate participation in their wider society, and a developmentally appropriate 'say' in decisions affecting their own everyday lives (see in particular UNCRC Articles 12 and 14).

Reflection: children's participation rights

How do you address children's participation rights within your setting, and how might you improve this aspect of your practice? Discuss this question with your peers and co-workers, considering where you might currently place yourselves on the 'ladder of participation', where you would like to be, and some ideas about how you might get there.

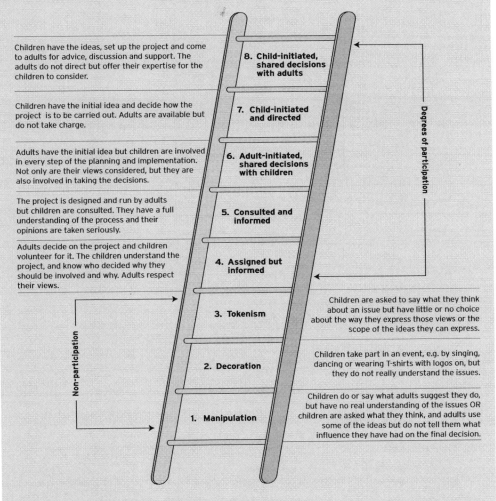

Children have the ideas, set up the project and come to adults for advice, discussion and support. The adults do not direct but offer their expertise for the children to consider.

8. Child-initiated, shared decisions with adults

Children have the initial idea and decide how the project is to be carried out. Adults are available but do not take charge.

7. Child-initiated and directed

Adults have the initial idea but children are involved in every step of the planning and implementation. Not only are their views considered, but they are also involved in taking the decisions.

6. Adult-initiated, shared decisions with children

The project is designed and run by adults but children are consulted. They have a full understanding of the process and their opinions are taken seriously.

5. Consulted and informed

Adults decide on the project and children volunteer for it. The children understand the project, and know who decided why they should be involved and why. Adults respect their views.

4. Assigned but informed

3. Tokenism

Children are asked to say what they think about an issue but have little or no choice about the way they express those views or the scope of the ideas they can express.

2. Decoration

Children take part in an event, e.g. by singing, dancing or wearing T-shirts with logos on, but they do not really understand the issues.

1. Manipulation

Children do or say what adults suggest they do, but have no real understanding of the issues OR children are asked what they think, and adults use some of the ideas but do not tell them what influence they have had on the final decision.

Degrees of participation

Non-participation

Figure 4.1 The ladder of participation
Source: Adapted from Wong *et al.* (2010).

Case study: the right to play

In 2007, American educational researchers Henley, McBride, Milligan and Nichols from Arkansas State University reflected on their nation's policy 'No Child Left Behind' (see www.understood. org/en/school-learning/your-childs-rights/basics-about-childs-rights/how-no-child-left-behind-affects-your-child) as follows:

> The playground at Maple Street Elementary School is quiet these days. The only movements on the swing sets are a result of a strong west wind edging the swings back and forth. The long lines that once formed for trips down the sliding boards are empty. There are no softball or kickball games nor are there any games of tag or duck-duck-goose being played. There won't be a fifth-grade musical this year. Children will not be learning to play the recorder nor will they be learning to march to rhythms or learn the traditional songs that have transcended the years of music instruction in elementary schools. There will be no art to display. Daddies' old long sleeved shirts that were handed down to children to cover up school clothes to keep from being stained with tempera paint and water colors are no longer needed. No, Maple Street Elementary School is not closing. It is squeezing every minute of the school day to meet the mandates of the [2001] No Child Left Behind Act (NCLB) ... Maple Street Elementary School is a metaphor for elementary schools across the nation ... With all the diversity among Maple Street's student body, the one commonality is that each student has affective and social needs that, according to some, are being compromised.
>
> (Henley *et al.*, 2007, pp. 56–7)

You have already read the similar commentary from some British experts relating to current early years policy in England on p.112. Here we meet some rights issues arising within the most developed nations in the world, which may, on the one hand, be taking their responsibility to provide their children with an education (Article 28) very seriously indeed, but in doing so to such an extreme extent and in such a monolithic manner, they may have now moved into a situation where the child's right to play and relaxation (Article 31) may be compromised by such policies.

Reflection

Consider the following questions:

- When we consider initiatives such as 'Every Child Matters' (UK) and 'No Child Left Behind' (US), are these principally about ensuring the rights of children within these societies, or about a state-driven attempt to 'socially engineer' adults who will fit into a consumer-driven, post-industrial society as uncritical consumer–workers?
- Are early years practitioners increasingly driven by a 'school readiness' agenda, interpreting statutory guidelines as an outcome-based curriculum (possibly driven by those who inspect the operation of early years settings)? If so, will this place our very youngest children in a uncompromisingly adult-directed environment, underpinned by relentless targets and an extensive programme of individual assessment?

In conclusion, EYGPs/EYTs need to gain a working knowledge of rights-based issues both nationally and internationally, and keep up with changes in this arena. Alderson (2008) gives a comprehensive overview of children's rights theory, practice and legislation as these impact on early years, which will help you to build on the brief summary above, and the UNCRC area of the UNICEF website posts regularly on ongoing developments: www.unicef.org/crc.

The emergence of the contemporary rights-based agenda also raises the issues of inclusion and equality of treatment; for example, consider UNCRC Articles 2 and 23. Such rights began to be represented in the legislation of most western nations over the second half of the twentieth century, with most developing a comprehensive set of rights-based legislation in the years leading up to 2000. Commentary on such legislation and its representation in practice can be found in chapter 7.

Conclusion

This chapter has addressed the following questions:

- How and why did legislation for children and families develop in England?
- What are 'human rights' and 'children's rights' and how are these protected through international policy?

We have offered a brief journey through a national history of legislation and policy for children and families, considering how the political beliefs of governments impact upon the regimes that they offer to care for, protect and educate children, and to help families to positively support and guide their children through the developmental period. The child protection and safeguarding aspects of this legislation are more thoroughly considered in chapter 3. We have explored the development of international rights-based policy, and its incorporation in British equality and inclusion policy and legislation will be further considered in chapter 7 with reference to early years practice examples.

How to keep up with such a relentless flow of legislation, policy and guidelines at both national and international levels is a challenge for all senior practitioners in childcare and education, across all ages and stages. In order to have ongoing knowledge of legislative and policy developments, it is necessary to keep up with current affairs, preferably by becoming a regular reader of a broadsheet newspaper (many of which can be accessed through inexpensive or free apps), but at the very least by a daily browse of a good-quality news website, such as those provided by the broadsheets and/or the BBC. **It is the responsibility of EYGPs/EYTs in every childcare/education setting to ensure that current statutory guidelines are being followed on an ongoing basis.** The local authority is always available to provide advice, and the leading practitioner in a setting should always maintain good relationships with their designated advisor. It is probably appropriate to close with the reminder that we offered in the first and second editions of this book: the advice on legislation and guidelines in this chapter, and, indeed, across the book as a whole can only be as up to date as the publication date stated on the imprint page. You should not, therefore, use this chapter as your only source of information, but as a springboard into an ongoing quest to seek social policy and inclusion information to inform the development of your own practice, and that of other practitioners in your setting.

Reflection: keeping up to date

How do you plan to keep up to date with current affairs and changes in the legislation and guidelines that apply to early years practice? Note the location of useful websites and resources in your continuing professional development portfolio; then ensure that you keep this list up to date. You may also find it helpful to search for relevant apps, and sign up to receive alerts from children and families policy websites. Some will also have Twitter feeds that you can follow.

Recommended reading

Alderson, P. (2008) *Young Children's Rights* (2nd Edn). London: Jessica Kingsley.

Baldock, P., Fitzgerald, D. and Kay, J. (2013) *Understanding Early Years Policy*. London: Sage.

House, R. (2011) *Too Much, Too Soon: Early learning and the erosion of childhood*. Stroud: Hawthorne Press.

Jarvis, P., Holland, W. and Swiniarski, L. (2016) *Early Years Pioneers in Context: Understanding theories about early childhood education and care*. Abingdon: Routledge.

Lovell, T. and Nation, L. (2016) *Social Policy for Early Years: Linking theory and practice*. Abingdon: Hodder.

Nutbrown, K. and Clough, P. (2014) *Early Childhood Education: History, philosophy and experience* (2nd Edn). London: Sage.

Journals

Children and Society

Children Now

Early Years – an International Journal of Research and Development

Early Years Educator

Educational Researcher

Nursery World

References

African Charter on the Rights and Welfare of the Child (1999) Retrieved from: http://acerwc.org/the-charter 1st February 2015.

Alderson, P. (2008) *Young Children's Rights* (2nd Edn). London: Jessica Kingsley.

Allen, G. (2011) *Early Intervention: The next steps*. London: The Cabinet Office.

Barnardo's (2008) *History of Barnardo's*. Retrieved from: www.barnardos.org.uk/who_we_are/history.htm 3rd May 2015.

BBC (2015) Queen's Speech 2015: free childcare access to double. Retrieved from: www.bbc.co.uk/news/uk-politics-32896284 28th May 2015.

Beveridge, W. (1942) *Report to the Parliament on Social Insurance and Allied Services*. London: HMSO.

Children, Schools and Families Committee (2010) *Fifth Parliamentary Report – Sure Start Children's Centres*. Retrieved from: www.publications.parliament.uk/pa/cm200910/cmselect/cmchilsch/130/13002.htm 3rd May 2015.

Coalition Government (2010) *The Coalition: Our programme for government*. London: The Cabinet Office.

Daily Telegraph (2013a) The Government should stop intervening in early years education. Retrieved from: www.telegraph.co.uk/comment/letters/10302844/The-Government-should-stop-intervening-in-early-education.html 3rd May 2015.

Daily Telegraph (2013b). Start schooling later than age five, say experts. Retrieved from: www.telegraph.co.uk/education/educationnews/10302249/Start-schooling-later-than-age-five-say-experts.html 10th January 2015.

DfE (2011) *Supporting Families in the Foundation Years*. London: DfE.

DfES (2003) *Every Child Matters*. Green Paper. London: The Stationery Office.

Eisenstadt, N. (2011) *Providing a Sure Start: How government discovered early childhood*. London: Policy Press.

Field, F. (2010) *The Foundation Years: Preventing poor children becoming poor adults*. London: The Cabinet Office.

Gov.uk (2014) Landmark Children and Families Act 2014 gains royal assent. Retrieved from: www.gov.uk/government/news/landmark-children-and-families-act-2014-gains-royal-assent 10th January 2015.

h2g2 (2009) *Children as Animals: Origins of anti-cruelty laws*. Retrieved from: http://h2g2.com/approved_entry/A640810 2nd May 2015.

Henley, J., McBride, J., Milligan, J. and Nichols, J. (2007). Robbing elementary students of their childhood: the perils of *No Child Left Behind*. *Education*. 128(1), 56–63.

Marr, A. (2007) *A History of Modern Britain*. London: Macmillan.

Moss, P. (2006) Listening to young children – beyond rights to ethics. In *Let's Talk about Listening to Children: Towards a shared understanding for early years education in Scotland*. Retrieved from: www.educationscotland.gov.uk/Images/listeningtochildren_tcm4-324433.pdf 7th December 2015.

National Head Start Association (US) (2015) About the National Head Start Association. Retrieved from: www.nhsa.org/about-us/mission-vision-history 3rd May 2015.

Roebuck, J. (1973) *The Making of Modern English Society from 1850*. London: Routledge and Kegan Paul.

Schwarz, L. and Boulton, J. (2007) *Parish apprenticeship in eighteenth century and early nineteenth-century London*. Paper presented at the Economic History Society Annual Conference, Exeter, 30th March 2007. Retrieved from: https://research.ncl.ac.uk/pauperlives/ehspapersummary.pdf 7th December 2015.

The Open University (2015) *Birth of the Welfare State*. Retrieved from: www.open.edu/openlearn/history-the-arts/history/history-science-technology-and-medicine/history-medicine/birth-the-welfare-state 3rd May 2015.

UNICEF (2008) *The Child Care Transition: A league table of early childhood education and care in economically advanced countries*. Retrieved from: www.unicef-irc.org/publications/pdf/rc8_eng.pdf 3rd May 2015.

UNICEF (2012) *Fact Sheet: A summary of the rights under the Convention on the Rights of the Child*. Retrieved from: http://www.unicef.org/crc/files/Rights_overview.pdf 7th December 2015.

UNICEF (2015) *History of UNICEF*. Retrieved from: www.unicef.org/about/who/index_history.html 3rd May 2015.

UNICEF (nd) *Children's Rights and Responsibilities* leaflet. Retrieved from: www.unicef.org/rightsite/files/rights_leaflet.pdf 3rd May 2015.

United Nations (1959) *Declaration of the Rights of the Child*. Retrieved from: www.unicef.org/lac/spbarbados/Legal/global/General/declaration_child1959.pdf 3rd May 2015.

United Nations (2012) *History of the United Nations*. Retrieved from: www.un.org/en/aboutun/history 3rd May 2015.

Wong, N., Zimmerman, M. and Parker, E. (2010) Typology of youth participation and empowerment for child and adolescent health promotion. *American Journal of Community Psychology*. 46(1), 100-14.

UK Government publications

DfES (1870) *The Education Act*. London: HMSO.

DoH (1870) *The Public Health Act*. London: HMSO.

DoH (1889) *The Children Act*. London: HMSO.

DoH (1908) *The Children's Charter*. London: HMSO.

DoH (1932/33) *The Children and Young Person's Act*. London: HMSO.

DfES (1944) *The Education Act*. London: HMSO.

DoH (1948) *The Children Act*. London: HMSO.

DoE (1980) *The Housing Act*. London: HMSO.

DfES (1988) *The Education Reform Act*. London: HMSO.

DoH (1989) The Children Act. London: HMSO.

Treasury (2003) *Every Child Matters*. Green Paper. London: HMSO.

DfES (2004) *The Children Act*. London: HMSO.

DfES (2006) *The Childcare Act*. London: HMSO.

DfES (2007) *The Early Years Foundation Stage*. London: HMSO.

DfES (2012) *The Early Years Foundation Stage*. London: HMSO.

DfE (2014) *Children and Families Act*. London: HMSO.

Section 2

Leading practice in the early years setting

5 Leading high-quality practice in children's learning and development from birth to seven years

Wendy Holland and Jonathan Doherty

CHAPTER OVERVIEW

This chapter will outline the role of the Early Years Graduate Practitioner/Early Years Teacher (EYGP/EYT) with respect to the strategies needed to lead high-quality practice that supports children's learning and development from birth to seven years. If we look internationally, we see that there are different approaches to this which provide an important, diverse context and these are the starting point for this chapter. For example, in Scandinavia, and in the Infant and Toddler centres and pre-schools of the Reggio Emilia region of Northern Italy, 'documentation' of evidence for pre-school children takes several forms, and formal schooling does not normally begin until after the child's sixth birthday. You can read a more detailed account of international perspectives in chapter 10. The focus on what 'evidence' to gather is also varied, based as it is on a profile of the individual child as physically active and socially capable, with a developing sense of empathy and fairness, and the ability to co-construct their own learning. This approach also views the adult as a *facilitator* rather than a *transmitter* of knowledge. To some extent this is in contrast to the increasing dependence on 'outcomes'-directed curricula we find in England, and to a lesser extent, in Wales, where the early years phase of education extends until the end of Year 1. In this chapter, we will focus on the English Early Years Foundation Stage (EYFS) and Key Stage 1 as it applies until the end of Year 1.

✔ What strategies are required to implement the cycle of planning, observing, assessing and recording of children's learning and development effectively?

✔ How might personalised provision for children based on secure understanding of child development and possible next steps in learning be effectively promoted in settings?

✔ How can high-quality practice that supports children's communication skills be achieved through the provision of language-rich environments?

The recommended reading list at the end of the chapter will introduce readers to a range of texts and online resources in which to read further on these topics.

Introduction: What strategies are required to implement the cycle of planning, observing, assessing and recording of children's learning and development effectively?

Reflection

If you are working in a country other than England, compare the examples below with practice within your own nation/region, considering similarities and differences, particularly whether any practice you identify as 'good' could be transferrable in some sense into your own practice.

In England, early years practitioners are expected to combine the facilitator and transmitter approaches, which brings particular challenges in managing the play-based framework of the EYFS (DfE, 2012a) and the subject-specific, outcome-driven expectations of the National Curriculum. The 'school readiness' agenda has placed more emphasis on 'directed outcomes', with the expectation that children (some as young as four years) will be gradually introduced to a more formal kind of transmission/teacher-led learning in 'readiness' for Key Stage 1 in schools. In this chapter we discuss how the uniqueness of each child must be addressed within a system that requires detailed measurement of attained 'outcomes' by the end of the Reception year. The adult must effectively balance the support and facilitation of child-initiated interests with adult-led activities.

Planning is the foundation of good teaching and learning. As an EYGP/EYT you will need to ensure that planning reflects each child's individual development needs. It should be flexible enough to respond to children's interests and be accessible and visible to staff and parents. There must be a clear understanding of the relationship between the different types of planning used in a setting. Three forms of planning relevant to both settings and schools are identified and discussed here.

- Long-term planning ensures that all seven Areas of Learning and Development in the EYFS are addressed. It usually covers a whole year and so includes a framework for the three school terms. It looks at the provision of resources for special occasions, celebrations, festivals, and visits either out of the setting or visitors to the setting, the overall balance of the curriculum, effective access to both outdoor and indoor provision and any special projects that may be undertaken with creative partnerships.
- Medium-term planning acts as a bridge between long- and short-term planning, covering a period from three to six weeks, or a half-term in the case of Key Stage 1. In the Foundation Stage, activities and themes tend to be of shorter duration, in line with children's changing interests and abilities. Medium-term planning considers access to and fair distribution of resources, the balance of topics and areas of focus within the areas of learning and development, and the ratio of child-initiated to adult-

led activities and experiences. In both long-term and medium-term planning, Key Stage 1 still retains its emphasis on discrete subjects such as English, mathematics, science, history and geography; however, an increasing number of primary schools are adopting more integrated systems such as the IPC (International Primary Curriculum), with its focus on a more integrated approach to topics (see, for example, this youtube video on the use of drama to support learning in maths: http://youtu.be/oOu16p4wyoE).

● Short-term planning usually has a time frame of one to three weeks. In the early years, the key factor is to ensure that the plan is flexible to allow children to follow their interests, as well as achieving their own personal targets. In some early years settings following the EYFS, short-term planning may change daily, dependent on the previous day's observations and assessments, reflecting perhaps a sudden development in an area of interest by the children.

For each of the above, planning still needs to retain flexibility. Inflexible adult planning can lead to transmission-based teaching and a *passive* learning environment for children. It also needs to be flexible enough to absorb and use those spontaneous moments of learning that occur daily with young children. At the same time, it needs to ensure that all children receive exposure to experiences and activities that promote each individual child's Learning Journey. Consider the vignette below which is a good example of a flexible approach to planning in the early years.

Figure 5.1 Flexible approach to planning in the early years

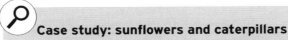

Case study: sunflowers and caterpillars

Sue, an early years educator in a nursery, had attended training on outdoor gardening activities. The head had been keen for a member of staff from the three to fives room to attend, as the setting had just finished re-designing some of the outdoor provision to include raised beds for the children to plant and grow seeds and bulbs. One project Sue developed involved the planting of sunflower seeds, initially in plastic cups filled with compost, which were nurtured by individual children at home, then duly planted out in one of the raised beds and further nurtured by Sue and the children. Sue had planned to link the event to the EYFS Areas of Learning and Development. She and Christine, the setting's EYGP, had discussed the timetable and planning for the three- to four-year-olds, as it had been agreed they would benefit from a slightly prolonged time of focused activity after lunch. The cut sunflowers were going to join a display of yellow objects in the room, which included a print of Van Gogh's painting of sunflowers. Sue had planned to look at one of the sunflowers in some detail, indicating in her planning the vocabulary she intended to introduce and the learning outcomes she hoped to achieve, which involved painting pictures of the sunflowers with thick brushes and thick paint.

The largest sunflower had been selected for examination, and placed on sheets of large white sugar paper on the floor. The tallest child in the group lay down next to it and the children estimated the flower was three times as tall as him. 'As tall as a giant', was one reply. Sue explained how the seeds in the seed head could be eaten, or planted, like they had a long time ago. She began to look at the flower, noting the 'hairs' on its long stem, its pale roots and the 'veins' in its leaves. 'We've got veins', said a boy, showing Sue his hands. 'Yes', she replied, then continued examining the sunflower. 'Yours are blue and knobbly', insisted the boy. This comment was ignored. Christine, who had been asked by Sue to observe the activity for the children's profiles, sensed some of the children had lost interest, and were no longer following the examination of the sunflower, but were concerned rather with something small and moving. A caterpillar had crawled from under a curled leaf and was slowly making its way to the edge of the paper. The children's interest in the sunflower immediately evaporated and all eyes focused on the caterpillar.

Sue tried several times to draw the children back to the focus of her careful planning, eventually looking to Christine for support. But Christine joined in with the children's interest, suggesting they made a 'home' of some kind for the caterpillar, and food for it to eat, gently persuading Sue that the sunflowers could be enjoyed another day, and the children could still experiment with thick brushes and thick paint. Sue was reluctant at first and concerned that her intended learning for the children and her planning would need to be fitted into another period of focused activity or discarded. She was eventually won over by the children's enthusiasm for the new class 'pet', whom they named Vincent 'after the man who painted sunflowers'.

Reflection

Sue's planning showed she had tried to think about the learning outcomes for the older children. Christine's gentle refusal to support Sue in continuing with the sunflower activity was indicating to Sue that children's interests need to be listened to. The caterpillar had caught their imagination and interest. The planned activity could take place another time, when the children would be happy to reengage with it. The resources Sue had prepared would not be wasted, as they could still form part of an activity in its own right. After this incident, Christine asked for Sue's help in developing the 'Vincent the caterpillar' project. Sue soon became caught up in planning activities and resources around the lifecycle of the butterfly.

- Do you agree with Christine's decision not to support Sue on this occasion?
- Could she have achieved her intentions in a different way?
- Do you think that Christine's lack of support for Sue's designated activity would help or conflict with the requirement to support Sue's development as a practitioner?
- Do you think it was important for Christine to illustrate the need to be flexible in planning?
- Did Sue plan and resource her project too rigidly in advance?

Observation is the means by which information can be gathered about each child. By doing close, regular observations, we can:

- determine children's particular interests, likes and dislikes through ongoing communication with children, parents and carers
- identify any special or particular needs
- establish levels of well-being and involvement
- gain knowledge of newly acquired skills
- assess individual progression
- plan next steps for personalised learning.

All of the above can be gained through regular, relatively informal participant observation, making notes while engaged in activities, talking with and listening to children. However, other forms of observation may be used; if there are concerns over a child's behaviour, event sampling may need to be employed and, by observing when a particular type of behaviour occurs, the triggers/causes of such behaviour identified (see chapters 2 and 3). Concerns about areas of possible deficit or delay could involve the use of more detailed target child and/or focal child observations (see chapter 2) in order to gather evidence to support further investigations by the Special Educational Needs Coordinator (SENCo). Another key focus for such observations would be to consider the balance between the amounts of ludic (imaginative) and epistemic (investigative) play in which the child engages (Hutt *et al.*, 1989), with a view to balancing this more carefully if the child is engaging in significantly more of one sort of play than the other.

On a broader level, observation can also highlight:

- gaps in resources
- an imbalance between child-initiated and adult-directed activities, as well as the quality and frequency of adult–child interactions
- lack of sufficient access to indoor and outdoor environments
- the need to provide more inclusive resources to acknowledge and celebrate the diversity of children in the setting and the unique individuality of each child
- exemplary practice that can be cascaded to others or the need for further training
- the input from parents and carers to support the child's Learning Journey.

Take a look at the story of Alice below.

Case study: Alice's progress

Alice, a twin aged three years, has been causing some concern. Her Key Person and Alice's mother have discussed how Paul, her twin brother, does all the talking for both of them. This practice seems to have increased since the arrival of their new baby brother. Alice's mother is particularly concerned about her language development and pronunciation, and has shared this with Jill, the setting's EYT. The twins are relatively new to the nursery setting and Alice is still not separating well from her mother, despite her brother being there. Concerns about Alice have also been expressed by other members of staff, so Jill has decided to do a narrative observation of Alice for the afternoon.

At the beginning of the session, Alice settles after a tearful parting from her mother. She joins her brother at the water; filling containers seems to calm her and her sense of well-being appears to improve. Her levels of concentration and involvement appear to be high as she attempts to pour water from one container into another. Chelsea, a four-and-a-half-year-old, comes to join them. She talks to Alice rather than Paul. Over the few short weeks Alice has been in the setting, she has tended to be more at ease with the older children.

Chelsea moves away to a painting easel and Paul decides it is time to play outside. Alice hesitates for a moment, then joins Chelsea who is humming to herself as she paints. The painting area is a favourite area for the twins, and Alice soon becomes absorbed in mixing colours on a palate, staying by herself at the easel when Chelsea has gone outside. She changes her brush from one hand to the other while mixing, then painting. Jill eventually draws up a small chair by the easel and looks at the painting Alice is involved in, asking Alice about her painting. Alice explains, with a reasonable amount of clarity, that it depicts a mother monster with a demanding baby monster. Jill records in her subsequent participant observation and evaluation that:

- Alice's level of well-being has been sufficiently high for her to feel confident to engage in activities on her own without Paul.
- She showed ease in the company of an older child.
- Her concentration and involvement while painting were sustained for longer than was usual for her.
- Her communication with the practitioner evidenced language skills to a degree she had not shown previously on her own, although some sounds were not yet fully articulated.
- The topic of the picture suggests that she is coming to terms with her mother's involvement with her baby brother.

Reflection

Think back to chapter 2 and the discussion there about forms of observation, including the use of the Leuven Involvement Scale for Young Children. How does the above practice compare with your setting's own strategies for observing children?

Observations in Key Stage 1 may use some or all of the above as well as observation pro-formas geared to specific areas such as Guided Reading or shared observations between the teacher and teaching assistant which can lead to differentiated provision for individual needs (Orlandi, 2014). How observations are recorded is usually dependent upon the requirements of individual settings and the provision they create for their children. The

EYFS (DfES, 2007) CD-ROM includes examples of basic pro-formas and templates for a child's Learning Journey which can be adapted for use when observing. For new practitioners these can provide guidance and help. Settings will also need to record effective knowledge of the three prime and four specific areas of learning and development outlined in the revised EYFS Guidance (DfE, 2012b) and their related aspects, as well as the Characteristics of Effective Learning.

Case study: Characteristics of Effective Learning

The EYFS summarises the Characteristics of Effective Learning as follows:

Playing and exploring – engagement
- Finding out and exploring
- Playing with what they know
- Being willing to 'have a go'

Active learning – motivation
- Being involved and concentrating
- Keeping trying
- Enjoying achieving what they set out to do

Creating and thinking critically – thinking
- Having their own ideas
- Making links
- Choosing ways to do things

Reflection

You may find it helpful to structure your observation notes as follows:
- Effectiveness of the context for learning.
- What did the child actually do (see points about gathering objective information in chapter 2).
- Links to Early Years Foundation Stage.
- How did the adult(s) support the learning?
- Potential 'next steps' for the child.

The only way that you will be able to develop your observation and evaluation skills is by plenty of practice. As we suggested in chapter 2, requesting feedback from experienced practitioners on your observations and evaluations will also be very helpful in further developing your skills.

Committing the observation to paper as soon as possible ensures reliability and validity. The perspectives of several members of staff, as well as parents and carers, provide triangulation of evidence for a child's profile. In Key Stage 1, a good working relationship between support staff and the teacher, where observations of small group work or individual children are regularly discussed, provides reliability as well as allowing for more appropriate, differentiated work to be planned. With the increase in the use of ICT, forms of recording other than written narrative are increasingly being developed. The use of iPads, digital photographs, video and audio recording, which can be shared with the family, all help to effectively build a child's profile and are to be encouraged.

Assessment, the next phase in the cycle is the essential analysis and review of what has been observed. James *et al.* (2006) believe all assessments have some common characteristics. They all involve:

- Making observations
- Interpreting the evidence
- Making judgements that can be used for decisions about actions.

Increasingly, many early years settings are now using computer packages to support assessment within the EYFS. Essentially, these provide an electronic version of Learning Journeys, and best practice is still when practitioners and also parents sit with the child and his/her Learning Journey and help them to reflect on what they did at the beginning, what they are able to do now, and what they might achieve in the future. This is a vital form of self-assessment for young children, as well as it being a celebration of what they have already achieved. To support continuing professional development and their ability to reflect on their own practice, EYGPs/EYTs need to have knowledge of alternative assessment systems including international systems (see ECD/PISA 2015, www.oecd.org/edu/school).

Pre-schools in Scandinavia cater for children from birth to six or seven years, and this extended 'childhood' is not generally assessed against specific outcomes for literacy and numeracy, but looks for growth in the child's physical skills, their creativity and, importantly, their social and emotional intelligence. In the Reggio Emilia Infant and Toddler centres and pre-schools in Northern Italy, children do not follow a National Curriculum and are not assessed against prescribed and standardised criteria. Their individual interests are well 'documented', through the use of observations, artworks, photographs, projects – recording the 'hundred languages' that Malaguzzi suggests children use to communicate (Edwards *et al.*, 1998). Adults are seen as facilitators and fellow researchers alongside children, and children are viewed through a community lens of the immediate community and not through distant government policy.

Underpinning all observation and assessment must be a secure knowledge of how children develop and learn. An understanding of schemas (Piaget, 1951; Athey, 1990; Atherton and Nutbrown, 2014) will support knowledge of important developmental stages (Pen Green, 2008). For example, how often has a transporting schema where a child is fascinated by moving materials from place to place not been recognised in a setting or at home, and been ignored or stopped because it is messy or inconvenient, instead of being supported and extended? There are a range of other methods of assessment alongside the EYFS Profile that the EYGP/EYT should become familiar with. We would refer readers to the recent *Development Matters* document (Early Education, 2012) for further guidance and to the *Characteristics of Effective Learning* (British Association for Early Childhood Education, 2011) to help deepen understanding of children's thinking and how features such as motivation and engagement impact upon learning. The use of the Scales of Involvement and

Well-being (Laevers, 1997, 2005) can help the observer assess the level of learning that is taking place on a continuum from deep to superficial.

The Infant/Toddler Environmental Rating Scales (ITERS) for children from birth to 30 months and the Early Childhood Environmental Rating Scales (ECERS) for children from two-and-a-half to five years (see www.ecersuk.org) are other important tools for assessment. These rating scales help when a setting wants to assess its provision holistically, by looking at such aspects as space and furnishings, personal care routines, listening and talking, activities, and interaction between parents and staff. These scales have been used in several high-profile early years research projects on both sides of the Atlantic over the past 20 years. They have recently been joined by a Sustained Shared Thinking and Emotional Well-Being scale (SSTEW, Siraj *et al.*, 2015) which 'goes much further in defining what the adults actually do that support both children's emotional well-being and their learning behaviours and attitudes – the characteristics of effective learning' (Thomson, 2015, online).

The EYFS (DfE, 2012a) introduced a new assessment: a Progress Check for two-year-olds, introduced to support this assessment through a combination of views from parents, practitioners and health visitors. The present EYFS Profile is a summative form of assessment, as it identifies the levels reached by a child at the end of the Foundation Stage, but can also be used in a formative way to inform the Year 1 teacher's planning to provide smooth transition to more formalised learning. The revised EYFS (DfE, 2012a) now includes a baseline assessment when the child enters Reception as well as the current EYFS Profile at the end of the Reception year, assessed on a three-point scale, where each individual child's progress is seen as: *emergent, expected* or *exceeding* the Early Learning Goals. For children who have made the transition to Key Stage 1 but are in need of interventions to support their attainment of the new level descriptors, P scales or an individual code to support their bespoke learning are suggested as the best practice (DfE, 2014a).

Reporting is the final element of the planning, observation and assessment cycle. Statutory arrangements allow for parents to receive a written summary of their child's progress and, where a parent requests it, a copy of the completed EYFS Profile. In Key Stage 1, schools have a statutory duty to inform parents annually of their children's progress, but many settings send out more frequent reports. Parents/carers will also be informed of the results of national tests at the end of Key Stages 1 and 2 as well as teacher assessments on their child's progress.

How might personalised provision for children based on secure understanding of child development and possible next steps in learning be effectively promoted in settings?

Personalised provision leads to effective personalised learning. The original EYFS framework describes it thus:

> The EYFS sets standards to enable early years providers to reflect the rich and personalised experience that many parents give their children at home. Like parents, providers should deliver individualised learning, development and care that enhances the development of the children in their care ...
>
> (DCSF, 2007, p. 9)

In order for the EYGP/EYT to lead and support practitioners in creating an 'enabling environment' for every child, thorough understanding of child development needs to be modelled to and expected of practitioners. Only by understanding the norms within a range of behaviours can the practitioner identify the needs of individual children, and become alert to potential deficit and delay. The EYFS framework (DfE, 2012a) provides a generous overlap between expected behaviours for children from birth to 60 months. The first 'norm' or age stage that begins at birth is structured as potentially extending to 11 months, with the next stage potentially starting at eight months, and so on (Early Education, 2012, also see chapter 2). However, the EYGP/EYT needs to ensure that the sequences that run through these norms are used with caution. For example, some babies will not crawl before they walk, and not all children will process language in exactly the same way, perhaps electing to be mute until they are ready to speak more competently.

The EYGP/EYT's responsibility in leading and supporting practice depends upon their ability to ensure practitioners take all these factors into consideration. Home visits before a child is admitted to the setting provide essential information about a child. In their home environments, parents often feel more relaxed, freely providing information about particular transitional toys, family language, and friendships that have been formed with children already attending the setting. For babies and very young children, it could focus on their likes and dislikes when having nappies changed, their feeding and sleep habits, and the way they prefer to be held or rocked. The home visit can also help the practitioner understand the child's position within the family, their relationship with other siblings, parenting styles, the family's position within the wider community, and any possible fears the parent might already have about their child; in addition, expectations parents/carers might have regarding the setting and 'education' in general can be identified. It can also create a particular bond between the practitioner and child. Seeing this new adult in the child's home environment builds trust and helps the child during the transitional phase from home to setting.

This information, combined with initial careful observations and assessments during the child's settling-in period, can help practitioners provide and plan for effective personalised provision for that child. Flexible planning around children's interests should ensure variations in practice to encompass and celebrate the diversity of children's backgrounds and experiences. The use of sustained shared thinking with children (Siraj *et al.*, 2015, also see chapter 2) as they create their products will demonstrate their understanding of process and give practitioners a clearer view of the next steps in provision needed for the child to progress. This may include revisiting an area of learning and development until they have successfully assimilated and then accommodated the process. Keeping profiles up-to-date is essential good practice, and regularly reviewing the content of the profile with individual children will help to personalise provision through aiding the child to self-assess, celebrate what they have achieved and consider their next challenge/step. In Key Stage 1, the need to share planning with support staff is vital for the effective and smooth functioning of the learning experience. Taking time not only to explain but also to listen to support staff, who often work closely with individuals and small groups, shows good practice and may result in planning which is a better 'fit' in the learning experience for the children with whom they regularly work. This may also include trainee teachers, as the case study below illustrates.

Case study: a lesson on 'shapes' with a mixed class of Year 1 and Year 2 children

Victoria, a final-year QTS (qualified teacher status) undergraduate, is being observed taking a maths lesson with a mixed class of Year 1 and 2 children in a small village school of 100 children. The range of abilities within the class of 28 children is wide and includes a child statemented for global delay, several 'looked after' children, some children with behavioural issues and a small group of children assessed as gifted and talented. The children have been placed into groups according to their abilities; each group is named – 'octagon' for the children who are perceived as being 'most able' through to 'circle' for the children with the lowest level of attainment. There are two teaching assistants supporting Victoria in this lesson; one is seated with the circle group, and the other with the octagon group. The room is quite cramped, with separate tables for each group, clearly limiting movement by children or staff.

Victoria's lesson is planned in detail. She begins the session by showing various shapes on the interactive white board which she feels the children have already covered, asking for 'quick fire' responses to her questions about the shapes. She gives quick positive feedback to correct responses. One of the children on the 'circle' table has difficulties in replying. She is told the answer by the teaching assistant sitting next to her, and repeats it. Victoria does not attempt to address the child's confusion, but keeps to her closely timed lesson plan (possibly because she is being observed and is clearly nervous). Glancing at her watch, she changes the visual stimulus and asks children from the different groups to come out and choose a small card from a box with a shape drawn on it. The child has to conceal the shape and then describe it. The first child to 'guess' the correct shape receives a 'house point'. The children on the octagon table gain the most points, and several other children begin to go off task. Victoria asks the children to take out their maths books and begin working with the sheets she has previously prepared for each group. She then proceeds to go around the groups, supporting them in their different tasks. She is marking as she goes, as well as giving formative feedback. The teaching assistant seated with the octagon group is unclear about the task and asks, 'do you want them to do tessellation?'. It is clear from Victoria's expression she is unclear what 'tessellation' means, and so has to spend some time explaining the task she has set for the octagon group. During these group extension activities she spends very little time with the circle group, relying on the teaching assistant to help them complete what look to be fairly simple 'matching' tasks, which most of the children achieve.

The issues begin when they are asked to draw the shapes in their books and label them; this results in several of the circle group going off task by talking and playing with some of the resources on the table. The octagon group finish their worksheets ahead of time, so Victoria tells them to get out their reading books. Victoria attempts to begin a plenary by asking the children to show a 'thumbs up/down' to indicate their understanding of the lesson. Some children clearly have not understood, but she pushes forward with the planned plenary, asking for certain children to come out and show the rest of the class what they have done, but is interrupted by the SENCo who needs to withdraw several children for a group assessment.

During her feedback, Victoria is defensive when asked about her differentiation of tasks. She admits she has taken the planning for the lesson from a standardised programme used by many schools. When asked how she would record her assessment of the lesson for individual children, she replied 'By marking their work … it seemed to go OK … most of them seemed to get it'.

How can high-quality practice that supports children's communication skills be achieved through the provision of language-rich environments?

To lead on high-quality provision, EYGPs/EYTs need to be able to create environments that support children's early language and actively promote language that is effective with children (Bernstein, 1976; Tough, 1974; Siraj-Blatchford *et al.*, 2002). From a baby's attempts at early vocalisation to the rapid fire 'why?' questions of the older child, children naturally engage in trying to communicate with significant others in their lives. The 2007 EYFS Practice Guidance suggested that effective practice in encouraging children's development in this area of learning requires positive relationships to be built with people who have meaning for them (DCSF, 2007, p. 39). Without the sense of security and trust such relationships engender, communication and language skills may not fully develop in the young child (see the account of language development in chapter 2; also see the story of the isolated child 'Genie' at www.youtube.com/watch?v=JOVY-52YmjE).

It is the EYGP/EYT's task to lead and support practitioners in creating such warm, enabling environments; for example, through trusting relationships with parents/carers, valuing and using their specialised knowledge of the child's daily routines and the forms of language used by the family that the baby or child responds to best. When a child comes from a home where the principal language spoken is not English, it can help to request tapes/CDs in the baby's home language. Ensuring the Key Person fully understands their role in promoting language and communication is essential in ensuring that babies and young children experience supportive, trusting environments in any setting.

Within such relationships, a baby will learn to link sounds and voices to the new routines of their day; for example, music being played during nappy changing, as well as the practitioner's calm voice, or a favourite story being read before they fall asleep. In a trusting relationship, children will more readily express feelings, thoughts and ideas. The EYGP/EYT needs to ensure that planning and organisation incorporate daily opportunities to explore language through rhymes, songs, poetry and stories, and for older children to access fiction and non-fiction materials, and that the language accessed is also reflective of the diverse nature of children's individual personalities and cultures. EYGPs/EYTs also need to model how a language-rich environment underpins not only the acquisition of language itself, but how language is embedded in all the Areas of Learning (e.g. how mathematical language helps children to problem-solve by estimating the number of sweets in a jar, the properties of shapes, the patterns in the world around them, etc.). Books and signs around the setting written in children's home language will enable children from diverse backgrounds to feel welcomed as part of the community. The Hundred Languages of Children suggested by Loris Malaguzzi (Edwards *et al.*, 1998) implies that children's communication is not limited to the use of speech, but is seen through dance, music, mark-making, drawing, modelling, painting, expression and body language, supporting the view that young children learn best when all their senses are engaged.

Case study: the Hundred Languages of Children

The child
is made of one hundred.
The child has
A hundred languages
A hundred hands
A hundred thoughts
A hundred ways of thinking
Of playing, of speaking.
A hundred always a hundred
Ways of listening, of marveling, of loving
A hundred joys
For singing and understanding
A hundred worlds
To discover
A hundred worlds
To invent
A hundred worlds
To dream
The child has
A hundred languages
(and a hundred hundred hundred more)
But they steal ninety-nine.
The school and the culture
Separate the head from the body.
They tell the child;
To think without hands
To do without head
To listen and not to speak
To understand without joy
To love and to marvel
Only at Easter and at Christmas.
They tell the child:
To discover the world already there
And of the hundred
They steal ninety-nine.

> They tell the child:
> That work and play
> Reality and fantasy
> Science and imagination
> Sky and earth
> Reason and dream
> Are things
> That do not belong together
> And thus they tell the child
> That the hundred is not there
> The child says:
> NO WAY. The hundred is there.
>   (Loris Malaguzzi in Edwards *et al.*, 1998, p. 3)

Reflection

Watch the video made by the United Way Center for Excellence in Early Education Demonstration School, Educare of Miami-Dade at www.youtube.com/watch?v=eqVH8ZwRXoU then consider how you could more effectively access the Hundred Languages of Children in your practice.

One way an EYGP/EYT can lead and support practitioners in promoting rich and inclusive language environments is through the use of 'conversations' and early 'proto-conversation' turn-taking with babies and toddlers (see chapter 2). Daily sessions with rhymes, songs sung in diverse languages and repetitive and familiar stories, linking sound to movement as children become more mobile, are essential. Song books can be created for parents to use at home to encourage familiarity with rhymes and language, accompanied by pleas for help from willing volunteers in compiling story sacks, songs and rhyme bags. As children progress they can be encouraged to 'read' a story to peers, or recreate a familiar story with such visual aids as home-made puppets and props and magnet boards, to listen to and act out story and rhyme tapes, as well as having access to both fiction and non-fiction books, big books, pop-up books, board books and interactive multimedia sources. Musical instruments can be used to emphasise the beat and rhythm of language, tapping out the beats, for example, in a child's name, trying to repeat a pattern played by an adult or peer. Later still comes the introduction of different uses of language for different audiences; the chance, time and encouragement to discuss, argue, share experiences, re-tell narratives in the correct sequence, showing an understanding of language patterns in stories.

Children in a rich linguistic environment with access to a range of printed materials will begin to link sounds to letters, using their growing phonic knowledge to write simple words. A reflective EYGP/EYT needs to be aware of contemporary issues around delivery of phonics and the use of government funding to schools for support of a discrete phonics programme. The link between nursery 'phonics', be it *Letters and Sounds* or other commercially available phonics programmes and the later phases, require the EYGP/EYT, where possible, to have knowledge of the phonics delivery in their main feeder schools for ease of transition and continuity of learning.

Case study: Zahir's world

Susan, the setting EYT, had been monitoring the profiles of the four- to five-year-olds who would be leaving the setting to go to school after the summer. She had already had a discussion with the Key Person responsible for Zahir, a four-year-old who would be leaving that summer. His Key Person, Josie, explained why his profile which had started so promisingly, with his observations showing a lively and active boy, interested and engaged in a number of areas of development and learning, suddenly seemed to plateau over the last few months. Around that time Zahir's mother had become seriously ill, and had been undergoing tests involving short stays in hospital. Zahir's aunt, who usually collected him, spoke very little English, and the dialect she spoke was not well understood by the member of staff who acted as interpreter in these situations. Zahir's father did speak good English, but on the rare occasions he collected Zahir he was in a hurry, reluctant to discuss the situation. Zahir had become isolated, preferring to engage in model building at the design and technology table. When other children offered to help or showed interest in his building, he would shout at them, often becoming excitable, using his home language. At times when the member of staff was asked to interpret, she would say he did not want anyone near, adding that he was too old to be using his home language in the setting environment, and the family should be helping to teach him English. While not openly defying the adults in the setting, he would only take part in focused activities reluctantly, refusing to communicate, except for the briefest of exchanges with other adults or children.

Story time was the only time he seemed to give his full attention, listening intently to the stories, but declining to take part. Susan decided to read the story in Zahir's room one afternoon. She took in a large empty cardboard box, telling the children they needed to listen carefully to the story so they would know what to do with the box afterwards. She read the story *This Is Our House* by Michel Rosen (1996), where a group of children from a block of high-rise flats find a large empty cardboard box. Zahir sat listening intently to the story. As soon as it had finished, he leapt up and said 'mine', attempting to put his arms around the cardboard box. Several other children began to argue and pull at the box. Susan got their attention by telling them they were behaving like the children in the story. The cardboard box was now also in need of repair. The children carried it over to the design and technology area and began to repair it, under Zahir's minimal instructions. The children trusted Zahir as he always built interesting models which others tried to copy. Susan began to take some pictures of the process with a digital camera, then remembered the camera had a video.

By this time, the group had decided not only to repair the box but to make it into something under Zahir's direction. Susan took digital images and video, but when she tried to show Zahir what she had taken and engage him in conversation, he looked away and continued with his task. The video, however, did catch his attention, along with the rest of the group. After they had been filmed for a while, Susan would stop filming and ask some children to talk to the camera. 'Like on the news', a child suggested. Susan agreed. Afterwards she showed the 'interview' back to them on the interactive whiteboard. Zahir had refused to take part until he saw the re-run, then he became animated, trying to explain his vision for the 'skyscraper house' his 'team' were building. In his excitement he slipped into his home language, then corrected himself, answering Susan's questions about windows, doors, lifts and stairs, as she probed how and why they were making a 'skyscraper house'.

Reflection

Assessing the situation, Susan noted the following:

- The issues around Zahir's behaviour should have been picked up earlier.
- This had resulted in a sad little boy developing defensive behaviour. His sense of well-being had been allowed to reach very low levels.
- No real attempt had been made to discuss or talk with members of Zahir's family.
- There were issues that needed addressing around staff in the setting and the use and encouragement of home language.

After discussion with the deputy manager the following course of action was decided:

- As well as the usual observations based on areas of development and learning, scales of well-being would be introduced.
- Better procedures for talking with and involving parents needed to be established. With only one part-time member of staff able to speak Urdu and Punjabi, the setting was limiting its ability to reach out to the increasingly diverse community it now served. The deputy manager said she would discuss with the manager the possibility of employing another member of staff with experience of highly diverse multi-lingual settings to work both in the setting and as a family support and liaison worker.
- Clear guidelines would be drawn up with regard to the use and encouragement of home language, and this would need to be reflected in the wider setting environment.

The number of children with English as an additional language in early years settings has grown rapidly in the first years of the twenty-first century, and many, mainly urban, settings now work with an increasingly diverse cohort of families with many different home languages, and it may be impossible to employ enough people to speak all the home languages represented in the setting. Read the article by Rose Drury, which is openly available on this link: www.tandfonline.com/doi/full/10.1080/1350293X.2013.814362, and then reflect on the above comments and assessments for Zahir. How would you have assessed the situation as an EYGP/EYT? Would you have taken the same course of action as above?

Conclusion

This chapter has explored a range of questions that focus on the knowledge, strategies and skills that EYGPs/EYTs need to lead high-quality practice from birth to seven years. In doing this, the chapter has also touched upon alternative approaches from other countries to give a wider perspective on what constitutes learning and development for children. Skills of engagement, observation and assessment that meet the individual needs of every child are vital regardless of context, in the UK or abroad. Through the modelling of such skills, EYGPs/EYTs will not only be engaged in high-quality practice themselves, but will also help to raise and develop the skill sets of other practitioners by leading practice.

What strategies are required to implement the cycle of planning, observing, assessing and recording of children's learning and development effectively?

Sound understanding of the planning cycle, and the skills to implement this are essential for all practitioners. This involves ongoing observation of children and the linking of information collected through various kinds of observation and sources to the formative assessment of each individual child's needs. Planning should allow for, in the short term, careful observation by staff of groups of children and the individual child to provide activities and experiences that promote learning for every child on their journey towards achieving the current Early Learning Goals (ELGs), and Key Stage 1 of the National Curriculum. In line with the play-based emphasis of the revised EYFS framework, planning needs to be flexible enough to accommodate children's individual interests. Triangulation of observations obtained by several members of staff, not only the child's Key Person, will provide the necessary reliability and validity.

Formative assessment of young children from birth to five years is an essential and statutory requirement of the EYFS framework (DfE, 2012a). At the time of writing, it appears that a new statutory baseline assessment process will be approached through the operationalisation of observation-based summative assessments on each child's entry to Reception. Assessment scales that recognise involvement and well-being as well as assessments against the areas of learning, will help to provide a holistic view of the individual child's development. The EYFS Profile (which may be removed in response to the imposition of baseline assessment) can also be seen as a summative document, detailing the level the child has reached in relation to the ELGs by the end of the Foundation Stage, which will help with the child's transition to Key Stage 1. Children in this first stage of the National Curriculum, in many cases, as research has shown (Whitebread and Bingham, 2011) still benefit from aspects of the play-based and flexible planning evidenced in the EYFS. This has to be 'married' with the more formal approach, especially in literacy and mathematics, that underpins the targets and outcomes of the revised National Curriculum (DfE, 2014b). The EYGP/EYT in Year 1 (Y1) needs to balance the requirements of the National Curriculum with the individual needs of the child through their understanding of child development and contemporary research.

It is essential that staff in Reception classes communicate what they know about each child to Y1, and as such, Y1 staff require some depth of knowledge of the EYFS; this is a level of multi-agency working (see chapter 3) that is fundamental to the ease of transition for each child from a play-based framework to a more formal transmission method of teaching. Knowledge of the ITERS, ECERS and SSTEW scales can also help the practitioner assess and improve the environment and support good practice.

Recording of observations and assessments can take many forms. Often settings design their own pro-formas, as do most schools. Reporting children's achievements and development to parents at least once a year has been and continues to be a statutory requirement. Other agencies, for example local authorities and Ofsted also require information such as EYFS Profile data from individual settings. Reporting also happens on a daily basis, between members of staff, between staff and parents and, most importantly, between practitioners and children, in order to help each child become self-reflective.

Reporting children's achievements in the National Curriculum is also multilayered, with the 'accountability' of school league tables influencing practice to a high degree (NUT, 2011).

How might personalised provision for children based on secure understanding of child development and possible next steps in learning be effectively promoted in settings?

Knowledge of child development, research and current initiatives is essential for personalised care and learning to take place. This has to be applied in conjunction with a sound understanding of the personal circumstances of each child. Bronfenbrenner's (1979) theory of the relationships within a family, between a family and settings and the larger world, and Baumrind's view of parenting styles (Oates *et al.*, 2005) show the necessity for the practitioner to be knowledgeable about each child's individual circumstances if effective personalised provision is to be established. Working with parents and carers to establish effective personalised learning for the child is essential, together with ongoing formative observation and assessment. This is now even more essential with the introduction of places for two-year-olds in maintained settings. The EYGP/EYT needs to ensure that staff are given training to improve their knowledge and understanding of the current needs of vulnerable children and families in poverty. Recent research suggests a lack of positivity and sensitivity when dealing with such vulnerable families (Simpson *et al.*, 2015). Sustained shared thinking between the practitioner and child helps extend the child's development and learning potential, through the use of open-ended questioning. Allowing time for a child to revisit projects and self-reflect must be built into the routines of the day, if effective personalised provision is to be achieved.

How can high-quality practice that supports children's communication skills be achieved through the provision of language-rich environments?

Practitioners need sound knowledge of the stages of language acquisition (see the EYFS Practice Guidance DCSF 2008; DfE 2012b: Literacy Programme, National Curriculum, 2014) for children from birth to seven years. The need for positive relationships to be established during the child's initial transition from home to setting is essential, with links to home provided by transitional toys, music or objects and culturally appropriate practice to reassure the child. Only in such supportive and enabling environments will children feel able to express themselves. The practitioner needs to recognise that children from birth to seven have the Hundred Languages of Children through which to communicate with others, the diversity and variety of which needs to be recognised and celebrated by the practitioner. The provision of a language-rich environment, through book corners, story sacks, role play, puppets and regular sessions playing with language through rhymes and songs, is essential for the development of a child's language. In Key Stage 1, more focus is given to the increased skills of phonic decoding of words, and the introduction of more complex grapheme/phoneme combinations. There is also the expectation that children at this stage should be able to read simple sentences, using their phonic knowledge to decode regular words.

The real acknowledgement of the diversity of languages within a setting, as well as the celebration of that diversity and difference, is important for establishing positive relationships and a confident sense of self in young children. The means to create music, dance and rhythm as ways of expression, both indoors and out, need to be resourced. Listening to children and taking their questions seriously, sharing their thinking as they engage in activities and experiences, both self-generated and adult-led, are important in encouraging the development of language-rich environments.

Recommended reading

Cooper, J. (2013) *The Early Years Communication Handbook*. London: Practical Pre-School Books.

Doherty, J. and Hughes, M. (2013) *Child Development: Theory and practice 0–11*. Harlow: Pearson.

Siraj, I., Kingston, D. and Melhuish, E. (2015) *Assessing Quality in Early Childhood Education and Care: Sustained Shared Thinking and Emotional Well-Being (SSTEW) Scale for 2–5-year-olds provision*. London: Trentham.

Whitebread, D. and Coltman, P. (Eds) (2015) *Teaching and Learning in the Early Years* (4th Edn). London: Routledge.

Wood, E. (2013) *Play, Learning and the Early Childhood Curriculum*. London: Sage.

Websites

Early Education: www.early-education.org.uk/development-matters

Nursery World: www.nurseryworld.co.uk

Reggio Children: www.reggiochildren.it/?lang=en

The Importance of Early Childhood Education: www.youtube.com/watch?v=tZhuBxOTXeM&list=PLOi8G vrHbwFGskqHQLXIT5DkAXk33Lesu

Too Much, Too Soon Campaign: www.toomuchtoosoon.org

References

Atherton, F. and Nutbrown, C. (2014) *Understanding Schemas in Young Children: From birth to three*. London: Sage.

Athey, C. (1990) *Extending Thought in Young Children: A parent–teacher partnership*. London: Paul Chapman.

Bernstein, B. (1976) *Class, Codes and Control*. New York: Routledge & Kegan Paul.

British Association for Early Childhood Education (2011) *How Children Learn: The characteristics of effective learning*. London: BAECE.

Bronfenbrenner, U. (1979) *The Ecology of Human Development: Experiments by nature and design*. Cambridge, MA: Harvard University Press.

DCSF (2007) *Statutory Guidance in the Early Years Foundation Stage*. Nottingham: DfES Publications.

DCSF (2008) *Early Years Foundation Stage Practice Guidance*. Nottingham: DfES Publications.

DfE (2012a) *Early Years Foundation Stage Statutory Framework*. Manchester: DfE Publications.

DfE (2012b) *Early Years Foundation Stage Practice Guidance*. Manchester: DfE Publications.

DfE (2014a) *SEND Code of Practice for 0–25 years*. Manchester: DfE Publications.

DfE (2014b) *The National Curriculum in England*. London: DfE.

DfES (2007) *The Early Years Foundation Stage*. London: DfES.

Early Education (2012) *Development Matters in the Early Years Foundation Stage*. London: Early Education.

Edwards, C.P., Gandini, L. and Forman, G. (1998) *The Hundred Languages of Children: The Reggio Emilia approach – advanced reflections*. New York: Alex Publishing.

Hutt, S.J., Tyler, S., Hutt, C. and Christopherson, H. (1989) *Play, Exploration and Learning: A natural history of the pre-school*. London: Routledge.

James, M., Black, P., Carmichael, P., Conner, C., Dudley, P., Fox, A., Frost, D., Honour, L., MacBeath, J., McCormick, R., Marshall, B., Pedder, D., Procter, R., Swaffield, S. and Wiliam, D. (2006) *Learning How to Learn: Tools for schools*. London: Routledge.

Laevers, F. (1997) Forward to basics! Deep-level-learning and the experiential approach. *Early Childhood Research Quarterly*. 12(2), 117–43.

Laevers, F. (2005) The curriculum as means to raise the quality of ECE: implications for policy. *European Early Childhood Education Research Journal*. 13(1), 17–30.

NUT (2011) *School Performance League Tables Too Narrow*. London: NUT Publications.

Oates, J., Lewis, C. and Lamb, M. (2005) Parenting and attachment, in S. Ding and K. Littleton (Eds) *Children's Personal and Social Development*. Oxford: Blackwell.

Orlandi, K.J. (2014) Addressing the attrition between the conflicting influences experienced by teachers on the interface between Foundation Stage and Key Stage 1. *Journal of Early Childhood Research*. 12(3), 294–307.

Pen Green (2008) *The Pen Green Framework for Engaging Parents*. Corby: Pen Green.

Piaget, J. (1951) *Psychology of Intelligence*. London: Routledge & Kegan Paul.

Rosen, M. (1996) *This Is Our House*. London: Walker Books.

Simpson, D., Lumsden, E., and McDowall Clark, R. (2015) Neoliberalism, global poverty policy and early childhood education and care: a critique of local uptake in England. TACTYC vol 35. No 1. 96–109. London: Routledge.

Siraj-Blatchford, I., Sylva, K., Muttock, S., Gilden, R. and Bell, D. (2002) *Researching Effective Pedagogy in the Early Years*. RB 356. London: DfES Publications.

Siraj, I., Kingston, D. and Melhuish, E. (2015) *SSTEW – Sustained Shared Thinking and Emotional Well-Being Scales*. Stoke-on-Trent: Trentham.

Thomson, R. (2015) New rating scale focuses on adult:child interactions. Retrieved from: www.nurseryworld.co.uk/nursery-world/news/1150247/rating-scale-focuses-adult-child-interactions   28th June 2015.

Tough, J. (1974) Children's use of language. *Education Review*. 26(3), 166–79.

Whitebread, D. and Bingham, S. (2011) *TACTYC Occasional Paper No 2. School Readiness: A critical review of perspectives and evidence*. TACTYC.

6 Promoting emotional security and positive behaviour

Wendy Holland and Jonathan Doherty

CHAPTER OVERVIEW

This chapter will outline the role of the Early Years Graduate Practitioner/Early Years Teacher (EYGP/EYT) in promoting emotionally secure environments and positive behaviour with children from birth to seven years. It examines their role in developing children's social and emotional competency through strategies which promote positive behaviour, self-regulation and independence with the aim that each child achieves their full potential. The chapter will address the following questions:

✔ What strategies develop children as confident and independent learners, so every child is capable of achieving their full potential?
✔ How can behaviour management strategies support children's social and emotional development and foster positive dispositions and attitudes?
✔ Can early years practice change the lives of children whose well-being or progress is affected by changes or difficulties in their personal circumstances?

Introduction: What strategies develop children as confident and independent learners, so every child is capable of achieving their full potential?

Current thinking proposes that every child's potential to achieve educationally is influenced by a number of factors. Increasing understanding of the plasticity of the growing brain, the effect of stress, early stimulation and the types of experiences in a child's life that foster social skills, problem-solving and thinking skills gives us some clear guidelines for enhancing educational potential (see chapter 2). The message is that far from potential being capped at birth, there are definite possibilities to enhance a child's trajectory in life (Greenspan and Greenspan, 2010). Early educators should create opportunities for children to develop their intellectual, communication, social and emotional capacities (Shanker and Downer, 2012). It is essential that practitioners have high expectations for every child so that each individual is enabled, with support, to achieve their true potential. We begin this chapter with a case study that illustrates how practitioners in one early years setting met a child's individual needs and put him back on an 'achieving' trajectory.

Case study: providing for John's individual needs

John had attended the daycare centre since he was two. Now at three years of age he was about to move into the attached nursery for three- to five-year-olds. John's older brother and sister were seen by parents and nursery staff as exceptionally able children; the label 'gifted' was applied to them, especially in relation to their early reading and number skills. As his parents had been vocal about their older children's achievements and 'gifts', they were equally open and forthright about their disappointment in John's apparent lack of literacy and numeracy skills. The setting had found John to be a quiet child, 'almost reclusive', and one member of staff had said, given to sudden short outbursts of 'difficult' behaviour. On looking through the new entrants' profiles, Angela, the nursery teacher, felt that, from her overview of the profile, John was making age/stage-appropriate progress in most Areas of Learning. What did concern her was his Key Person's commentary about his reclusive nature and sudden acts of aggression. Often he would soil himself. The soiling was seen by his parents as a particularly 'backward' step, even after Angela tried to explain that transitions sometimes had this effect on a child and they needed to be patient. John's parents got into the habit of expecting to talk at length on a daily basis to his Key Person, often making comparisons between him and his elder siblings. When his Key Person discussed this with Angela, she suggested the Key Person made more regular close observations of John. These highlighted his interest in dinosaurs as well as his skills on the computer and on the outdoor apparatus and a particular interest in den building. John's parents, however, were not positive in response to these reports as they wanted to see evidence of his writing and mathematical skills.

In discussion with John's Key Person, Angela suggested adopting an approach where children were filmed engaging in play-based activities, and this material was then used in discussions with parents/carers to provide insight into learning through play. She suggested they should include film of John building one of his special dens, which could then be used to inform parents during the twilight sessions that had been arranged for parent consultations. John's parents were regular visitors at the twilight sessions, and after watching the evidence, their views began to change. This resulted in more praise and celebration of the activities their young son engaged in and, while still remaining proud of their older offspring, they began to accept and enjoy John's uniqueness. Slowly, this had a positive impact on John's behaviour, and his aggressive outbursts and soiling gradually began to lessen. Over time John showed an improvement in his attitude to learning, his behaviour, and showed again his love for learning and for life.

Reflection

As an EYGP/EYT, what are your next steps for John, to ensure momentum is maintained and he keeps on this achieving trajectory?

Knowledge of child development

The first strategy we offer to ensure every child can achieve his or her full potential is to have a sound knowledge of child development. Throughout this book, we argue that practitioners need in-depth knowledge of all the areas of human development – cognitive, linguistic, emotional, social and physical. Teachers, early years practitioners and professionals working with children must be aware of the processes and factors that influence the ways in which children grow, think, learn new skills, acquire knowledge and interact with others (Doherty and Hughes, 2014). This knowledge encompasses the expert observers of children's cognitive development such as Piaget, Bruner and Vygotsky, and of emotional and social development like Freud, Erikson and Bowlby. It allows those who work directly with children to interpret the areas or domains of development and see the connectedness between these areas. Knowledge of theoretical frameworks in child development allows interpretation of children's thinking and actions on a daily basis and is a vital bridge between theory and practice.

Knowledge of the individual child

Secure knowledge of the individual child through home visits, or through meetings with parents and carers is the second strategy. If a home visit is not possible, and in a busy Reception class where ratios are less flexible, there may be insufficient staff to provide cover, or if the visit is not wanted by the parent/carer for any number of reasons, the practitioner needs to allocate time to talk with those parents/carers to gain a fuller picture of the child's prior knowledge, experience and interests. Knowledge of previous learning and of the different experiences in a child's life provide a fuller picture of the individual which then allows practitioners to influence learning and development through developmentally appropriate practice relevant to the child. Gaining such knowledge, however, takes time and energy. The detail needed is not found in a single pro-forma that a parent or carer might have hastily or anxiously filled in when the child first attends a setting, or from a brief observation of the child during the initial settling-in period. In order for the information to be detailed and meaningful, a holistic review of the child's experiences needs to be undertaken. Ideally, this holistic view would begin with a home visit before a child attends the setting. Much information can be gained from such a visit. For example:

- How the child relates to the significant others in their home environment.
- How they communicate with parents/carers, younger or older siblings.
- The quality of such relationships: are they warm, affectionate, supportive?
- What kind of behaviour management strategies does the parent/carer use?
- What kinds of parenting style(s) does this suggest and how can we provide support and balance of experience for the child?
- What transitional comfort objects does the child use, and what techniques work best when they are comforted in the home?

Parents do feel at ease in their home environment and better able to talk about their child's particular likes and dislikes, or the important routines of their day. They may also discuss concerns they might have. The practitioner is not there to judge, but to gain as complete a picture of that child as possible. Studies such as EPPE showed it is what parents do to support their children's development and learning and how they do it that is more important than other influences (Sylva *et al.*, 2003). Within the security of the home, rather than the strangeness of a new setting, the practitioner, hopefully, will be able to create the beginnings of a positive relationship with the child that will transfer when that child eventually arrives at the setting. Leaving a toy or book for the child to enjoy and bring with them during their settling-in period is one way of helping to build warm and respectful relationships with young children. Recognition that the parent/carer is the child's first and enduring educator, who has intimate knowledge of the child allows the practitioner to create engaging environments that reflect the child's interests and support learning.

The ongoing strategy for each child must include planning for personalised provision alongside regular focused observations, and assessments. Flexible planning based on a secure knowledge of each child allows provision to be differentiated. Readers should refer back to the section on the planning, observation and assessment cycle in chapter 5, and the section on observations in chapter 2. The cycle is essential to inform practitioners of children's individual interests and needs as they change and develop. Triangulation of team observations, through discussion at daily planning meetings, guides the planning of appropriate and challenging adult-led, child-led and adult-extended activities within rich, supportive and well-resourced provision and provides for the individual needs of children. Careful observation also identifies not only developmental stages but the levels of an individual child's self-esteem and involvement (see the Leuven scales of well-being and involvement in chapter 2 and the SSTEW scale of Sustained Shared Thinking and Emotional Well-being in chapter 5). Establishing positive relationships which take into account children's levels of well-being and involvement, as well as practitioners' levels of engagement and support is another effective strategy for success.

A further strategy to enhance potential is to build respectful and supportive relationships between practitioners, parents and children. The starting point for this is knowledge of the emotions that children develop and the broad timescale within which these typically develop. From birth, babies show signs of all the emotions; by two the infant is guided in their emotions by close adults and by seven children are developing their own strategies for regulating their emotions and using language to express themselves. The bond existing between a child and their parents is the most critical of all. According to evolutionary theories of attachment, babies are hard-wired to form attachments, and human beings are biologically disposed to respond positively to children's emotions. What adult can ignore the cry of a baby in distress, for example? Bowlby's attachment theory (Bowlby, 1969) proposes that a sense of security is at the heart of emotional attachment (see chapter 2). Mothers have a genetic blueprint that programmes them to respond positively to their baby and it is this synchrony of action that produces attachment (Doherty and Hughes, 2014). The crying baby cries to have its basic needs met, usually hunger, cold or thirst, and the adult responds. It is a kind of 'relationship dance' between the two and gives the child a sense of identity and of the place they occupy in the world. Such interactions help build the emotional architecture of a child's brain (Langston and Doherty, 2012). It is through relationships that young children experience the world around them and build important skills of self-confidence, resilience, temper control and conflict resolution. Relationships also build motivation to learn and achieve.

A climate of trust and warm, caring relationships builds positive values, attitudes and behaviour. This is achieved through careful listening and communication, valuing children's ideas and contributions. In support of these relationships, routines in the setting should develop *shared* control of the environment. The ideal ethos is one where children interact positively with each other and the environment. They show inner confidence, manage their feelings and display self-control. Their relationships with each other and with adults are caring, in a setting which is their community. Children are encouraged to take responsibility for their actions, becoming independent and confident individuals. In a Reception class these routines might include welcome, lunchtime, story time, reading in the book corner and home times (Harnett, 2002). By modelling respect and value for and of each child, you will raise a child's self-esteem and create the beginnings of a positive, trusting relationship that will enrich both adult and child. From such a safe, supportive base with their confidence high, children will assess risk and be motivated to engage with any appropriate challenges they are set. The Social and Emotional Aspects of Learning (SEAL) programme (DfES/ Primary National Strategy, 2005) is still being used in schools and provides comprehensive resources and ideas to help young children feel good about themselves.

A broad knowledge of 'best practice'

The final strategy we offer in this section to ensure that every child is successful is to learn from the best practice embedded in other international approaches to early childhood care and education. As an EYGP/EYT you should be knowledgeable about best practice in other countries and reflect upon the principles that underpin those practices. The Reggio Emilia pre-schools in northern Italy are a good example of this. These settings promote the picture of the child as 'rich' in imagination and abilities, a curious and determined investigator and researcher of the world around them. Emphasis is placed on adults and children learning together, of valuing each other's opinions and viewpoints. The welfare of young children is seen as the collective responsibility of the community, creating feelings of 'ownership' among all those involved.

Case study: the Reggio Emilia approach

Created by the women of Reggio Emilia and documented by Loris Malaguzzi, the early pedagogical framework known to the world as 'Reggio Emilia' is a pluralistic approach to early childhood education and care that involves children, parents, teachers, administrators and politicians. It took its influences from social constructivism (e.g. Vygotsky, 1978), and aims to develop children's knowledge through a collaborative partnership. The child is viewed as rich in potential, strong, powerful and competent and able to develop their own theories about the world – a self-confident explorer/investigator with a sense of curiosity and the freedom of spirit to venture beyond the known or given. They are believed to have the capacity to explore such ideas in collaboration with other children and adults, using a 'hundred' languages with which to express themselves, including sign, art, dance, etc., all of which are equally valued (see chapter 5).

Children are encouraged to be aware of the present, build on the past and look to the future, and priority is given to setting aside the necessary time for children and adults to discuss, debate and reflect. Revision and reflection are considered central to children's learning. They are encouraged and expected to concentrate for long periods of time from a very young age, while caring adults spend much time documenting, interpreting and sharing information with colleagues and parents. There is no set curriculum; both children and adults are viewed as researchers, and adults give great respect to children's theories and hypotheses, allowing children to make mistakes. It is common to find an artist in residence in Reggio Emilia settings, working with the children to express their ideas in art and craft forms.

Practitioners are expected to try to understand children's learning processes rather than acquire skills and knowledge that they will then expect to 'transmit' to children in turn; the practice of teaching is not seen as being about how to transmit information, but about developing understanding of how children learn. Practitioners are seen as facilitators and researchers. A question like: 'Where does the water come from?' (perhaps asked by a young child seeing water pouring from a tap) might lead to the child's being challenged to find out. Donning hard hats, young children between three and six years, accompanied by practitioners/facilitators, might begin a field trip to investigate the setting's plumbing system and develop a project around the properties of water. The Reggio Emilia pre-school approach sees the environment as a *third teacher*, where the environment is carefully planned and resourced to encourage light and space and challenges the children to use it imaginatively and autonomously, with free-flow movement both indoors and out.

Reflection

Reggio Emilia practice is distinguished by its rejection of hierarchical staff structures, externally imposed policies, manuals and curriculum guidelines. If we in the UK are committed to high expectations of children and their achievements, how can we provide similar environments rich in resources and potential?

What problems might a Reggio approach create within a system that runs on the statutory guidelines of the Early Years Foundation Stage (EYFS)?

How can behaviour management strategies support children's social and emotional development and foster positive dispositions and attitudes?

How children behave is strongly linked to their emotional states and the emotional experiences they have in early childhood. This includes beliefs about themselves and their world and includes self-esteem, confidence and capacity to hope (Brearley, 2001). To respond to children's behaviour effectively as an EYGP/EYT requires the ability to be open and honest and self-reflect. Webster-Stratton (2000) argues that practitioners need to be able to distinguish between their own feelings and thoughts, as well as be aware of their negative and positive thoughts in any conflict situation; in essence, they need to be able to manage themselves. See chapter 2 to further consider the importance of practitioner behaviour in creating a secure and nurturing environment for young children (Sims *et al.*, 2006).

Case study: modelling positive behaviour

Watch this Australian Television Advertisement

www.youtube.com/watch?v=KHi2dxSf9hw

Consider the possibility that children in your setting may see poor behaviour modelled by adults, particularly where there may be disagreements between practitioners about how to do things.

Reflection

What steps could you and your colleagues take to ensure consistently positive role models? This does not mean that adults have to be perfect, but that they do need to consistently attempt to 'do the right thing' and be willing to apologise and make amends if things go wrong.

You could start by making a list of your personal strengths and areas to work on. List the resources you have already and those you will need. Identify the changes you can make and those you think are outside your control. Chaplain (2003) describes strategies for behaviour management such as checking you are being understood, communicating in verbal and non-verbal ways, looking and feeling confident yourself and having a belief in yourself.

Knowledge of child development

A sound understanding of child development lays the basis for successful practice and is the second behaviour management strategy we propose. By the time a child enters school, self-regulation should be evident in most children's behaviour. This can be seen in the length of time the child can concentrate on a task, and how he or she ignores distractions in the classroom and resists impulsive behaviour like shouting out. They should demonstrate a level of resilience when challenges are not solved straightaway and can seek out adult and/or peer help to help them solve these. Some children are unable to self-regulate and problems of reactivity occur: the child becomes anxious, over-excited or distracted. Shanker and Downer (2012) remind us that in self-regulation one must recognise that physiological and emotional factors are involved, and that it is an ongoing process. For example, issues around summer-born children (especially boys, who may typically learn in more 'active' ways) need to be weighed against behavioural expectations in settings and schools. The more formal daily requirements of the Reception and Year 1 classroom may well prove to be difficult for such young children. Labels of 'disruptive', 'lacks the ability to concentrate', 'continually off task', can result in such children being described as 'difficult', when it is the higher level of maturity being demanded of them, and pedagogical techniques that do not suit their current learning style, that are the key issues.

Practitioners need a clear understanding of age/stage norms so that behaviour strategies are appropriate. They should pay attention to *emotional competency* (Denham, 1998). It is through the development of the child's emotional competency that empathy, self-control, perseverance, social awareness and sensitivity are encouraged (Goleman, 1995). Research suggests the emergence of a rudimentary empathy in children as young as two (Knafo *et al.,* 2008). From three years, the child begins to be able to express more complex social emotions, for example attempting to comfort a person who is obviously upset. Some will be more emotionally expressive than others, and between four and five years more obvious personal and emotional styles begin to emerge (see the temperament section in chapter 2). 'Theory of Mind' emerges at this stage, an emerging ability to understand that other people have 'minds', feelings and an internal self; an understanding that the needs and feelings of those around them may be different from their own.

Case study: Theory of Mind

Psychologists have been studying 'Theory of Mind' in young children using various tests for nearly 50 years. This video shows children dealing with the crayons–candles problem:

www.youtube.com/watch?v=8hLubgpY2_w

The lack of Theory of Mind can be theoretically linked to the feature of the Pre-operational Stage of child development that Piaget called 'egocentrism' (see chapter 2); at this point, schema development is in a state of immaturity that does not allow children to take into account any view of the world apart from their own, both in the physical and social sense.

Reflection

Consider what impact such a view of the world would have upon children's behaviour in a setting. As a preliminary reflection, you might consider how people might drive a vehicle if they had no effective concept that other people's thoughts and intentions might be very different from their own!

Along with a growing appreciation of themselves and 'others' as distinct and different, children placed in regular social situations outside the family environment need to develop the skills to organise and/or control their own emotions and behaviour to facilitate their interactions with peers. Maccoby (1980) describes the basically impulsive nature of young children's behaviour and their limited ability to sustain attention. The average attention span in physical play is identified as:

- 30 seconds at two years
- 42 seconds at two and a half years
- 55 seconds at three years.

Sensitive management

Young children's impulsive behaviour needs understanding and sensitive management. The two-year-old experiencing the emotional 'storms' that are frequent at this age needs to be soothed and calmed before re-engaging with others in the world around them. The 'coping strategies' that children themselves develop in order to control and organise their behaviour are not simply maturational, but influenced by their social environments in both negative and positive ways. The EYGP/EYT must be aware of any cultural or social stereotyping that may happen in a setting, between children, staff and/or parents or carers. Research has shown that children as young as two and three years develop an understanding of and reactions to skin tone and gender which can result in cultural/racial stereotyping or, for example, gender stereotyping of types of play or toys or behaviour. Any of the above can have a definite and sometimes lasting effect on children's self-identity and consequently on their behaviour and emotional competence.

Helping children to rationalise and talk through their feelings is a key technique. By engaging in this process, children begin to identify how they and others are feeling, come to realise the impact of their actions on others, and start to find solutions to problems without conflict. There are times, for example in the case of bullying, that practitioners might need to use other strategies. The use of empathy or persona dolls is an effective resource, where issues relating to behaviour management can be addressed. If a child is being bullied, or is the one being aggressive to others, this can be explored through the use of the doll, without specifically identifying the child/children involved. This allows for the unacceptable behaviour to be effectively discussed without 'naming and shaming' or embarrassing either the child being bullied or the child doing the bullying, building an awareness that, while the *behaviour* will not be tolerated, the child as an individual is still valued. To act otherwise would damage the child's sense of self-esteem and self-worth, and could well lead to progressively more 'difficult' behaviours as a result. Often, while the doll is being passed round for 'comfort', the child responsible for the unacceptable behaviour will console the doll and offer advice.

Effective planning

If the day is over-planned or divided into too many routines this may result in children having insufficient time to establish themselves or settle into areas of provision, or time to finish or reflect. Alternatively, if too much time is allocated to very young children being expected to sit still, for example during overlong 'circle' or 'carpet' times, this too can lead to conflict and behaviour management issues. Planning, like the behaviour strategies themselves, needs to be age/stage appropriate. Again, involving children in the planning can have a positive effect, with ownership creating respect for and interest in the planned activities. Involving children in the behaviour management strategies, where they have to take some responsibility for their implementation, is also successful. A 'kindness' tree, where children discuss and elect who they feel has done a kind act that day, a 'happy smile' chart, where children decide, depending on their feelings about a particular incident, to display a happy or sad face, or the shared responsibility for a class pet, all provide children with the chance to reflect, take responsibility for their behaviour and act autonomously.

Planning must also include the environment. The EYFS, in its promotion of 'Enabling Environments', clearly states the importance of what is sometimes called 'the third teacher' (see the earlier reference to pre-schools in Reggio Emilia). Ensuring that the environment has enough space, light and resources both indoor and out for children to explore and meet surmountable challenges can be a stabilising factor in behaviour management. Overcrowding around an area of continuous provision, a common problem in busy early years settings, can be remedied by establishing 'fair' rules with the children on the numbers allowed access at any one time. Children's input in helping to create 'class rules' also shows positive results. Scarce or poorly planned resources can again cause unnecessary conflict. If the scarcity cannot be remedied very quickly, for example the provision of extra tricycles in the outdoor

Pearson Education Ltd/Malcolm Harris

area, then, again, rules for fair use of the equipment need to be clearly established. The use of a visual reminder, for example a large egg-timer, again with the children's cooperation, helps reinforce fairness and responsibility in turn-taking.

The EPPE research (Sylva *et al.*, 2003), in considering the features of 'excellent' settings, found they had adopted discipline/behaviour policies where staff supported children in rationalising and talking through their conflicts, using a problem-solving approach, supported by a strong behaviour management policy which all staff understood and to which they all adhered. In the less effective settings it was found that there was often no clear response to children's misbehaviour and/or conflicts and, on many occasions, children were simply told to 'stop' or distracted from their behaviour without being helped to consider the consequences of their actions. In terms of leading and supporting practice, EYGPs/EYTs need to ensure a whole-team consistency in implementing behaviour policies/strategies. This, of course, requires discussion, a feeling of ownership on the part of staff, and agreement with the philosophies on children's behaviour that underpin the policies created. The relevance and age-appropriateness of behaviour policies/strategies is key when considering effective practice. Asking a two-year-old to 'say sorry' will have little meaning for the child, who may not even be able to understand the words 'why did you do that?' This is developmentally inappropriate, in the sense that it is aimed at a child too young to be able to articulate reasons for his/her actions. The issue is then exacerbated when adults presume a lack of reply to the admonition is evidence of stubbornness and a determination to 'be naughty'!

Age appropriateness needs to be built into every successful behaviour policy, especially as within many early years settings practitioners are dealing with the full age range across birth to five years. Every school is legally required to have a behaviour policy. Governors are responsible for setting general principles that inform this policy and must consult with the head teacher, school staff, parents and pupils when developing it. Head teachers are responsible for developing the policy in the context of this framework. They decide the standard of behaviour expected of pupils at the school and how that standard will be achieved, the school rules, any penalties for breaking the rules and ways of rewarding good behaviour. Our case study below shows the problem Joshua had in his Reception year and the way in which the school approached his situation.

Case study: Joshua and the Early Years Foundation Stage

Joshua soon acquired the label 'disruptive' during his first term in the Reception class of his local school. The school was situated in the middle of a large council estate which still boasted high-rise flats. Joshua lived in one of these blocks with his parents and three elder brothers. As an August-born child with no previous nursery experience he had entered the Reception class aged four years one month. The school had been struggling, but was coming out of 'special measures' after the last Ofsted inspection. Now the school systems were deemed to be working more effectively, even though staff still felt under constant pressure to meet unreachable targets. The Reception teacher had been advised by the head teacher to adopt a more 'school readiness' approach. This meant allowing less outdoor time, which Joshua loved, and introducing more adult-led activities and longer carpet time. Joshua had not reacted well to the changes.

During the extended 30-minute sessions, he would often hit out at his 'talking partner', or run away from the focused, adult-led extension activities that followed. Joshua's behaviour deteriorated, resulting in one parent accusing him of bullying her daughter. His mother was sent several letters to attend school for a discussion. Her reaction had been to keep Joshua away from school. When the School Welfare Officer managed to find her at home and inform her of the consequences of Joshua's absence, his attendance improved. But by this time, the Reception year was drawing to a close, and when he returned to school after the summer holidays, his newly qualified Year 1 teacher complained to colleagues 'it's like he's "settling in" all over again'.

She had, by that time been warned about Joshua; his name had been coming up in staffroom conversations all year. From her experience on placements, she presumed that a 'firm but fair' approach would work. He might be the youngest in the class of 30 transitioning from Reception, but he'd had a year of 'play', now it was time to work. Joshua, however, did not respond well to this strategy. In spite of his teacher's best efforts to differentiate work for the 'below national standard' group, to which Joshua had been allocated, he continued to be off task and disruptive in most lessons. The school's behaviour policy of rewarding individual and group effort did not have the hoped for effect on Joshua. Sometimes, when his poor behaviour led to a group sanction (his group being held back at playtime, for example), he appeared not to care. The few friendships he tentatively made soon failed; as a result he became isolated and even more aggressive. The Year 1 teacher apologised when handing over Joshua's achievement record to the Year 2 teacher, who on reading his profile, thought it was time that a statement of special needs should be considered in Joshua's case.

Reflection

Consider how practice could have been improved to support Joshua's learning and development during his time in Reception and Year 1, using the concepts of:

- Knowledge of child development
- Knowledge of the individual child
- Effective planning.

Schools very much subscribe to the idea that the key to good behaviour is through good teaching. Guidance produced by the Teaching Agency states that 'teachers who plan and teach dynamic, stimulating lessons based on sound assessment and excellent subject knowledge are likely to experience fewer difficulties with behaviour' (Teaching Agency, 2012, p. 1). Readers are referred to a very informative DfE document, *Behaviour and Discipline in Schools. Advice for headteachers and school staff*, which provides advice to head teachers on developing the school behaviour policy and explains the powers members of staff have to discipline pupils. The document states that it is for individual schools to develop their own best practice for managing behaviour. Many schools have developed excellent systems of behaviour management from managing low-level disruption to dealing with more challenging behaviour in classrooms. Often the simplest systems are the most effective. The Government's behaviour champion Charlie Taylor is a strong advocate of this and he has developed a simple checklist for the Department of Education (DfE, 2011) to improve behaviour in schools, which we present below.

Case study: Charlie Taylor's behaviour checklist for teachers

Classroom

Know the names and roles of any adults in class.
Meet and greet pupils when they come into the classroom.
Display rules in the class – and ensure that the pupils and staff know what they are.
Display the tariff of sanctions in class.
Have a system in place to follow through with all sanctions.
Display the tariff of rewards in class.
Have a system in place to follow through with all rewards.
Have a visual timetable on the wall.
Follow the school behaviour policy.

Pupils

Have a plan for children who are likely to misbehave.
Ensure other adults in the class know the plan.
Understand pupils' special needs.

Teaching

Ensure that all resources are prepared in advance.
Praise the behaviour you want to see more of.
Praise children doing the right thing more than criticising those who are doing the wrong thing (parallel praise).
Differentiate.
Stay calm.
Have clear routines for transitions and for stopping the class.
Teach children the class routines.

Parents

Give feedback to parents about their child's behaviour – let them know about the good days as well as the bad ones.

Reflection

- If you were asked to lead on behaviour policy in your setting, how would you use this checklist, tailoring it to the age and stage of the children with whom you are working?
- How would you go about ensuring ownership of this from all staff?
- Do you think it is appropriate to have such a tightly defined approach for children under seven? If not, what are your objections?

Can early years practice change the lives of children whose well-being or progress is affected by changes or difficulties in their personal circumstances?

In the previous section we proposed that children's behaviour is linked to beliefs about themselves and the world around them. If that view is tainted with negative views about themselves and others from an early age, they spiral downwards with deficit views of themselves and their well-being. You can connect this to the concept of John Bowlby's 'Internal Working Model' in chapter 2. The recent SSTEW scale (Siraj *et al.*, 2015), with its emphasis on emotional well-being referred to in chapter 5, reflects concerns about the lower levels of well-being of children in the UK compared to other western countries; see chapter 10. A 'good childhood' and notions of well-being are linked (Layard and Dunn, 2009). Messages continue to be sent out to the public in research reports and the media that the UK is not a happy place for children to live (Adams, 2013). Well-being, childhood and education are high on political agendas and link also with the wider society. Our nation's future depends on our children. They deserve the best education and the best start in life. Nurturing their potential through high-quality care and education, encouraging them to play and explore, and to have high expectations for them is everyone's business.

Family issues

Family breakdown, low educational attainment, unemployment, debt, drug and alcohol dependency, and crime may combine to cause multiple disadvantages that affect family life. EYGPs/EYTs need to be aware of the complex issues that many families face nowadays and the effect that any combination of these can potentially have on the child. Examples include issues arising from relationship breakdown, which may involve the child observing poor conflict resolution strategies. There may also be the need to deal with the complex emotions involved in the process of accommodating step-parents and step-siblings in blended families and/or living 'separately' with each parent in different households. When an adult leaves the family home permanently, young children often struggle with the emotions created by separation or bereavement, and where adults are also traumatised by the same event, adults in the setting environment can be key players in supporting the child through the experience. Other emotional upheavals can be associated with the birth of a sibling, a mother's post-natal depression or the long-term illness or disability of a family member. Young children will not be able to articulate the emotions which accompany such changes and transitions, and may respond with uncharacteristic and 'troubled' behaviours. It is the setting's responsibility to provide a calm and supportive environment for a child having to deal with such changes, and the child's Key Person should expect to lead in this respect. Children should be encouraged to express their fears and frustrations, through, for example, the use of empathy dolls/puppets and stories.

Parents/carers who are themselves experiencing some of the trauma of the above changes may not want to talk or communicate, and may also be in need of help, advice and support (see chapter 3). Establishing trusting relationships that support the child and his/her family is important not only in the everyday sense, but also when families are going through difficult periods and transitions, and it is a very unusual family that does not experience such events at some time. If a trusting relationship is created initially, the practitioner is in a position to help and support both the child and the family, by listening and then helping them where necessary to source appropriate specialist help. In leading practice, the EYGP/EYT needs to ensure that practitioners know how best to offer help and support, but also the appropriate boundaries in such sensitive situations (see chapter 3). However, where practice is driven by externally imposed targets and outcomes, it can be very difficult to tailor practice to individual children. This issue is further discussed in chapters 4, 5 and 10.

Reflection

In May 2015, the National Association of Head Teachers conference warned that schools are now 'feeding and clothing pupils' (www.bbc.co.uk/news/education-32540801).

You may be able to connect this situation to the work of the McMillan sisters in London, which you read about in chapter 1.

Consider how living in such poverty impacts upon the emotions and behaviour of children, and how the imposition of over-ambitious national targets for a very narrow set of 'achievements' may additionally exacerbate the situation.

Children as independent social beings

Requirements to sensibly oversee children's relationships and behaviour should not over-extend to a situation where staff presume that children need constant adult intervention. For example, constant adult interruptions in disputes in an early years setting or primary school playground can damage children's growing abilities to negotiate their own social contracts (Jarvis *et al.*, 2014a). Consider the case study example below.

Case study: Nathan's playtime

Five-year-old 'Nathan', one of the Reception class boys, was one of the most active children within my observation sample, and was frequently to be found engaged in highly active play. However, when it came to his turn to be the focus of one of my focal child observations, he was involved in an incident at the beginning of the relevant play session where he mistakenly hurt another boy in play fighting. His actions were mistaken for real aggression by the supervising adult, which resulted in a 'time out' punishment. When this was over, Nathan sought out the boy he had accidentally injured, apologised and explained that the incident had been an accident; the boy accepted the apology. Nathan then asked the boy to come with him to speak to the supervising adult and tell her what had happened. She listened to what they had to say, and asked the boys to shake hands, which they did. Nathan then walked away alone, still looking upset and sucking hard on his thumb (which had been in and out of his mouth since the situation arose). He continued to look rather morose, while Chris, one of his closest friends, jumped around him, clearly trying to entertain. Nathan turned around and smiled at Chris, but continued to stand quite still in the middle of the playground, with his thumb in his mouth.

(Jarvis *et al.*, 2014b, p. 7)

Reflection

Jarvis *et al.* comment on this incident:

Playtime is useful even when it is not 'fun'! I recorded a reflection in my observation notes, that the socially sophisticated measures that Nathan took to try to rectify his accident over a period of half an hour (albeit with the typical 5-year-old stress-diffusing mechanism of a thumb firmly in his mouth) would have been beyond the social repertoires of some adults. Whilst Nathan's experiences certainly did not make for a pleasant play period for him, it can be strongly argued that many such playground-based social events, even those which have quite negative results, are highly developmental experiences for the child concerned.

(Jarvis *et al.*, 2014b, p. 7)

'Nathan' was a very socially successful child, who was one of the older children in his cohort, and had settled well into school. With this in mind, consider how you might have dealt with this incident keeping in mind your knowledge of the child, and your knowledge of child development theory. Do you think that Nathan 'behaved badly'? Consider your reasons for your response to this question.

Conclusion

This chapter has explored a range of questions that focus on children's social and emotional development, behaviour and well-being.

What strategies develop children as confident and independent learners, so every child achieves their full potential?

High expectations for all children should be established from the beginning, and these expectations must be effectively communicated to colleagues and children in settings and to parents, in order to make them a shared aim. Possible stereotypes or misconceptions about each child's abilities should be challenged. The EGYP/EYT should have realistic expectations based on prior knowledge, and respect for and commitment to meet each individual child's needs in a working partnership with parents/carers. When children feel supported and respected, they are more likely to achieve their potential. Sound knowledge of the principles, theories and research underpinning child development is essential, as is a secure knowledge of the individual child, and effective planning with regard to these two underpinning factors. Secure knowledge of the individual child can be gathered through home visits, and meetings with parents and carers, and within the setting, ongoing observations and assessments. The careful planning of personalised provision from the basis of this knowledge means that the learning journeys of every child within a setting can be effectively supported. Positive relationships which take into account children's levels of well-being, their interests and past experiences will raise a child's self-esteem and set them on an achieving trajectory as confident independent learners.

How can behaviour management strategies support children's social and emotional development and foster positive dispositions and attitudes?

Behaviour is linked to emotional states, and these are created to a great extent by emotional experiences in early childhood. Practitioners need to reflect on their own preferences and dispositions, in order to best manage themselves and the behaviours of children effectively. Promoting children's self-control and independence requires planning for regular opportunities that foster children's social and emotional skills. Children need opportunities to be responsible, and make decisions, errors and choices, while continuing to feel secure in the belief that adults will be there with help and support if the situation becomes too difficult for them to manage. In this sense, practitioners must support children to talk through conflicts and seek resolutions that are fair and equitable.

Children need to learn to develop skills of negotiation in problem-solving with their peers, and it is crucial that adults model such skills appropriately, not only when they are working with the children, but also when they are communicating with each other in environments where children are present. The example of 'Nathan's playtime' indicates that adult intervention must be carefully judged to ensure that it does not actually de-skill children in such an important area. Settings should aim to set a tone of high expectations with regard to individual behaviour at all times, and consistently apply a behaviour policy that has clear boundaries and concise rules, and one that sets reasonable, age-appropriate expectations.

Can early years practice change the lives of children whose well-being or progress is affected by changes or difficulties in their personal circumstances?

Against an international backdrop of more inclusive societies which foster human rights for each individual, the UK has much work to do to ensure that children are happy and confident. Whilst this is a global commitment, it is a formidable challenge to translate somewhat abstract 'feel-good' aims into everyday practice for those who work with young children and families on a daily basis. The rhetoric talks about best outcomes for all children, but there is still much tension in aligning the EYFS with the increasingly outcomes-driven agenda that pervades the education system in the UK. If practice is dominated by policy which is uninformed by child development theory, it is very difficult for practitioners to engage in fully effective planning, regardless of the knowledge that they have constructed with respect to the individual children in their care. This issue is further discussed in chapter 10.

Recommended reading

Brazelton, B. (2015) *Learning to Listen: A life caring for children* (2nd Edn). Boston, MA: Merloyd Lawrence Books.
Dukes, C. and Smith, M. (2009) *Building Better Behaviour in the Early Years*. London: Sage.

Dunlop, A. *et al.* (2008) *Positive Behaviour in the Early Years.* Available at: www.gov.scot/resource/doc/238252/0065411.pdf

Mathieson, K. (2012) *Understanding Behaviour in the Early Years.* London: MA Education.

National Strategies Supporting Children with Behavioural, Social and Emotional Difficulties: Inclusion development programme. Available at: www.foundationyears.org.uk/wp-content/uploads/2011/10/Inclusion_Development_Programme_Behaviour_Emotional+Social_Difficulties.pdf

Sunderland, M. and Armstrong, N. (2003) *Helping Children with Low Self-Esteem.* London: Speechmark.

Websites

A website on supporting children's well-being: www.childrenssociety.org.uk/what-we-do/research/well-being

Help with using persona dolls: www.persona-doll-training.org

Some 'expert guides' from Nursery World: www.nurseryworld.co.uk/challenging-behaviour

Dr Maria Robinson on managing toddler tantrums (video): www.educationscotland.gov.uk/video/p/video_tcm4637491.asp

References

Adams, K. (2013). Childhood in crisis? Perceptions of 7–11-year-olds on being a child and the implications for education's well-being agenda. *Education 3–13.* 41(3), 523–37.

Bowlby, J. (1969) *Attachment and Loss.* New York: Basic Books.

Brearley, M. (2001) *Emotional Intelligence in the Classroom.* Carmarthen: Crown House Publishing.

Chaplain, R. (2003) *Teaching without Disruption in the Primary Classroom: A model for managing behaviour.* London: RoutledgeFalmer.

Denham, S.A. (1998) *Emotional Development in Young Children.* New York: The Guilford Press.

DfE (2011) *Getting the Simple Things Right: Charlie Taylor's behaviour checklists.* London: DfE . Retrieved from: www.gov.uk/government/uploads/system/uploads/attachment_data/file/283997/charlie_taylor_checklist.pdf 11th July 2015.

DfES/Primary National Strategy (2005) *Excellence and Enjoyment: Social and emotional aspects of learning.* Nottingham: DfES Publications

Doherty, J. and Hughes, M. (2014) *Child Development: Theory and practice 0–11* (2nd Edn). Harlow: Pearson.

Goleman, D.P. (1995) *Emotional Intelligence: Why it can matter more than IQ for character, health and lifelong achievement.* New York: Bantam Books.

Greenspan, S. and Greenspan, N.T. (2010) *The Learning Tree: Overcoming learning disabilities from the ground up.* Boston, MA: DaCapo Press/Lifelong Books.

Harnett, A. (2002) Developing children as independent and confident learners: personal, social and emotional development, in I. Keating (Ed.) *Achieving QTS: Teaching the Foundation Stage.* Exeter: Learning Matters.

Jarvis, P., Newman, S. and Swiniarski, L. (2014a) On 'becoming social': the importance of collaborative free play in childhood. *International Journal of Play.* 3(1), 53–68. Available at: www.tandfonline.com/doi/pdf/10.1080/21594937.2013.863440

Jarvis, P., Brock, A. and Brown, F. (2014b) Three perspectives on play, in A. Brock, P. Jarvis and Y. Olusoga (Eds) *Perspectives on Play: Learning for life* (2nd Edn), pp. 2–38. Abingdon: Routledge.

Knafo, A., Zahn-Waxler, C., Van Hulle, C., Robinson, J.L. and Rhee, S.H. (2008) The developmental origins of a disposition toward empathy: genetic and environmental contributions. *Emotion.* 8, 737–52.

Langston, A. and Doherty, J. (2012) *The Revised EYFS in Practice: Thinking, reflecting and doing!* London: Featherstone/Bloomsbury.

Layard, R. and Dunn, J. (2009) *A Good Childhood: Searching for values in a competitive age*. London: Penguin.

Maccoby, E. (1980) *Social Development: Psychological growth and the parent–child relationship*. New York: Harcourt.

Shanker, S. and Downer, R. (2012) Enhancing the Potential in Children (EPIC), in L. Miller and D. Hevey (Eds) *Policy Issues in the Early Years*. London: Sage.

Sims, M., Guilfoyle, A. and Parry, T. (2006) Child care for infants and toddlers: where in the world are we going? The First Years – Nga Tau Tuatahi. *New Zealand Journal of Infant and Toddler Education*. 8(1), 12–19.

Siraj, I., Kingston, D. and Melhuish, E. (2015) *SSTEW – Sustained Shared Thinking and Emotional Well-being Scales*. Stoke-on-Trent: Trentham.

Sylva, K., Melhuish, E., Sammons, P., Siraj-Blatchford, I., Taggart, B. and Elliot, K. (2003) *The Effective Provision of Pre-School Education (EPPE) Project: Findings from the pre-school period*. London: Institute of Education.

Teaching Agency (2012) *Improving Teacher Training for Behaviour*. London: HMSO.

Vygotsky, L. (1978) *Mind in Society*. Cambridge, MA: Harvard University Press.

Webster-Stratton, C. (2000) *How to Promote Children's Social and Emotional Competence*. London: Paul Chapman/Sage Publications.

7 Creating environments for play and learning

Wendy Holland and Jonathan Doherty

CHAPTER OVERVIEW

This chapter will outline the role of the practitioner in establishing and sustaining purposeful learning environments. We argue that it is the ultimate responsibility of the setting's practice leader to ensure that environments reflect high-quality provision. We give some examples of creative partnerships, to illustrate the potential of this approach to promote learning. In such environments the child's sense of creativity and natural curiosity is fostered and every child's ideas and contributions are valued. Environments need to be developmentally appropriate to the needs of every child and, where necessary, resources can be adapted to reflect diversity and promote inclusive practice. The chapter will address the following questions:

✔ How can the 'Characteristics of Effective Learning' support the establishment of warm, supportive and purposeful environments that promote play and learning?
✔ How can outdoor play and creative partnerships with outside agents such as artists 'in residence' develop children's learning and foster creativity?
✔ How can practitioners ensure that children are provided with flexible routines that meet individual needs, in well-resourced environments that take account of diversity and encourage inclusive practice and provision?

The recommended reading list at the end of this chapter will introduce readers to a range of texts and online resources for further reading on these topics.

Introduction: How can the 'Characteristics of Effective Learning' support the establishment of warm, supportive and purposeful environments that promote play and learning?

> Adults can admire their environment; they can remember it and think about it – but a child absorbs it.
>
> (Maria Montessori, 1967)

Enabling learning environments that stimulate play and learning embrace not only indoor and outdoor contexts, but also the emotional context. Throughout this book there are many references to the important role that practitioners play in establishing warm attachments with children to foster their emotional well-being and development. Leaders and practitioners have a huge responsibility to create stimulating environments of high quality, as it is the environment that can either enable or disable children's progress. Children learn from their environment and the people in it. They build a sense of themselves from the attitudes and values of the significant people around them. Caring adults who are responsive to and interested in the children in their care help them to develop a positive self-image. Strong partnerships between practitioners, parents and carers are also crucially important.

In the best settings adults organise the day to focus on the needs of *each* child. There is an ethos where children are welcomed warmly and adults show they value each child as unique. Every child is treated as an individual. Each has a Key Person who knows the child and family well, in order to ensure the child's welfare, learning and development needs are met. Adults listen and respond to children sensitively and this in turn enables them to make good progress in all areas of learning. In the right emotional environment, children will feel accepted. They try new things out. They express how they feel and explore the physical environment with confidence knowing that others around them will support them. They take risks. The importance of the emotional environment is summed up in the following quote:

> The environment is more than physical space because it contains the emotions of the children who spend time in it, the staff that work there and the parents who leave their children there. The emotional environment is an invisible measure of 'feelings' – sometimes it can have a 'feel-good' factor where the children, staff and parents feel positive, and at others it can have a 'not-so-good' feel about it when children, staff or parents are down or unhappy. Maintaining positive feelings is important for staff, children and parents, but equally if they feel safe in the emotional environment children can express their feelings safely, knowing that their parents or staff are nearby to help them if they feel overwhelmed by these.
>
> (Early Years Matters, 2015, online)

What strategies are needed to create safe, welcoming and nurturing environments for learning that foster the emotional aspect? We offer three:

1   Ensure that there is a high level of involvement and overall sense of belonging for children and families.
2   Respond appropriately and positively to children's needs and preferences.
3   Respect and value children's interests.

Children thrive in the context of the environment and the relationships with others around them. This reflects Gura (1996) in her description of the two contexts of learning: the inner aspect and the outer or social context where learning takes place. *Development Matters* (Early Education, 2012) provides guidance on enabling environments through the 'Characteristics of Effective Learning' that underpin the seven Areas of Learning in the Early Years Foundation Stage (EYFS). These are playing and exploring, active learning, and creating and thinking critically.

Playing and exploring

Wood (2010) writes that early childhood education is underpinned by traditions which regard play as essential to learning and development. The famous playwright George Bernard Shaw wrote, 'We do not stop playing because we grow old. We grow old because we stop playing'. Play is a multi-layered and complex process. The term itself is likely to spark off heated discussions, and reaching agreement on what it actually means cannot be taken for granted! Its subtlety and complexity are often masked when observing children and it takes a skilled practitioner to unpack its layers of complexity and uncover the meanings it has for children. Play is freely chosen by the child, and is under the control of that child. It is the child who decides how to play, how long to sustain the play, what the play is about and who to play with. Tina Bruce's 12 Features of Free-Flow Play (Bruce, 1991) continue to influence practitioners in settings and develop their understanding of play in action. Bruce said that 'play cannot be pinned down, and turned into a product of measurable learning. This is because play is a process [which] enables a holistic kind of learning, rather than fragmented learning' (in Ward, 1998, p. 22). More recently, Hughes (2010), summarising the views of a number of play theorists, informs us how play facilitates important processes that are connected with learning:

rehearsing practising repeating imitating
exploring discovering revising extending
problem-solving combining transforming testing

The role of play is significant in children's social, emotional and intellectual development. It develops children's physicality through the acquisition of physical skills and helps with their assessment of risk. They learn to develop strategies to deal with challenges, and to interact with others, to manage social relationships and be creative. Play is a potent facilitator of language. Watch a child at play and listen. Often you will hear them talking, at times to themselves, not to those around them. Self-talk is that way they work out challenges, talking through their strategies in their head and supporting narrative thinking. At other times language is supported in communicating what they are doing with adults who respond to their ideas. In play they demonstrate high levels of cognitive self-regulation and the very highest levels of learning. Important dispositions to learning such as intrinsic motivation, perseverance and a 'can do' approach are also fostered. Play is about enjoying learning. It is about developing children's curiosity and their intrinsic urge to explore and find meaning. It happens in the home, outside and in classrooms.

It is serious business. The relationship between play and early learning which is the focus of this chapter is not well understood by educators or parents. Pressures to achieve in school often result in a content-heavy curriculum and intense teaching throughout the school day, leaving little or no place for play. Many parents subscribe to the view that in school children are there to work, not to play. Many teachers battle with including play in their classroom pedagogies. Practitioners can lack the skills and confidence to make play integral to learning and pedagogy (Nutbrown and Clough, 2014). Educators need to 'know enough about play to be both its advocates and its sceptics – (to) recognise play's potential without romanticizing it and reducing it to fuzzy, simplistic slogans' (McLane, 2003, p. 3). As authors we go even further and propose that there is actually no distinction between play and learning. In this heightened age of attainment and recording children's achievement against a narrow interpretation of what this means, the need for practitioners to understand and celebrate play in early years settings and schools has never been more urgent. Ofsted confirms the value of play as 'the natural, imaginative and motivating contexts for children to learn about themselves, one another and the world around them' (2015, p. 8). In their good practice survey which explored perceptions of teaching and play in the early years, inspectors visited a sample of successful early years providers to observe the interplay between teaching and play and evaluate the difference chosen approaches were making to the learning and development of disadvantaged children, especially two-year-olds. The report summarised that schools and settings visited did not see teaching as separate from play or infer teaching to mean one fixed view of how things should be done. Leaders did not view their work in such black-and-white terms, believing that to do so would prevent the flexible approach needed when addressing young children's individual needs. They saw teaching as the different ways in which adults, consciously or otherwise, helped children to learn (Ofsted, 2015, p. 4).

Play in the EYFS is about engagement. In relation to the Unique Child this involves:

1   *Finding out and exploring.* With babies this is primarily through their senses and following their natural curiosities about things and people around them.
2   *Playing with what they know.* This involves acting and role play and representing meaning and personal experiences.
3   *Being willing to 'have a go'.* This involves actively searching out new challenges and taking risks.

Each area of learning must be implemented through planned, purposeful play and through a combination of adult-led and child-initiated activity. In responding skilfully to support children's learning, knowing a range of appropriate strategies will help practitioners make decisions about which are likely to be most effective and in which contexts. Let us provide some clarification of terms at this point. *Child-initiated activity* has many characteristics in common with play, as it is decided upon completely by the child. It is based on the child's motivation and remains under the child's control. It may involve play of various types, or it may be seen by the child as an activity with a serious purpose to explore a project or express an idea. It is set within certain expectations within early years settings in relation to use of space, time and its purposes. *Adult-led activities* are those which adults initiate. These activities are not play, and children are likely not to see them as play, but they can be playful. Here, activities presented to children are as open-ended as possible, with elements of imagination and active exploration that will increase the interest and ensure motivation. As well as focused activities with groups of children, adult-led activities include greeting times, story times, songs and tidying up. Wood (2010) proposes a model of integrated pedagogies which combine the benefits of child-initiated and adult-directed activities. In this, she argues that play is always structured by indoor and outdoor environments, the curriculum, ratios, the resources available and the values and beliefs of the adults. Such integrated approaches to pedagogy, which include flexible planning, observation, documentation and reflective dialogue, enhance the potential for co-construction of knowledge between children and adults. This is because educational goals are formed around children's patterns of interest and their motivations.

Reflection

Play through the birth to seven age range is best resourced and supported by skilled and knowledgeable adults who skilfully combine a range of pedagogical approaches. This includes providing opportunities for:

1   Free, child-initiated play which can be directed and sustained by children according to their interests, capabilities and dispositions.
2   Structured play between adults and children, which creates opportunities for modelling play skills and knowledge.
3   Directed play and playful activities with a particular purpose or outcome.
4   Co-constructed play between adults and children, where the adult acts as a sensitive co-player in line with the children's intentions and meanings.
5   Free and directed exploration of materials and resources, which may include some direct teaching and modelling of new or challenging resources.

Consider:
● How and why is play different for a three-year-old and a seven-year-old?
● How does this look in practice?
● Do the conditions for learning change in terms of the mix of play/child-initiated/adult-directed play?
● What difference does the environment make?
● Is progression in play different according to context? How might it differ between a daycare centre, a childminder's home or a Reception class?

Active learning

Children are naturally curious. They seek out 'hands-on' and 'brains-on' activities and their innate exploratory tendencies use their senses to investigate the world around them. This is how they master resources and build knowledge and skills. They are highly motivated learners who learn by engaging in the world. Active learning is about the dispositions and attitudes that define their motivation. In the EYFS the three foci of active learning are:

1   Being involved and concentrating. You can see this when children stay on task and are not distracted. They are highly energised and fascinated by an activity for a period of time.
2   They keep trying and show persistence and bounce back after difficulty or setbacks.
3   They achieve what they set out to do.

They enjoy meeting new challenges and are proud of meeting their goals. Their intrinsic motivation provides their reward, rather than seeking praise or approval externally from others. This view of the child as an inherently *active* learner should underpin practitioners' attempts to personalise and individualise provision.

Active learning in schools involves children in investigative approaches to their learning. There is often collaborative group work going on which involves children sharing ideas and experiences together and using language. They generate their own targets and learn to evaluate their success with help from peers and adults. Teaching mathematics/numeracy in a Year 1 classroom, for example, uses real contexts for learning. In teaching about money, this might typically involve setting up a shop in the classroom where children can experience first-hand buying and selling transactions and the value of currency. This can be extended beyond the classroom doing exactly the same in shops in the local area and involving parents. Teachers report how such approaches put no limits on children's learning. The authors interviewed the head teacher of a primary school recently about active learning in her school and she had this to say:

> Active learning is an approach to teaching and learning we strongly support in school. It's about learning by doing and finding out meaning. That leads to real understanding. Staff support this of course by asking open questions, getting the children really interested in something, then having good resources and setting them off to explore it. You can see it for some children that they stay with things for longer. They don't give up as quickly. Staff here love it, and so do the children. We use it in any subject and it is great for cross-curricular work. We think it raises the bar on children's attainment.

Creating and thinking critically

The idea of fostering thinking is certainly not new (Nisbet, 1990). It is arguably a central aim of education. Findings from cognitive psychology overturn earlier notions of children's limited thinking capacities. Current research findings indicate that people learn best if the pedagogical approach is rooted in social constructivism (see chapter 2). This requires that

Pearson Education Ltd/Jules Selmes

learners actively seek out meaning, which helps to *construct* knowledge of the world through interactions with other people, in partnership with practical actions in the physical environment. Children have a rudimentary ability to think and reason along the same lines as adults; however, they need to develop skills of reflection (which psychologists refer to as metacognition – which means 'thinking about thinking'). They also need to build concrete experiences in order to build their understanding of the world and the way that it 'works' (see Piagetian theory in chapter 2). Incremental experience is crucial for knowledge construction and to help develop self-reflective and self-regulatory skills (Goswami and Bryant, 2007). Creative thinking involves children developing their own ideas, making links between these and devising strategies to put them into action. When creating, they find new ways to solve problems and new ways of doing. When they make links between ideas they are involved in prediction and practical experimentation, which helps them to begin to understand cause and effect. They generalise from information and experience in order to search for trends and patterns. They apply learning in new contexts and new ways. This approach requires 'What if?' questions, 'Why?' and 'How?' and always asking the unusual and unexpected questions! They play with ideas and explore possibilities. They try alternatives and experiment. By keeping open minds they can adapt and modify their ideas to achieve creative results.

Critical thinking is concerned with reflecting critically on ideas and actions and making perceptive observations. Children evaluate what they have done and review progress. They ask questions such as, 'Is this a good ...?' or 'Is this what is needed?'. They invite feedback and use this to help explain their ideas and ways of doing things. The work of McGuinness (1999) is helpful in identifying the types of mental processes that are used in critical thinking. These are:

- Collecting information
- Sorting and analysing information
- Drawing conclusions from the information
- Brainstorming ideas
- Problem-solving
- Determining cause and effect
- Evaluating options
- Planning and setting goals
- Monitoring progress
- Decision-making.

Is this characteristic of learning something that can realistically be seen and indeed be promoted in classrooms? Most certainly. The interview transcripts that follow from research in schools carried out by the authors confirm this.

Case study: critical thinking

Interviewer: Can you tell me how you develop children's critical thinking in your classroom?
Year 1 teacher: I think a lot of teachers are very good at it (critical thinking) here. I know one class teacher who has a Question of the Week to get the children thinking. He doesn't pose it. He invites the children to come into school with a question. The children like it because they set the question for the rest of the class to answer. Thinking skills are given priority here. I think about what thinking is going on, what cognitive approaches. I'm sure I could do it better though. If I have a focus in my head I let the children lead it. I feel I can learn from the children.

Interviewer: Do you believe that thinking skills are possible for primary-aged children?
Year 2 teacher: Yes, it is there as a preparation for doing, then the critical thinking which is like the evaluation of what they are doing, their achievements.

Interviewer: Do you see any constraints to this?
Year 2 teacher: When I've done it deliberately I asked them about it in terms of what they learned. They said they worked a lot harder! They had to be very strongly led but you could definitely see the difference.

Reflection

How do you help children engage in critical thinking, and how would you ensure that this is age- and stage-appropriate? You may find looking back on the concept of 'sustained shared thinking' in chapter 2 helps you with this reflection, particularly how it can be flexibly used in a range of environments, with children at different stages of development.

Stimulating and purposeful learning environments need to be appropriately and adequately resourced and planned for. The effective practitioner should ensure that children have choice, not only in which activity/experience they decide to engage, but whether to do so on their own, with their peers or with adults. Sufficient space and time are vital prerequisites in an enabling environment where a range of activities should be on offer, some of which may be planned and led by adults, based on their knowledge of children's current interests, learning styles and stages of development. Such a rich, enabling environment, where practitioners allow children to dictate the pace and length of focus, and sensitively and subtly intervene and support, provides a safe, secure dispositional milieu in which children can develop and learn. Each early years setting will have its own unique milieu, presenting to children a particular view of what it means to be an active learner in that particular environment. Effective practice establishes a place where children will develop and learn in their own unique ways. The flexibility of such a play environment encourages the development of 'playful minds ... the most suitable approach to future life in our fluid, multi-media, global society' (David and Powell, 2005, p. 1).

Pearson Education Ltd/Jules Selmes

How can outdoor play and creative partnerships with outside agents such as artists 'in residence' develop children's learning and foster creativity?

Play and learning in outdoor environments

Children learn best when using their physicality within an active approach to learning (Cooper and Doherty, 2010). The outdoor environment brings an added layer of pedagogical responsibility as it is in these spaces that practitioners must exercise more courage, trust and faith in children and in their own decisions (Wood, 2013). The EYFS clearly reinforces the need for opportunities that enable children to develop and learn in indoor and outdoor contexts. Outdoor provision needs to have the same depth and breadth of engagement by practitioners as indoor provision. Children play and express themselves differently outdoors and, if practitioners are to create environments that harness the uniqueness of each child, outdoor provision needs to be planned so that children are inspired, challenged and intrigued, providing an environment just as 'enabling', with as much thought and planning as the indoor environment. In resourcing the outdoor environment the following should be available:

- A space large enough to promote vigorous heart fitness
- Large apparatuses that offer challenging climbing opportunities
- A space for wheeled toys
- Small apparatuses such as beanbags and hoops
- Different surfaces
- Quiet areas for reflection with blankets or mats
- Places to hide
- A wild area to explore
- A garden.

(Doherty and Brennan, 2008)

Case study: Forest Schools

The Forest School approach to outdoor provision, developed in Denmark, is gaining increasing recognition in the UK in schools and early years settings as powerful environments to promote play and learning. Many benefits have been demonstrated through this approach. The Forest Schools ethos supports practitioners by encouraging their use of resources, self-discovery and problem-solving. For children, deep-level learning and the ability to turn discoveries into new knowledge or skills can stem from Forest School experiences (Blackwell and Pound, 2011). It addresses the 'nature deficit' that many children may experience in today's society and encourages self-initiated learning with children engaged in experiencing a variety of skills like den-building, treasure trails, bushcraft, environmental art, planting and growing produce, as well as adult-supervised activities such as building woodland fires, cooking and learning to work with knives. Children with language difficulties particularly seem to benefit, as research suggests children make significantly more utterances when outdoors; through improved communication they also develop their emotional literacy. This more kinaesthetic and flexible approach to learning experiences develops children's ideas and respect and appreciation for the natural environment (Cook, 2008). Natural woodland environments provide opportunities for social and emotional development. Physical prowess is enhanced with advantages in fine and gross motor skills, balance and coordination. These environments have an obvious contribution to make to the management of risk and through the physical challenges associated with climbing trees and fire building; for example, a respect for the environment. The nature of resources in outdoor environments creates a situation where children work with what play workers refer to as 'loose parts' (Play England, 2009) – natural items that can be used in a number of ways, or crafted to fit various purposes, rather than manufactured toys made for very specific purposes. This makes such play inherently creative.

Pearson Education Ltd/Jules Selmes

Reflection

What elements of the Forest School could you import into your setting? You will see in chapter 10 that it is not usually a good idea to simply import practices from other cultures without considering the consequences; the best idea is to consider what aspects might work in the environment of your setting and how you are going to operationalise them. Through this process, it is possible to make gradual ongoing changes.

The creative use of movement, which involves all the senses – hearing, vision, taste, smell and touch, can lead to the extension of verbal and non-verbal means of communicating for a child. Such movement aids expression, balance, flexibility, strength and confidence. Research has shown how essential movement itself is for children's growth and development. Greenland (2000) suggested that human beings do not just live in their heads but, as playful physical beings, in their whole bodies, while research suggests babies and young children are biologically driven to seek the physical experience that will most benefit their particular stage of development.

The movement-based learning involved in children's schemas such as transporting, connecting, trajectory and rotation is well fitted to outdoor provision where the space to move and explore safely can be offered. With provision that is flexible and versatile, children can re-create and change their environment imaginatively, taking ownership of their play milieu. Provision should offer and resource a wide range of holistic experiences for children outdoors, including areas where play is active, boisterous and noisy, and others that are calm and allow children space and time to reflect.

Outdoor environments offer the unique opportunity for risk-taking and for children to understand how to manage risks. Pound and Miller (2011) remind us that such environments place emphasis on both physical and personal development, and of the parallels between being willing to engage in physical and emotional risk-taking. Not exclusive to the outdoors, risk-taking is integral to play itself, but some practitioners are concerned that the outdoor environment is a potentially dangerous one. Some children actively seek out exciting and challenging play that has risks, and if they are under-challenged in physical play, they can quickly become bored with their experiences and this may lead to using equipment in inappropriate or dangerous ways (Doherty and Brennan, 2008). Clearly the message here is that practitioners need to balance appropriate challenge with sound risk assessment. Careful planning and monitoring is essential to make outdoor learning experiences safe, rewarding and purposeful. Children desire to push boundaries, try things out, and experiment with ideas and the unknown (Tovey, 2010). This is a life skill and rather than try to tightly control it or eradicate it, adults need to help children weigh up risks in their physical play activities in the outdoors and understand their bodies' capabilities and limitations. To deny children opportunities to engage with risk is to deny them something that is an important part of life.

Case study: planning for outdoor provision to support learning and development

Rachel, the manager of a private daycare setting housed in a large Victorian detached property, discussed with her Lead Practitioner, Alice, how best to improve the outdoor provision. Babies and young children attending the setting currently accessed the outdoors by being taken on regular trips to a nearby park and play area, as well as spending a limited amount of time with tricycles, scooters and prams on a small tarmac area at the front of the building. Alice felt some changes could be made relatively cheaply, as she had a number of contacts locally who could supply larger equipment such as tyres and milk crates, and suggested to Rachel that one of the trees in the grounds of the house could be made into a sitting log with sections cut for use as stepping stones. She also discussed re-organising the staffing rota, to ensure that outdoor play could be accessed more regularly. At a staff meeting, Alice discussed the proposed rota changes for outdoor provision, whereby one member of staff would be involved in a focused activity, while another practitioner monitored the children's play generally, with some flexibility if the numbers of children accessing the outdoors increased. Alice also suggested that the staff in each room took it in turns to plan for a whole week's outdoor activities.

Alice reminded staff of the balance between indoor and outdoor provision that good practice demands in the EYFS. She suggested that some of the older children could help with tidying away equipment and felt the new arrangements should be trialled for a short period. The overgrown areas were fenced off temporarily and Alice modelled good practice by planning and implementing the first two weeks' outdoor activities. After each group had been responsible for one week's outdoor provision, staff met to discuss how they felt the new arrangements had gone. Alice also reminded staff that it was not expected that the outdoors would exactly 'mirror' indoor provision, and that planning should include alternatives for differing weather conditions. She suggested all-weather clothing should be purchased for the children, and it was also agreed that she and another member of staff would attend training on planning and resourcing outdoor provision currently being run by the local authority. After attending this training, the following recommendations were made:

- Soft surfacing should be laid for a new climbing frame and separate slide.
- The area around the trees and shrubbery should be pruned back and cleared and plants inspected for 'safety', but left for such uses as a den-making area, treasure hunt trail, and digging and planting activities.
- A veranda at the side of the play area should be made safe and roofed to provide cover in wet weather.
- A new shed should be situated next to the play area for storing equipment. Alice said this could be made multifunctional, by painting one wall of the shed with blackboard paint to encourage mark-making, and hanging instruments on another wall to encourage musical activities outdoors.

Reflection
- How do you feel Alice handled the changes proposed for the outdoor provision?
- Did Alice model good practice long enough for staff to adapt their practice?
- Did she give sufficient guidance on the new planning?
- How could staff have had more input on the expectations for outdoor provision set out in the EYFS practice guidance?

Creative Partnerships

Creativity flourishes through the dynamic interplay between teacher and child in an enabling environment where children's contributions are valued and innovation is encouraged. Writers like Jeffrey and Craft (2003) argue that practice that fosters creativity in learners must involve the construction of a learning environment that is appropriate for the children in it. Malaguzzi (1993) reminds us that being creative is not something separate but integral to ways of thinking, knowing and making choices. Jeffrey suggested that creative practitioners have skill in drawing upon a repertoire of approaches to facilitate children's learning, saying that they 'devise, organize, vary, mix whatever teaching methods and strategies they feel most effectively advance their aims' (1997, p. 74). It is therefore not only children we want to be creative: the same should be true for adults, too! Adults have a key role here and facilitate creativity by setting up environments that allow play, exploration, creativity and learning to flourish. These are environments where adults welcome children's ideas and build upon them, integrating creative problem-solving into all aspects of the curriculum, and which, moreover, emphasise 'process' alongside 'product'.

The Creative Partnerships initiative was aimed at introducing creative approaches to the arts and culture into educational settings, bringing creative workers like artists and scientists into settings and schools to work with teachers to inspire children to think and act creatively and assist directly with learning. It was England's flagship creative learning programme from 2002 to 2011, designed to develop the skills of children and young people across England, raising their aspirations, achievements and life chances. We feel that the benefits of such creative partnerships with their focus on creativity are many and include:

- Children gain confidence.
- They learn new skills that are not simply 'task-related'.
- They grow in emotional intelligence through learning to communicate their feelings and ideas to their peers.
- They have increased awareness of difference and diversity.
- They learn to collaborate and work as part of a team.
- The environment is seen as an effective 'third teacher'.
- There is a depth of interaction as a result of children being given time and space to pursue their interests.
- The emphasis is clearly on process and not on outcomes.
- Children are encouraged to make judgements, become absorbed and be persistent.

The programme worked with over one million children and over 90,000 teachers in more than 8,000 projects in England (see www.creative-partnerships.com). In 2011 funding was withdrawn but the impact of the programmes was significant, not merely on arts education but on learning generally. In their critical review of Creative Partnerships, researchers Thomson and colleagues (2012) found evidence for this approach encouraging enjoyment and engagement in schools and showing improvements in attendance and motivation. The researchers found the programmes produced benefits in the areas of well-being and citizenship, and there were also professional learning gains for teachers.

Many settings and schools continue to work in partnership with experts from the world of culture and the arts, many of whom live and work in the local community. Having an artist 'in residence' in a setting has many advantages relating to children's learning and creativity. Adults need to feel 'delight and curiosity in discovering artistic opportunities ... the more the child feels the pleasure of the practitioner, the more willing they are to let their own pleasure show' (Théâtre de la Guimbarde). There is a need from the beginning of the partnership to establish that the artist is sympathetic to the setting in terms of its ethos and principles regarding children's learning and development as well as having an ability to communicate with and listen to children effectively. Practitioners and artists need to reflect by sharing their perceptions on what is or is not working within a particular project and why. Adults also need to reflect upon how much they themselves are learning from such creative experiences, demonstrating Vygotsky's observation that 'teachers' and 'learners' often construct learning together. Having an artist in residence, as well as introducing new skills and experiences often produces very dynamic environments for children: a potter's wheel, creating sculptures, drawing and painting with unusual media can also help practitioners look afresh at the environment and seek to make it attractive and stimulating.

Associated activities add a vibrancy to the environment. Storytelling by children, with props they have made, encourages listening skills in the audience and speaking skills in the storyteller. As well as helping a child's creativity, stories can also give us insights into influences and anxieties or actual events which the child is trying to make sense of. Using photographs to record a process or achievement, or to confirm an acquired skill, is sometimes seen as an end in itself. However, photography can be used as an art form, by both children and adults. A camera can provide the child with autonomy; they choose what they wish to photograph, and they can choose whether or not to use the resulting photograph as a 'product' or permanent record. The authors observed children on a visit to the park to feed the ducks taking photographs of the patterns left by their trainers in the mud, not the ducks they were going to feed! Photographs can be used to help communication with parents, support metacognition in children by recalling their previous experiences, and, if there is no common language, photographs can be a clear aid to communicating meaningfully.

The spontaneous expression of children's imagination through a range of different media, helped by an artist's perspective, demonstrates the innate human drive to explore, develop concepts and solve problems that all children have: 'through their imagination children can move from the present into the past and the future, to what might be and beyond' (Duffy, 1998). Children thrive in an environment that fosters connections rather than separations. Making mistakes and trying again should also be built into the process, with no pressures to produce a perfect result. Only through such first-hand experience can increasing competence and the confidence to accept new challenges be developed. The same starting point will and should have different outcomes for individual children, if practitioners apply the principles of good practice in the EYFS.

Case study: an artist in residence

A local authority setting had managed to secure funding to work with a local artist. The Lead Practitioner, Cathy, was very enthusiastic about the thought of working with an artist for a two-week period. The theme that the setting focused upon was seasonal change, considering the changes that were taking place in nature, particularly in terms of light and dark. The idea was that the techniques introduced by the artist would allow the children to express their ideas around this theme.

During the first week, Sue, the local artist, focused on showing the children how to create a simple weaving frame from wood and string, and then demonstrated the principles of weaving with strips of ribbon and material. The older children, especially a group of four-year-old boys, enjoyed using the hammers, saws and tools to create the weaving 'looms', but a few lost interest in the weaving process itself. The older girls persisted, creating loose, interesting patterns from two or three lines of weaving with various materials. Eager to have 'evidence' of the artist's involvement with the children, Helen, another practitioner in the setting, emphasised how important it was for the children to 'finish' their work. On seeing this, Cathy spoke with both Sue and Helen, separately. She reminded Helen that it was the process of weaving that should be the focus and not the product. With Sue, she thanked her for her contribution, talked about how the weaving activity had helped some of the children with their fine motor skills as well as extending knowledge in other areas of learning like the turn-taking and conversation that had taken place with the 'communal' piece of weaving Sue had initiated. Lastly, she commented on the need to focus on process rather than product.

At a staff meeting the next week, Cathy asked for observations from staff about how they had found the experience. Staff had found it beneficial, that Sue had been very supportive and full of suggestions, and said they would look more creatively at how they used resources, and that the presence of a 'creative' mind in their midst had stimulated creativity within the children.

Reflection

- What do you see as the benefits of working with a local artist such as Sue in this case study?
- Do you think the issue about finishing work was dealt with correctly in this case? What would you have done?
- The 'light and dark' theme became rather lost in the process, as the children focused on the weaving techniques. Do you think that this was a problem, or not?
- What next steps would you plan for the setting to build on this initial work?

How can practitioners ensure that children are provided with flexible routines that meet individual needs, in well-resourced environments that take account of diversity and encourage inclusive practice and provision?

Meeting the individual needs of all children will help every child reach their full potential. Children today are growing up in a rapidly changing world and one of increased diversity. Diversity is about difference. It is an evolving concept in early childhood and represents the acknowledgement that difference is complex and that it exists in some way for every child (Petriwskyj, 2010). It recognises individual differences and accepts and respects each individual regardless of their gender, age, ethnicity, socio-economic status, ability, religion or beliefs. Children from an early age should understand that people may have views and beliefs different to theirs but which need to be respected. They should begin to know about their own cultures and have a developing respect for these and the beliefs of other people. Culture is quite dynamic and changes across generations. It involves habits and traditions as well as customs, food, music and artefacts of other people and countries. Celebrating cultural diversity is recognised as part of everyday practice in early years and much valued, but the commitment to it is relatively recent in British society (Baldock, 2010).

Leaders and practitioners have a responsibility to ensure positive attitudes to diversity and difference in settings so children learn to value diversity in others and make a positive contribution to society. Good outcomes for children are achieved when their diverse strengths, interests and cultural practices are understood and fully supported. This includes professionals having high expectations for all children and breaking down barriers that might hinder their success. By focusing on the uniqueness of each child and their interests, the effective practitioner can create an environment whose resources reflect the diversity of cultures and beliefs of the wider community – ensuring this through artefacts, books, activities and experiences that are shared with parents/carers. Children will feel their cultures and beliefs are celebrated and valued. Providing labels and print in the environment written in children's home languages will help children come to understand the importance of print, and will also make parents/carers feel more welcome. Dual-language books that are commercially available or made by the children and shared with their peers and family also promote a sense of self-esteem.

World music and stories in different languages available on audio tapes for children to access and share, dolls and puppets representing a range of ethnicities and cultures, clothing representative of several cultures available in role-play areas, foods from different cultural cuisines prepared and available at the snack table for children to taste and discuss, as well as the celebration of special festivals, are all examples that settings using good diversity practice adopt. *Learning for All: Standards for racial equality in schools* (Commission for Racial Equality, 2000) states that effective provision will help schools ensure that:

- all pupils achieve their full potential
- expectations of all pupils are equally high
- all pupils have access to and make full use of the facilities and resources
- all pupils are prepared for life in a diverse and multi-ethnic society
- an environment that has a positive ethos on diversity is developed within the school.

Inclusion and diversity are integral to effective provision, and in order to ensure inclusive practice, schools and settings must develop their ethoses, policies and practices to include all learners with the aim of meeting their individual needs. Nutbrown and Clough propose:

1   Inclusion has an operational rather than conceptual focus.
2   Inclusion is always in a 'state of becoming'.
3   Inclusion can/must only be known by its outcomes – not its rhetoric.
4   There are as many versions of inclusion as there are people to be included.
5   Cultures, communities and curricula are, by definition, exclusive.
6   Inclusion must not be imposed from without.
7   Inclusion is ultimately about how people treat each other.

(Nutbrown and Clough, 2013, p. 5)

There is a statutory requirement for practitioners within the EYFS to provide holistic and inclusive provision for young children. Early years practitioners already do this extremely well. This recognition is reflected in the words of Chizea and colleagues: 'The pre-school model of society, in which all members have something to offer and in which all members can find the level of support they need, can provide an inclusive approach to the needs of all children' (Chizea *et al.*, 1999, p. 5).

Inclusion is a basic human right and championed by international legislation. (Readers should refer to the Universal Declaration of Human Rights, the Convention on Human Rights and the UN Convention on the Rights of the Child.) International governments are working towards a more transformative education agenda where inclusive education and education for all meet. Whilst this is a global commitment, it is a formidable challenge to translate policy into everyday practice for those who work with young children and families on a daily basis. The model of inclusive education that we advocate as authors argues that it is the environment that disables, and settings and schools either create obstacles or open doors to participation and learning through their culture, policies, organisation and structures, and their curriculum and content. Therefore, the preferred model is one that seeks to reduce barriers that might hinder a child from being an equal participant in society. This has relevance to all ages and stages of development, by placing responsibility on settings to promote participation, to make learning accessible to all children and by challenging discriminatory practices.

A strength of good inclusive practice is that it challenges stereotypes and misconceptions of all kinds. This includes the possibly lower expectations that parents/carers, practitioners and children themselves may have about what is possible or achievable. A new parent might perhaps be finding it hard to adjust to their child attending the setting and may be overprotective. This may well be preventing the child from settling in and taking full advantage of all the setting offers. It is the practitioner's task to explain this sensitively to the parent. It may be that an inexperienced practitioner is 'taking over' children's activities, thinking they are helping children who are 'struggling', when what they are really engaged in is the celebration of their own artistic talents! Again it is the practice leader's duty to model and explain good practice, while not dampening enthusiasm. There is an important role for the EGYP/EYT in the referral process for children who may need specialist support from other services.

The emphasis on inclusive practice which is central to the Children and Families Act (2014) which saw the removal of previous *Early Years Action*, and *Early Years Action Plus* has been cascaded to settings and schools regarding SEN (Special Educational Needs) assessments. If the child already has a statement, the setting needs to support parents while conversion to a new Education, Health and Care Plan (EHCP) is put in place. This should ensure that the additional financing needed will support the expected individual outcomes for each child.

In 2014 a new Code of Practice came into force in England spanning the years from birth to 25. The Statutory Guidance document makes explicit objectives to improve outcomes for children with SEN through high aspirations and expectations. It states that all children are entitled to an education that enables them to 'achieve the best possible educational and other outcomes and become confident young children with a growing ability to communicate their own views and ready to make the transition into compulsory education' (DfE, 2015, p. 79).

Have we gone far enough? There have been some recent concerns raised and a number of criticisms about inclusion education policies in this country. Ofsted reported earlier that whilst a number of mainstream settings meet individual needs well, others do not. Full participation in the mainstream life of a school or setting is difficult, and progress of a significant number of children with SEN is inferior to that of their peers. In the current climate of league tables and performance statistics, there are clear pressures on teachers and practitioners through the EYFS and through the National Curriculum to achieve good results. This can lead to inadequate provision of learning opportunities and even the reluctance of some settings to accept children with special needs. As Nutbrown and Clough (2013) point out, one of the challenges of an inclusive agenda is allying this with an educational standards agenda. Both are important: inclusion is a vital plank in the platform of social justice and raising achievement is a goal for all educators. Demands coming from competing discourses need to be reconciled to make it possible for the development of successful inclusive practices, and for all children to reach their potential (Nutbrown and Clough, 2013).

The effective practitioner, nevertheless, has to strive for and promote inclusive, anti-discriminatory practice by:

- Identifying and addressing any practices that are discriminatory within the setting
- Promoting self-esteem and positive group identity
- Valuing children for their individuality and ensuring a sense of belonging
- Respecting where children come from, what they achieve and what they bring to the setting.

Practitioners working in early years settings and schools are committed to providing equality of opportunity and striving to provide inclusive practice to promote equal opportunities for all children. In creating inclusive environments that foster learning for each child, practitioners need to consider appropriate and flexible routines which incorporate a balance of child-led and adult-initiated experiences and opportunities, as well as routines that allow children time to follow their interests and support particular individual needs. Routines need to be created that are flexible enough to reflect the different kinds of access to and time spent in the setting by individual children, thus promoting the very necessary sense of continuity for the child between home, the setting, and possible other provision that the child attends. Routines need to be flexible enough to take into account the important links between home and the setting, whether it be the feeding and sleeping patterns of babies and infants reflecting the patterns and practice of home, or attempting to embed children's interests, however transitory, into short- and medium-term planning. How to plan for the unexpected is a skill the effective practitioner needs to develop and, when children's interests take hold, planning and routines need to be flexible enough to accommodate them. Planning and routines also need to support children at particularly vulnerable times, such as the transition from pre-school to mainstream settings, or at times when their personal circumstances are temporarily difficult, for example the arrival of a new sibling, or the ill-health of a parent, or a death in the family (see chapter 6).

When organising and resourcing the environment, the effective practitioner needs to take into account the free flow of play between indoor and outdoor provision. They have to ensure that all children have equal access to such provision and that the resources reflect the diversity of the wider community. If physical changes to buildings are required for children with particular disabilities, then, within reason, this must be swiftly undertaken in order to ensure that practice is inclusive. To meet children's particular needs, materials and space may need to be adapted, so they have equal access to indoor and outdoor provision safely. Tracking rails and tactile symbols can help the visually impaired child negotiate the indoor environment with more autonomy. Outdoor provision, using the senses of touch, smell and sound, perhaps through the building of a sensory garden, would support inclusive experiences. The use of an extensive range of communication systems in a setting including PECS (see www.pecs.com), Makaton, British Sign Language and Baby Sign (see www. underfives.co.uk/signs.htm) helps hearing-impaired children and children on the autistic spectrum to feel included. Simple, practical additions like ramps or widened door openings give children using wheelchairs and walking aids easy access to indoor/outdoor provision.

Case study: 'Cherry Trees'

'Cherry Trees', a large nursery for three- to five-year-olds, had to deal with a complex issue relating to special educational needs. A set of four-year-old identical triplets, all of whom had been identified as being on the autistic spectrum had recently been admitted. Their mother, a single parent, had met with the nursery's Lead Practitioner Elizabeth, and Pat, the setting's SENCo (Special Educational Needs Co-ordinator) and expressed the wish that the triplets should remain together and not be separated into different areas. Pat was supported by an Early Years Practitioner with special needs training and several teaching assistants, and the setting policy was to try and include children with SEN as much as possible in the daily routines, including free-flow play within the continuous provision, withdrawing the children into a small group only at the beginning and end of the day. Each child was usually allocated a class base and attempts were made to involve them at story or circle time, with support. Some staff felt concern at the prospect of the triplets being in one class base even with support. As the triplets displayed differences in terms of their current placement within the autistic spectrum it was felt, in order to meet individual needs, it would be beneficial to separate them.

Elizabeth and Pat discussed this with their mother, Pauline, who was resistant to the proposal at first, but eventually agreed to a trial period. Over time, Tom, the triplet who showed the least overt autistic behaviours managed to gradually access circle and story time within his class base. Initially his support worker would sit beside him, but after a period she was able to move away, as long as she remained in view. This had an effect on the rest of his play and involvement, as he gradually began to accept other children into his personal space. Peter, the triplet with most complex needs, was placed in a class base managed by a teacher whose initial degree was in art, where his obvious talents for drawing and painting were stimulated and praised. As time went by he began to quite happily access group times for short periods. Stephen, the triplet with the greatest need for cognitive and emotional support, preferred to play and explore in a one-to-one situation with a trusted adult, and would actively seek out only the company of his brothers. Elizabeth regularly co-ordinated with the boys' Key Workers and subsequently collated and communicated all these developments on a daily basis to Pauline via a home–school diary to reassure her that the triplets were happy, and enjoying their time in the setting.

Reflection

- In this practice example, do you feel the mother's wishes were sufficiently respected?
- Do you feel the solutions reached supported each triplet's individual learning journey?
- Was this a case of the triplets fitting into existing routines or a genuine attempt to meet individual needs?
- Have you experienced a similar difficulty in trying to meet individual needs within inclusive provision? If so, how did you deal with this?

Policy changes reflected in the current and previous Education and Children Acts reflect progress from the early medical model of disability diagnosis to a contemporary social model. The former is characterised by defect or impairment and with labelling (exclusively carried out by medical practitioners and psychologists), focused upon attempts to restore or rectify perceived 'deficits'. Conversely, the latter aims to empower individuals by emphasising their rights to be independent and make choices, including the choice to be different. As we argued above, it is the environment that disables, and settings and schools either create obstacles or open doors to participation and learning. Therefore this model is one that seeks to reduce barriers that might hinder the child from equal participation in society. This places responsibility on leaders and practitioners in settings to promote participation, make learning accessible to all and challenge unequal practices.

Case study: autism as difference not deficit

Watch American academic and autism activist Temple Grandin talking about how her mind works, and the problems she has experienced with the 'normalisation' agenda in her social milieu, education in particular:

www.youtube.com/watch?v=fn_9f5xOf1Q

Naoki Higashida, a 13-year-old boy with high-functioning autism says:

So how do people with autism see the world, exactly? We, only we, can ever know the answer to that one! Sometimes I actually pity you for not being able to see the beauty of the world in the same way we do. Really, our vision of the world can be incredible, just incredible …

When you see an object, it seems that you see it as an entire thing first, and only afterwards do its details follow on … But for people with autism, the details jump straight out at us first of all, and then only gradually, detail by detail, does the whole image sort of float up into focus.

Every single thing has its own unique beauty. People with autism get to cherish this beauty, as if it's a kind of blessing given to us.

(Higashida, 2013, pp. 91–2)

Reflection

Would it change your practice if you thought about conditions such as autism and ADHD as differences rather than deficits? Consider this from the perspective of 'knowing the child' that you met in Chapter 5, and consider what modifications you might make to your setting or classroom, including what you might do if you were not bound by curriculum outcomes/standards.

Conclusion

This chapter has explored a range of questions that focus on the important role of the environment in promoting play and learning. In it we have suggested a number of strategies and approaches to resourcing environments that take account of diversity and encourage inclusive practice and provision.

How can the 'Characteristics of Effective Learning' support the establishment of warm, supportive and purposeful environments that promote play and learning?

The opening question to the chapter focused on the three types of environments: emotional, indoor and outdoor. We used the 'Characteristics of Effective Learning' underpinning the seven Areas of Learning in the EYFS – playing and exploring, active learning, and creating and thinking critically – to discuss how these each contribute to establishing purposeful and stimulating environments for children. The section finished with a brief discussion on the Forest School approach and we described how this ethos supports practitioners by encouraging their use of resources, self-discovery and problem-solving, and for children, deep-level learning and the ability to turn discoveries into new knowledge or skills.

How can outdoor play and creative partnerships with outside agents such as artists 'in residence' develop children's learning and foster creativity?

Outdoor play is by its less constricted nature inherently creative, allowing children to play with objects as 'loose parts', creating uses for them from their imaginations. We considered the concept of the Forest School, and asked you to consider how elements of this might be brought into your own setting. Partnerships with the community are a feature of good practice for schools and settings. In this section we introduced the Creative Partnerships initiative as an example of one way of bringing arts into education. Having an artist 'in residence' in a setting has many advantages relating to children's learning and creativity. In this approach the environment is seen as an effective 'third teacher'.

How can practitioners ensure that children are provided with flexible routines that meet individual needs, in well-resourced environments that take account of diversity and encourage inclusive practice and provision?

Leaders and practitioners have a responsibility to ensure positive attitudes to diversity and difference within settings so that children learn to value diversity in others and make a positive contribution to society. The ultimate responsibility for ensuring high-quality practice in this area lies, as always, with the lead practitioner in the setting. By focusing on the uniqueness of each child and their interests, the effective practitioner can create an environment where resources reflect the diversity of cultures and beliefs of the wider community.

In creating inclusive environments that foster learning for each child, we argued that practitioners need to consider appropriate and flexible routines which incorporate a balance of child-led and adult-initiated experiences and opportunities, as well as the need for routines that allow children time to follow their interests and support individual needs.

Recommended reading

Eaton, C. (2014) *Enabling Environments on a Shoestring: A guide to developing and reviewing early years provision*. London: Early Education.

Ephgrave, A. (2015) *The Nursery Year in Action: Following children's interests through the year*. London: Sage.

Hodgman, L. (2011) *Enabling Environments in the Early Years: Making provision for high quality and challenging learning experiences in early years settings*. London: Practical Pre-school/MA Education.

Knight, S. (Ed.) (2011) *Forest School for All*. London: Sage.

White, J. (2011) *Outdoor Provision in the Early Years*. London: Sage.

Websites

Two websites to consider the features of forest schools:

www.foresteducation.org

www.forestschools.com

British Sign Language and Baby Sign: www.underfives.co.uk/signs

Picture Exchange System (PECS): www.pecs.com

References

Baldock, P. (2010). *Understanding Cultural Diversity in the Early Years*. London: Sage.

Blackwell, S. and Pound, L. (2011) Forest schools in the early years, in L. Miller and L. Pound (Eds) *Theories and Approaches to Learning in the Early Years*. London: Sage.

Bruce, T. (1991) *Time to Play in Early Childhood Education*. London: Hodder & Stoughton.

Chizea, C., Henderson, A. and Jones, G. (1999) *Inclusion in Pre-School Settings: support for children with special needs and their families*. London: Pre-School Learning Alliance.

Commission for Racial Equality (2000) *Learning for All: Standards for racial equality in schools*. London: CRE.

Cook, J. (2008) Setting up a forest school. *The Teacher*. November, p. 43.

Cooper, L. and Doherty, J. (2010) *Supporting Development in the Early Years Foundation Stage: Physical development*. London: Continuum.

David, T. and Powell, S. (2005) Play in the early years: the influence of cultural difference. in J. Moyles (Ed.) *The Excellence of Play*. Maidenhead: Open University Press.

DfE (2015) *SEND Code of Practice*. Retrieved from: www.gov.uk/government/uploads/system/uploads/attachment_data/file/398815/SEND_Code_of_Practice_January_2015.pdf 21st July 2015.

Doherty, J. and Brennan, P. (2008) *Physical Education and Development 3–11: A guide for teachers*. London: Routledge.

Duffy, B. (1998) *Supporting Creativity and Imagination in Early Years*. Oxford: Oxford University Press.

Early Education (2012) *Development Matters in the Early Years Foundation Stage (EYFS)*. London: Early Education/NAECE.

Early Years Matters (2015) *Enabling Environments*. Retrieved from: earlyyearsmatters.co.uk/index.php/eyfs/enabling-environments/emotional-environment 10th July 2015.

Goswami, U. and Bryant, P. (2007). *Children's Cognitive Development and Learning* (Primary Review Research Survey 2/1a). Cambridge: University of Cambridge.

Greenland, P. (2000) *Hopping Home Backwards: Body intelligence and movement play*. Leeds: JABADAO Publications.

Gura, P. (1996) An entitlement curriculum for early childhood, in S. Robson and S. Smedley (Eds) *Education in Early Childhood*. London: David Fulton.

Higashida, N. (2013) *The Reason I Jump*. London: Sceptre.

Hughes, F.P. (2010) *Children, Play, and Development* (4th Edn). Thousand Oaks, CA: Sage.

Jeffrey, B. (1997) The relevance of creative teaching: pupils' views, in A. Pollard, D. Thiessen and A. Filer (Eds) *Children and Their Curriculum: The perspectives of primary and elementary children*. London: Falmer.

Jeffrey, B. and Craft A. (2003) *Creative Teaching and Teaching for Creativity: Distinctions and relationships*. Paper presented at the British Educational Research Association National Conference on Creativity in Education, 3rd February. Open University Centre: The Open University.

Malaguzzi, L. (1993) History, ideas, and basic philosophy, in C. Edwards, L. Gandini and G. Forman (Eds) *The Hundred Languages of Children: The Reggio Emilia approach to early childhood education*. Norwood, NJ: Ablex Publishing.

McGuinness, C. (1999) *From Thinking Skills to Thinking Classrooms: A review and evaluation of approaches for developing pupils' thinking*, DfEE Research Report No. 115. Norwich: HMSO.

McLane, J. (2003) *'Does not.' 'Does, too.' Thinking about play in the early childhood classroom*. Occasional Paper No. 4. Chicago: Erikson Institute.

Nisbet, J. (1990) *Teaching Thinking: An introduction to the research literature* (Spotlight 26). Edinburgh: SCRE.

Nutbrown, C. and Clough, P. (2013) *Inclusion in the Early Years*. London: Sage.

Nutbrown, C. and Clough, P. (2014) *Early Childhood Education: History, philosophy and experience* (2nd Edn). London: Sage.

Ofsted (2015) *Teaching and Play in the Early Years – A Balancing Act? A good practice survey to explore perceptions of teaching and play in the early years*. London: Ofsted.

Petriwskyj, A. (2010). Diversity and inclusion in the early years. *International Journal of Inclusive Education*. 14(2), 195–212.

Play England (2009) *Playwork and the Early Years Foundation Stage*. Retrieved from: www.playengland.org.uk/media/99820/0907-playwork-partnerships-early-years.pdf 21st July 2015.

Pound, L. and Miller, L. (2011) Critical issues, in L. Miller and L. Pound (Eds) *Theories and Approaches to Learning in the Early Years*. London: Sage.

Thomson, P., Coles, R., Hallewell, M. and Keane, J. (2012) *A Critical Review of the Creative Partnerships Archive. How was cultural value understood, researched and evidenced?* Nottingham: University of Nottingham/Arts and Humanities Research Council.

Tovey, H. (2010) Playing on the edge. Perceptions of risk and danger in outdoor play, in P. Broadhead, J. Howard and E. Wood (Eds) *Play and Learning in the Early Years*. London: Sage.

Wood, E. (2010) Developing integrated pedagogical approaches to play and learning, in P. Broadhead, J. Howard and E. Wood (Eds) *Play and Learning in the Early Years*. London: Sage.

Wood, E. (2013) *Play, Learning and the Early Childhood Curriculum*. London: Sage.

8 Partnership and leadership in early years

Jane George, Pam Jarvis and Wendy Holland

CHAPTER OVERVIEW

In this chapter we are going to address the various ways in which Early Years Graduate Professionals/Early Years Teachers (EYGPs/EYTs) can develop effective working relationships with other adults and act as leaders of practice and innovation in order to ensure that outcomes for children are enhanced and improved. The chapter will deal firstly with working with parents and carers, move on to some tips to help with leading practice for an Early Years Team within a setting (which is further explored in chapter 9 in terms of continuing professional development), and conclude with a brief consideration of multi-agency working with staff from other professional groups and backgrounds. The skills, knowledge and values which support the achievement of these aims will be considered, as well as how research supports effective practice.

The chapter will address the following questions:

✔ What strategies are needed to ensure that effective working partnerships with children and their families are valued and embedded in practice in order to promote children's well-being, learning and development?
✔ What strategies can help EYGPs/EYTs to build and lead teams in early years practice?
✔ In what ways can the EYGP/EYT lead practice to ensure that multi-agency teamworking is understood, valued and used effectively in supporting children's particular needs, both among professionals and within the setting and external agencies?

The recommended reading list at the end of this chapter will introduce readers to a range of texts and online resources in which to read further on these topics.

Case study: Josh's family

Josh, a three-year-old, whose family had recently moved into the area, began attending afternoon sessions at a nursery school set in a reasonably affluent urban area of a city. His Key Worker, Level 3 practitioner Eve, noticed how his mother, Fran, who brought him to the sessions, seemed very reserved and reluctant to engage in conversation, making her younger child, a 10-month-old daughter, the excuse for a quick departure. By contrast, his father, who sometimes collected Josh at the end of the session, was talkative and generally pleasant, sometimes apologising for being a little late. Josh appeared to settle into his new surroundings quite quickly, and formative observations soon began to show he had good communication skills and a facility for problem-solving.

At the commencement of one session, determined to share an observation with Fran, Eve attempted to draw her into conversation, but the younger child was crying and Eve quickly saw that Fran was on the verge of tears herself. Josh was also not as happy to leave his mother as usual, so Eve tried to distract him with his favourite activity of constructing with the large hollow blocks. She mentioned the incident to the nursery teacher, Pat, who suggested a meeting with Fran at a less hectic time than the session 'meet and greet'. Eve commented that she might mention this to Josh's father when he called to collect him that afternoon, but he was even later than usual, so late that Eve had been on the point of phoning Josh's home contact number.

On looking through Josh's profile, which was accompanied by some notes from the family's health visitor, Pat learned that the family had moved to the area to be nearer Fran's family due to Fran complaining of 'constant tiredness' following the birth of her daughter. Pat continued her efforts to meet with Fran, and when this was finally accomplished the following week, Fran appeared distressed and at times near to tears during the meeting. Pat asked whether Fran had seen her GP about the tiredness, but Fran replied that the family had only just become registered locally and had been trying to self-medicate with 'tonics'. Pat continued to encourage Fran to see her GP, and by the end of the meeting, Fran promised that she would do so.

The following week, Fran thanked Pat for her help, with the additional information that she was now being treated for mild post-natal depression. As the days went by, both Eve and Pat noticed that Fran began to appear less stressed and exhausted and was more willing to stay and talk about Josh's achievements, as well as communicating through the home–school diary. After the summer holidays, Fran volunteered as a parent-helper, as after hearing of her illness, her mother now regularly cared for the baby for one day a week. After Fran's daughter also started attending the nursery, she made a successful application to become a part-time teaching assistant in one of the local primary schools, and began studying for a foundation degree in Early Years Practice.

Reflection

This is a story of a very common situation affecting young families, which in this case had a happy ending. However, we can see how Pat's sensitive professional intervention allowed her to act as an enabler to help this family over a problem that was having an effect upon all of its members, including the children. It is not unusual for children like Josh to feel reluctant to leave a parent who is distressed or who they intuit is 'in trouble' in some way (even if they don't understand why or how). In this way, children are not so different from adults, although they are likely to lack the language to communicate that 'something is wrong at home' or to ask for help.

One of the authors of this chapter has a vivid memory of how children feel in such situations, when her own father was very seriously ill; in this case an aunt and adult cousin stepped in with both practical and emotional support. However, the school she was attending at the time did not acknowledge the situation she was living through at all, although all the adults were fully aware of it. This is an example of how important the 'soft' elements of early years practice are in preventing family dramas becoming full-blown crises, and how very outdated the 'I'm a teacher not a social worker' attitude has become.

If Josh had been your key child, how would you have tried to work with this situation? You will find a technique called 'Critical Incident Analysis' in chapter 9; working with a family like Josh's would be a very good example for you to use in the exercises that we suggest.

What strategies are needed to ensure that effective working partnerships with children and their families are valued and embedded in practice in order to promote children's well-being, learning and development?

Stable, healthy families are at the heart of strong societies. It is within the family environment that an individual's physical, emotional and psychological development occurs. It is from our family that we learn unconditional love, we understand right from wrong, and we gain empathy, respect and self-regulation.

(Centre for Social Justice, 2010, p. 6)

The above quote suggests that the family is central and familiar, but 'the family' can have several meanings (for example, see Table 8.1). In fact we could be said to live in several 'families'; the nuclear family, the extended family and the ancestral family, to name a few, all of which impact upon a child's development. The EYGP/EYT needs to be aware of the possible forms 'the family' might take when trying to meet the needs of individual children. The practitioner could be working with a relatively new mother who is unsure of her own parenting skills, wary of the 'public' nature of the setting and feeling she is being judged on these emerging skills, a young father who has been given the job of taking the baby to the setting and is desperate to get on his way, or possibly even a grandmother bamboozled and/or annoyed because 'it wasn't done like that in my day'. Many caring adults feel threatened by institutional contexts, by the agendas they feel are set by practitioners without sufficient consultation, and the incomprehensible jargon used between professionals. This sense of insecurity is sometimes aggravated by the media 'hype' which criticises parents for working too many hours, for allowing children unsupervised access to the internet, for being lone parents or divorced ... the list is long. Practitioners need to be wary of being influenced by media headlines that may lead them to blame carers for being too busy, stressed, disorganised, defensive or having poor relationships with their children, and try instead to empathise and see life from the carer's perspective.

Table 8.1 The family in time

The family of the past	The family of the present	The family of the future
Was a traditional/extended family in the pre-industrial and early industrial period (to the early twentieth century). Was a 'unit of production' in the pre-industrial period – working life was carried out in or nearby the home, often with the whole family 'pitching in'. Was a family of many brothers and sisters – parents had several children, but expected to lose one or two due to high infant mortality. From the mid-twentieth century onwards, contraception and better health care reduced the number of children born, but increased life expectancy. Marriage was for life, but the typical lifespan was shorter than today. The Industrial Revolution (1800–50) brought the change of 'going out to work' for the adults of the family. After World War II (1945 onwards) many families moved to new, single family-sized houses in the suburbs and the cultural stereotype of the nuclear family with the 'instrumental' commuter father and 'expressive' housewife mother became the 'norm'. The liberalisation of divorce laws in the Divorce Act (1969) was followed by a growing divorce rate (1970–90), and a subsequent rise in the number of single-parent, single-parent + grandparent(s), and reconstituted or blended families.	The liberation of women, including the rejection of full-time housework and childcare for paid work has brought about the development of the 'symmetrical family' where parents of both genders take equal roles (theoretically, but don't forget the female 'triple shift', i.e. paid work/ housework/childcare). There is a growing rate of children born outside formal marriage (1980–present), and falling marriage rates. There has been a rise in alternative family lifestyles (e.g. gay families, friendship group 'families'). The typical family tree structure of the modern family is 'beanpole' like, with many single- and two-child families but longer-lived members. The need to provide childcare for working women has been firmly on the agenda since the early 2000s, particularly the balance between the amounts paid by the family and the taxpayer for such provision. You will see from the content of other chapters in this book that no clear resolution has yet been reached on this question in the UK nations, and we currently look towards Scandinavia for further inspiration. Fertility techniques have been piloted that allow women to consider older first-time child-bearing, and there has been a rise in the average age of first-time parents.	*This obviously has to be based on logical prediction.* A continuing rise in 'alternative' family lifestyles. Growing flexibility in gender partnerships focused upon shared child-raising, often outside formal marriage. Emerging roles for older people, as the lifespan extends and people remain healthy and active for longer, and the statutory retirement age continues to rise. These may possibly be associated with provision of care for grandchildren/great grandchildren while parents are working. Expansion of artificial fertility techniques and associated legislation may eventually allow completely 'test-tube' babies via the use of artificial wombs, and stem cell fertility techniques may additionally allow same-sex couples to genetically co-parent their own child. As the 'baby-boomer' generation born 1945–65 moves towards the end of its working life, society will have to consider how to fund the final years of this large demographic group, both in terms of pensions and health care. Uncertainty in international financial markets, particularly Britain's relationship with the European Union, and the eventual fate of the Euro will be likely to have some effect upon this.

Case study: a grandparent's perspective

One of the authors of this chapter found the detailed handover of her grandchild from the setting quite strange at first. Her children had only attended a church hall playschool prior to being admitted to school in the late 1980s/early 1990s, where arriving and departing had been a far more casual process. After the 'culture shock', however, she began to avidly read the daily report on her grandson and talk to him about it on the way home. This grandmother rapidly grasped that such information sharing was a positive process, presenting her with a number of opportunities to engage with her grandson's development. However, some grandparents, or parents may continue to find the whole reporting system worryingly intrusive or threatening if their knowledge of children's services principally depends on reports in the tabloid press. There may also be additional associated issues if the family do not read or speak English.

Reflection

Discuss how you explain to adults new to the setting about the daily processes involved. Do you consider your entire community of practice, which is likely to include parents, other family members, unrelated carers (e.g. child minders) and the perception of your setting that they take with them into the wider community? How do you make provisions for families who do not speak/read English, and those with other diverse additional needs?

The leader of practice in a setting needs to establish agreed policies while building a trusting partnership with parents and other relevant adults providing care for the child. All practitioners also need to be aware of the impact of environmental factors on how a family functions (see Bronfenbrenner's view of the bi-directional influences on a child and their family in chapter 2, which helps to illustrate the complexity of such influences). Obvious factors such as employment, health and housing will impact on the functioning of every family within the setting's neighbourhood. Ghate *et al.* (2002) describe the characteristics of families who may be 'at risk' (see chapter 3) as a result of 'poor' environments, 'poor' in this sense meaning not just poverty but also environments that do not have 'optimal parenting' conditions. While acknowledging that not all materially poor families live in poor environments, they suggest there is a strong link between 'geography' and 'deprivation'. The Coalition Government 2010-15 made a start on focusing provision in the early years towards the *child in the family* in the Children and Families Act 2014 (see chapter 4). Whether the subsequent Conservative Government, elected in 2015 is committed to the provision of the funding that is required to make this work in practice remains to be seen.

The multiplicity of factors involved in working with families shows the implausibility of trying to formulate one policy that will work to create a 'partnership' with all families. Early dialogue is essential and needs to be maintained (see chapter 7). Such dialogue also has to be meaningful for both practitioners and families. It should empower families by providing accessible and non-threatening information, advice, support and ideally, personal development. It should raise awareness about facilities and services through user-friendly media; how, for example, will adults with limited reading skills feel if most information is only available in printed form?

The best services in the world will not necessarily enhance parents' ability to cope unless they are perceived as helpful and acceptable ... to ensure that parents feel in control of the type of support they receive and the way in which it is delivered.

(Ghate *et al.*, 2002, p. 262)

These authors go on to suggest that problems arise when parents no longer feel 'in charge' of their children, in the sense that they are in some way handing them to someone else who will take over their care. In order to feel secure, they need to feel that there is a partnership in which the parents are the 'senior' carers.

Case study: blaming the family?

In June 2015, the newly elected Conservative Government announced plans to change the way that 'living in poverty' is calculated, using 'a range of other measures and indicators of root causes of poverty, including family breakdown, debt and addiction', which it will put together in a 'children's life chances strategy' (*The Guardian*, 2015, online). Scottish Social Justice Secretary Alex Neil says that this development will 'cast children adrift'. Tam Baillie, Scotland's Children's Commissioner says that the plan is a 'scandal' and that the Conservative Government 'just doesn't care' (BBC, 2015a, online). At the time of writing (mid-2015), the calculation that the government are going to use to define poverty has not yet been revealed, but however this situation develops, it appears that EYTs and EYGPs in the UK will play an important role in offering support to families in crisis in the foreseeable future.

Reflection

'"Where's your Mama gone? Where's your Mama gone?" Used to sing that to the kids when Monica f***ed off, never a dry eye in the house, all shot off upstairs howling they did.'

This is a quote from the hit TV series *Shameless*, from the principal protagonist, single father 'Frank Gallagher'. The programme relies on stereotyping a 'troubled family' within a range of humorous situations and interactions, and popular media of this type are likely to have informed some of the ideas that your staff carry around with them when they think about the concept. How would you, in modelling positive behaviour (see chapter 7), help them to see past this type of 'popular culture' response?

Support for parenting

Research has demonstrated convincingly that parental involvement makes a huge difference to children's achievements (e.g. EPPE, 2004). The role of all practitioners involved with children in the early years should be to support all parents to become the best parents they can be, and not to replace the parent in any way. The impact of parental involvement can also have tangible benefits for early education and care settings and the wider community through the creation of a 'triangle of care' between parent, child and practitioner. In this section we will consider how the EYGP/EYT can support the development of parental involvement in their child's learning and development in the setting and beyond. We will do this by examining some examples of good practice in relation to parental involvement, including the work of the Pen Green Centre (PGC) in Corby and the Parents Early Years and Learning (PEAL) Project. We will also be considering international evidence found in the approach to partnerships with parents and families taken by the pre-schools in the Reggio Emilia district of Northern Italy.

In creating open and trusting partnerships with parents, EYGPs/EYTs need to be able to reflect on their own values and beliefs in relation to parental involvement. As the DfE suggests in its *Know How* guide to the statutory EYFS Progress Check at Two (DfE, 2012), some practitioners, in attempting to build partnerships with parents, may find certain parenting styles have a closer cultural fit with their own views, and they clearly need to reflect on the subsequent potential for bias. EYGPs/EYTs need to be prepared to move beyond traditional deficit approaches, which appear to suggest that the professional's principal role is to compensate for some kind of inadequacy on the part of the parent, so do beware of operating within a 'disadvantage' culture (see the 'blaming the family' box above). Such a 'deficit' model can lead to the creation of a partnership where the parent is expected to be a junior, passive partner, which may eventually lead to resentment if they feel that their leading role has been usurped by the professional. Reay (1998) suggests that this 'deficit' view can be particularly problematic in practitioners' perceptions of the abilities and interests of working-class parents, in relation to their child's development and education. She further suggests that although both working-class and middle-class mothers invest time, effort, money, thought and emotion into their children's development and education, the difference that emerges tends to be the *effectiveness* with which middle-class mothers are able to access, shape and facilitate their child's care and education due to their greater 'cultural capital' (Bourdieu, 1977).

Case study: a glass floor?

Government-sponsored research suggests that children from middle-class homes may have brighter employment prospects than children from working-class homes with higher abilities and achievements. Reasons cited include being able to place children in more prestigious schools, giving children greater confidence that shines through in interview situations and having connections that allow children to get a start in their career. Suggestions made to address such social inequalities include education and support for parents at an early stage in the child's life. The glass floor concept suggests that some children may 'look up' at opportunities that remain unattainable to them, because aspects such as accent, interaction skills and inability to access a career 'network' create an invisible barrier to progress (DfE, 2015).

Reflection

You may currently be wondering what this has to do with working with children in the early years. The answer is that it has a lot more to do with working with their parents. If parents are offered opportunities when their children are young, they are most likely to carry their children with them. The authors of this chapter were all offered opportunities through adult education chances that emerged in the 1970s and 1980s through what is nowadays known as 'widening participation', particularly due to a growing recognition during this time of the need for gender equality in education and employment. All of us have experience of simultaneously studying and parenting, and all feel that our children benefited from this background, in its illustration of what achievements are possible through self-development.

We will follow the self-development thread through more thoroughly in chapter 9. But at this point in the book, we are going to ask you to consider what opportunities your setting might be able to offer for parents to develop their knowledge and skills. You could get some hints from the example of the Pen Green Centre in Northampton (see below).

It is clear that the home environment remains critical to young children's development and learning, whatever the quality of the professional setting; while the idea of the parent as the most effective and enduring educator may be over-quoted, it is nevertheless very true. As such, effective teachers and practitioners need to understand each child's background and early experiences through both acknowledging the child *within the family* and incorporating the child's early experiences in learning activities. The surest way to achieve this, as suggested at the beginning of this chapter, is through the development of an open, honest and authentically respectful relationship with the child's parents and other carers.

True parental involvement needs to reflect a model of empowerment (Whalley, 2007). This model seeks to promote a parent's sense of being an active participant and co-educator in their child's learning and development rather than a passive recipient of information from professionals; this reciprocal relationship also enables the professional to become an active learner. This approach underpins the work at the Pen Green Centre (PGC) set up by Whalley and her associates in 1983, where such a model is used to enable parents to develop skills in critical reflection so that new knowledge and understanding can be co-constructed with their children and with the professionals employed in settings; indeed, the PGC has a reputation for later employing and further developing parents who they have initially trained through their innovative parent partnerships. The PGC was set up in Corby, an English town in Northamptonshire, in response to ongoing social and economic decline in the area. It was one of the areas which relied on heavy industry for its wealth creation and that suffered greatly from the Thatcher government policies of the early 1980s (see chapter 4). Teachers and social workers in the area proposed that the upheavals and subsequent poverty experienced by families were resulting in poor outcomes for local children. Pen Green was subsequently set up with a strong vision to provide a service which would 'honour the needs of young children and celebrate their existence. It would also support families, however they were constituted, within the community' (Whalley, 2007, p. 3), see www.pengreen.org.

Case study: Parents Involved in Children's Learning

The Pen Green practitioners set up a programme called Parents Involved in Children's Learning (PICL). It operated by:

- Informal chats at 'drop off' and 'pick up' times
- Home visits, particularly to share information about the child's learning in the centre
- Home/setting exchange, encouraging parents to share information about their child's learning at home, and creating portfolios contributed to by both parents and practitioners
- Holding very regular events and sessions where parents, children and practitioners were all present
- Encouraging parents to join in with the work of the setting; for example, going on trips with the children
- Involving parents in the assessment of their children; for example, by discussing the judgements that were made and agreeing them
- Videoing the children's activities in the setting and sharing the video with parents, along with a discussion of how to support 'next steps'.

(C4EO Archive, 2015, online)

If you compare the above with some of the advice in chapters 5, 6 and 7, you will see that a lot of this practice has now entered the mainstream. Involving parents in assessment is not as well developed as some of the other strategies, however.

Reflection

Do you think the formality of nationally administered assessments in the English EYFS and National Curriculum mitigates against the involvement of parents? If so, what changes do you think might address this issue? If you consider this from your own professional perspective at this point, you should get some further ideas on this point from chapter 10.

PEAL (see www.peal.org.uk) is another programme based on collaboration with parents: a consortium project run by the National Children's Bureau (NCB), Coram (formerly the Thomas Coram Foundation for Children) and the London Borough of Camden. These partners collectively developed a training programme for practitioners to help them work with families to ensure that parents are involved in their children's early learning. PEAL advocates the following elements as central to partnership working with parents:

- Authentic relationships
- Communication and partnership
- The exploration of what is effective practice in the early years.

PEAL supports practitioners in beginning the process of involving parents; this includes establishing the setting's values in relation to parental involvement, opportunities for parental involvement and helping the practitioner to reflect upon any skill or knowledge gaps they may have in relation to working with parents in this way.

Parental involvement has been at the heart of the collective early years experience of children within the European context for centuries, initially informally, and then by the formation of cooperative groups from the post World War II period until the present. The first pre-schools in Reggio Emilia, for example, were founded by parents and a range of opportunities for involvement continue to be offered to parents. 'Parent participation enables a communication network that leads to fuller and more reciprocal knowledge as well as to a more effective search for the best educational methods, contexts and values' (Malaguzzi, 1997, p. 28).

> The central focus is on the relationship between children and adults. The [school] ... should be seen not as a single system, but as ... a system of relationships and communication among children, teachers and parents ... a living organism that pulses, changes, transforms, grows and matures.
>
> (Rinaldi, 2005, p. 85)

In the Reggio Emilia approach (Malaguzzi, 1997), induction programmes for new parents ensure that parents are familiar with the layout of the building, the staff and, most importantly, that they understand the values, principles and philosophies which will shape their children's early learning experiences. Parental participation is nurtured through a range of methods to stimulate parents' interests and enable them to connect with the work of the setting. A day book, for example, uses photos to capture the children's significant experiences during the day. Extensive communication round the 'documentation' of children's learning and development is also an area where parents help by giving input and suggestions for future planning. They, alongside the teachers, are seen as co-researchers with their children and facilitators of their own children's learning journeys.

In England, the introduction of the Progress Check at Two, which involves close cooperation and dialogue between a child's Key Worker and their family, can, if it is effectively administered, also be seen as a partnership 'in action'. For this Progress Check, a practitioner will assess the child against the three Prime Areas of Learning and Development and the Early Learning Goals. The child's parents are then invited in for a discussion of their child's progress, and any concerns at this point are discussed with a view to possible intervention; for example, support with speech and language from a trained professional.

The examples given in the *Know How* guide (DFE, 2012) stress the importance of the parents' contribution, and the need for an open and transparent discussion. Some critics of the Progress Check at such an early age suggest, however, that this could be seen as 'pathologising' disadvantaged families (Brock and Rankin, 2011), and the process remains controversial.

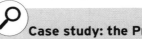

Case study: the Progress Check

Amy, aged two years, two months was the youngest of four children, her sisters being aged eight, 10 and 14. Amy's mother was single, in her mid-40s, and not easy to talk to. During the three months Amy had been attending the setting, her mother was usually in a hurry, as she'd told Amy's Key Worker, EYGP Julie, on numerous occasions, because she was 'holding down two jobs'. The older sisters had all attended the setting prior to Julie's arrival there; the younger two were now at the local primary school, and according to their mother, were all doing really well. This made it all the harder for Julie to discuss issues of concern she had around Amy's lack of expressive language. Amy seemed to understand, but she rarely spoke, and would often push other children away if they tried to engage with her. When Julie carried out Amy's two-year Progress Check, she judged that Amy's progress was best captured by the EYFS descriptors for the 16-22 month band.

When Julie finally managed to arrange a meeting with Amy's mother, she met great resistance to the suggestion that Amy was 'behind' in her language. 'All the girls have been the same, they took their time talking, then I couldn't shut them up!' Julie tried to sound a little more determined about the benefits of getting early 'help' for Amy, but she could see that Amy's mother was adamant there was nothing wrong with her daughter's speech, insisting, 'She understands everything me and her sisters say to her'. Julie began to feel awkward and unsure, but in keeping with the concept of the parent as the 'first best educator' she realised that she did need to genuinely listen to parents' opinions and show her willingness to act upon them. As such, it was agreed that Amy should have more time to 'develop her language skills', and that Julie would meet again with Amy's mother in six weeks' time.

Julie, who had recently completed her honours degree in early years with a research project that involved many in-depth focal child observations (see chapter 2), carried out a series of narrative observations on Amy, and by chance, the final observation took in the arrival of Amy's mother. This particular day, Amy's eight-year-old sister had come along, too. She immediately picked Amy up, and started talking at her, rather than to her, not waiting for any verbal response from the child. Julie's impression was that she saw Amy very much as an animated 'dolly'. Amy smiled and pointed to the home corner. This was all the excuse her eight-year-old sister needed to go in and play, and the way she organised Amy's play reminded Julie of a stage magician and his 'glamorous assistant'. It was clear that Amy's needs were being almost immediately anticipated, and the babbling, when it did happen, was immediately understood and acted upon, clearly to Amy's satisfaction.

It was also clear that Amy did indeed understand what was being said to her. When her sister said 'let's see what you've painted today', the two-year-old tugged her sister's arm, leading her to where the day's 'art work' was laid out for parents to collect.

Reflection

- What would you do now, if you were Julie, keeping in mind the need to work with the family?
- On balance, do you think the Progress Check might have been useful here, in terms of raising an issue that might have been missed or sidelined had the national requirement not been in place?

Examination of research findings that identify and exemplify current good practice may help support practitioners in developing their own partnerships with parents, for, as Siraj-Blatchford and Manni (2006) suggest, good practice, effective pedagogy and strong partnerships with parents/carers must be complementary if a child's learning and development is to be rich and empowering. Discussions with other professionals both within and beyond their settings may also support the development of successful ideas and practices (see below, and chapter 9). The practitioner's own understanding of what parental involvement is and how it can be achieved needs, however, to be grounded in the specific practice within their own setting and the families that attend it through ongoing dialogue with all stakeholders.

What strategies can help EYGPs/EYTs to build and lead teams in early years practice?

Caution needs to be used when considering theories around team building, teamworking and team management, as most of these derive from a business perspective; see Rodd (2007). Early years setting leaders have traditionally been expected to adapt their role on a daily basis, moving between the direct care and education of children to leading practice and being a member of a team, to leading and line-managing the team. The demarcation lines between being a team colleague, a manager and a leader are blurred to say the least.

However, expectations with regard to roles in early years practice are continuing to grow, while expectations of teachers to work *with* teams of support workers, and to support their professional development rather than to just simply allocate work *for* them have emerged from more enlightened, democratic ways of working in early years classrooms (see chapter 9). All leaders of early years practice need to be aware that there is an ongoing emphasis on accountability, alongside expectations of excellent practice. So, from this perspective, we need to investigate what is meant by *leadership* and how this differs from the more traditional model of the *management* of a setting/classroom and its staff.

Whalley (2005, p. 10) suggests that effective leaders within the context of early years settings demonstrate the ability to:

- Enhance the learning and development potential of the children
- Encourage, enable and empower parents in their roles as parents and primary educators
- Develop and enhance the skills and knowledge and understanding of staff, including other leaders and potential leaders.

She proposes that reflection is critically important in order to avoid becoming 'role precious', to be open to innovation in practice, and to be able to work effectively across professional boundaries.

An EYGP/EYT can demonstrate all of the above without necessarily line-managing any members of staff within a setting. Research indicates that there is no single behaviour, trait or style which defines 'good' leadership behaviour. Goleman (2000, p. 5) specifies six leadership styles:

- The *Coercive* leader demands compliance
- The *Authoritative* leader mobilises people towards a vision
- The *Affiliative* leader creates an appropriate emotional climate
- The *Democratic* leader builds consensus through participation
- The *Pace-setting* leader expects excellence and self-direction
- The *Coaching* leader develops people for the future.

He adds:

> According to the data, the authoritative leadership style has the most positive effect on climate, but three others – affiliative, democratic, and coaching – follow close behind. That said, the research indicates that no style should be relied on exclusively, and all have at least short-term uses.
>
> (Goleman, 2000, p. 5)

Case study: one style of leadership

One of the authors of this chapter leads a team in a Further and Higher Education College. She reflects: 'You aspire to be a particular type of leader when you are able to work within the boundaries of your "ideal self"; however, you do have to adapt your style to suit:

- The individual(s) you are working with at any given time
- The actual situation/task you are trying to manage
- The culture of the organisation in which you are all working
- The relationship that exists between yourself and the people or person you are trying to work with at the time
- Other people involved in the situation, for example, children, parents, wider community.'

She says 'whilst I aim to be a pace-setting, affiliative, democratic leader who coaches future leaders, circumstances sometimes force me to become an authoritative, coercive leader, which I find very uncomfortable'.

Reflection

Consider your own personal style as either a current or future leader and record your thoughts on this in a professional journal (see chapter 9). Consider situations which tend to move you from your ideal style, to see if there is a pattern and/or trigger. Might there be any ways that you can guard against this?

Goleman goes on to propose that the most successful leaders have strengths in the following emotional intelligence competencies:

- Self-awareness
- Self-regulation
- Motivation

services where a united effort is more likely to succeed in the complex arena which centres around children, families, their relationships and their feelings.

If such an organisational climate is to be empowering and effective it needs to reflect some or all of the categories suggested by Siraj-Blatchford and Manni (2006) in their ELEYS project report (see above).

The importance of the team

You can use theories around the identification of specific roles within a team as an effective team-building tool: they can help to reinforce your understanding of the fact that everyone is bringing something to the team, and that you all need each other if you are to be successful. A good team leader will work to individual strengths and preferences. Although preferred roles are relatively unchanging over time, most people can happily perform two or three roles, sometimes simultaneously – particularly important in small settings.

Alongside having the right mix of roles and personalities, teams also need other pieces of a complex situational 'jigsaw' to fall into place. We cannot assume that individuals will recognise that they are expected to be working *together*; therefore, the team leader may need to allow reflection time for team members to recognise their interdependence as well as their independence. They also need to be aware of the tendency of individual personalities to gravitate towards particular roles within teams, and when/how to utilise this tendency to best effect.

Case study: the Belbin team

Belbin (2010) proposed that the nine principal roles that people take in teams are as follows:

Plant: the creative ideas generator. While this is a very productive role within a team, plants sometimes need to be supported to engage with an initiative once the ideas-generation stage is over, rather than throwing out yet more ideas for change, and not to get into fruitless arguments with other plants about who has the better ideas.

Resource Investigator: the wheeler and dealer, who seeks the means to action the ideas in the outside world. This too, is an important role if well directed, but this 'type' may get too involved in the relationships and 'deals', losing sight of the finer details of the project.

Co-ordinator: the chairperson, who looks for 'the big picture'. Co-ordinators can help to broker decisions and focus other team members on their roles, but if they become too firmly entrenched in the role they may become unpopular in the team, being perceived as too keen to delegate all the work and too manipulative.

Shaper: the achiever and goal setter, who enthuses the other people in the team to keep going and to focus on agreed targets. They sometimes need to be reminded that some team members may become more discouraged by obstacles than they do, and not to act as a 'slave driver' when the going gets rough.

Monitor/Evaluator: the analyst, who can stand back and give a fair overview of how a project is progressing. They are very good at giving cool appraisals but may come across to other team members as unenthusiastic and critical.

Teamworker: the social leader, who can broker conflicts between team members and defuse conflicts. Teamworkers can, however, become so involved with other people's perspectives that they lose the ability to be decisive when necessary.

Implementer: the keenest activist in the project, implementers can take ideas and turn them into actions. They are loyal, responsible and diligent, and may take on jobs that others reject in order to progress a project. They may become inflexible once they have decided upon a course of action.

Completer/Finisher: the quality control inspector. Completers are very valuable team members towards the end of a project as they have a keen focus on detail. They may, however, irritate other team members by wanting everything 'just so' at points in a project where this is not yet possible, and this may lead to completers failing to delegate tasks when they should do so.

Specialist: the expert. Specialists are very useful team members when they are able to work in areas that reflect their own expertise. However, their interest in a project may be very 'one-dimensional'; once the focus moves outside their specialist area, they lose interest, which may create accusations from fellow team members about 'not being onside'.

Reflection

You can read more about Belbin's theory in his book *Management Teams* (Belbin, 2010). Before you get carried away with this theory, however, you should reflect that real people are unlikely to be one 'pure' type, and that different environments are likely to bring out different qualities in different individuals. While one of the authors of this chapter is most obviously a 'plant', for example, she can think of teams in which she has responded as a 'specialist' and others in which she has acted as 'implementer', this book being a good example of the latter!

With this warning in mind, consider a team in which you currently work, and teams in which you have worked in the past. Can you put names and faces to the various roles outlined above?

The above points shed some light on teamworking within a particular organisation, but EYGPs in particular are frequently called upon to work with professionals outside the remit of the individual setting in looser 'team' constructions; EYTs may also find themselves in this position if they are employed within an academy, a local authority or national advisory service, or if they become involved in a multi-agency safeguarding case (see chapter 3). The next section deals with such 'multi-agency working'.

In what ways can the EYGP/EYT lead practice to ensure that multi-agency teamworking is understood, valued and used effectively in supporting children's particular needs, both among professionals and within the setting and external agencies?

For some settings, particularly those which include services in the social care or health arenas, inter-professional working is quite routine. Schools may conversely have a more 'separatist' atmosphere, where teachers work in classrooms, and counsellors, family support workers and pastoral staff are more likely to be located in offices, only coming into classrooms on an occasional basis. Health and social care staff are often peripatetic to schools; for example, nurses, doctors and social workers. For some settings, such as private daycare, accessing external agencies can be somewhat problematic as a result of limited resources and heavy workloads.

However, the vision of effective multi-agency working is underpinned at statutory level by the Childcare Act 2006. Margaret Edgington maintains that early childhood practitioners have always worked within a multi-disciplinary context because

> Services for children and families have been developed by professionals holding a range of qualifications within the disciplines of education, social work and health, and are (variously) funded by and organised by the local authority, by private enterprise or by the voluntary sector.
>
> (Edgington, 2004, p. 2)

In a speech on working with families, Prime Minister David Cameron also called for multi-agency working within the children's workforce to become more effective, proposing that recent safeguarding tragedies (see chapter 3) have been largely due to situations in which 'no-one ultimately took sufficient responsibility, in a complex landscape of multiple agencies and protocols' (Prime Minister's Office, 2015, online).

One of the key problems with multi-agency working is that simply having or being exposed to a range of professional expertise does not equate to integrated working, nor can we simply assume that those professionals work in collaborative ways to achieve shared outcomes for children and families. As we noted earlier, the Childcare Act 2006 (see chapter 4) and associated legislative frameworks now put a duty on early years services (education, social and health services in particular) to work in synthesis, but there is no clear statutory guidance to help practitioners in this endeavour.

The challenges to effective integrated teamworking are not to be underestimated; they involve bringing together staff from a range of cultural and social backgrounds, and frequently involve overcoming professional and/or cultural practice barriers to work towards common goals, maximising the benefits to children and families. Professions tend to create 'communities of practice' (Lave and Wenger, 1991, and see chapter 9) in which certain ways of doing things and expressing ideas using specialist language may exclude others. Profession-specific language used in the workplace may be unfamiliar to those from a different profession, for example, teachers use acronyms such as SATs (Standard Assessment Tasks), EBD (Emotional/Behavioural Disorder), etc., which may not be familiar to health workers, whereas the Emergency Services phonetic alphabet (e.g. Alpha, Bravo, Charlie, Delta, etc.) may be everyday parlance to health workers, but not at all familiar to teachers. One of the authors of this chapter, a teacher and a psychologist, was only very recently introduced by a social worker colleague to the very useful process of creating family genograms, which are not used in education or the social sciences. Hence it can sometimes be difficult for practitioners from different professions to work together seamlessly. These are not inconsequential issues and they need to be addressed sensitively if we are to be successful in multi-agency working to the benefit of children and families.

Reflection

Consider how much more difficult it may be to lead a multi-agency team of Belbin's 'types' than it might be if these people were working in a unitary professional environment. What additional challenges might there be?

Evidence from the study by Wigfall and Moss (2001) suggests that there are common barriers to effective teamworking:

- Loss of individual professional identity
- Competitiveness
- Poor communication, leading to feelings of isolation and resentment
- Lack of shared vision and shared understanding of desired outcomes.

These factors can be exacerbated by poor management and weak organisational structures and/or the use of inappropriate leadership styles.

Frost suggests that the drive towards effective multi-agency working needs to be balanced with the development of practice within individual professions and settings:

> Efforts to improve children's services systems should focus on positive organisational climates rather than on increasing inter-organisational services co-ordination. This is important because many large-scale efforts to improve children's services systems have focused on inter-organisational co-ordination with little success and none to date have focused on organisational climate.
>
> (Frost, 2005, p. 21)

Reflection

It has been suggested that there should be a cohesive set of standards for social workers (BBC, 2014); whether or not these would be aligned with the teachers' standards is not yet clear. What do you think that the impact of highly specified 'targets and outcomes' driven practice in multiple branches of the children's workforce might be upon multi-agency working, particularly if these are not effectively co-ordinated?

Case study: Majid's hearing

Majid had just turned three and a half years old when he arrived at his new setting, a nursery class within a primary school. He and his parents had moved because of his father's new job; a move from Birmingham where there had been extended family, to a strange city, with few friends. Majid's mother spoke little English, relying on his father to interpret in most situations. The father had been unable to be there during the home visit, so the nursery had sent Nabeela, a bilingual teaching assistant. The house had boxes in each room, waiting to be unpacked, and Majid was swinging from the curtains, as his mother nervously told him to stop. He was finally distracted by Nabeela as she unpacked a basket of toys, and called him over.

Nabeela subsequently managed to engage Majid's mother in conversation to find out Majid's interests, as well as the necessary information about dietary requirements, home routines, his health and well-being, and if he had had his two-year Progress Check. His mother looked unsure at the last question, but then nodded. Having tried to speak to Majid and getting little response, Nabeela asked if Majid was confident in using his home language. His mother answered that Majid had 'difficulty in saying some words'.

After the visit, Rachel, the nursery teacher, prepared all the documents in readiness for Majid's arrival at nursery. She had made sure there were some of Majid's favourite resources available (dinosaurs and trains) on the day of his first visit. As Rachel began to observe Majid, she realised he was being quietly aggressive to some of the other children, nipping them or pushing past them to get to a toy he wanted, and he rarely reacted when his name was called. Rachel became concerned when Majid didn't respond to Nabeela's gentle requests for him to have 'kind hands', and as he rarely turned at the mention of his name, began to wonder about his hearing.

Further observations indicated that Majid tended to breathe with his mouth open, which Rachel had previously observed in children who had been found to have congestion in the nose and sinuses. This was further confirmed by a speech therapist who regularly visited the nursery to work with another child. She additionally suggested that the problem had most likely led over time to Majid becoming 'flat tongued', which would require correction. She left some simple activities for Rachel to carry out with Majid, such as helping him sip through a straw and learning to breathe with closed lips, and blowing his nose. She also suggested his congestion might be affecting his hearing.

When Nabeela communicated this development to Majid's mother, the response was alarm, and a refusal to engage in further conversation about the matter. The next morning, Majid's father brought him to the nursery, wanting to know why his son had been seen by 'some specialist' without his consent, adding that there was nothing wrong with his son. With Nabeela's help, Rachel tried to explain why she had spoken to her multi-agency colleague, and that any official referral would naturally have to be agreed with his parents. That seemed to mollify his father, who remained adamant that his son did not need to see any 'specialists', adding it was Rachel's job to teach Majid English.

Rachel discussed the situation with the school's EYFS leader, who suggested she and Rachel meet with Majid's parents. It took several proposed meetings before Majid's parents turned up, during which time Majid's language had not improved significantly, and his behaviour had worsened. His father's body language spoke his disapproval, but after listening to the professionals, his manner softened and he finally agreed, not only to speech and language interventions but to a hearing test being carried out, to see if Majid's 'constant colds' were having some impact on his hearing.

After this meeting, Rachel made formal referrals to both the Speech and Language and Hearing Impairment teams. However, there was quite a long delay before Majid's hearing test. The speech therapist offered to speak with the local peripatetic teacher for hearing, in support of the nursery's referral, but this did not result in the provision of additional services for Majid.

Nabeela was now Majid's Key Worker and provided some extra support for him, which did improve his speech in his home language. Rachel made several more phone calls before Majid was finally assessed, shortly before his fourth birthday. The result of the hearing test showed some depression in hearing in his right ear that would need to be monitored and might require minor surgery if it didn't improve. He was then formally referred for additional speech and language support. By this time Rachel was certain that Majid would not meet several of the language targets in his upcoming EYFS summative assessment.

Reflection

Do you think Majid's situation could have been handled more effectively? Do you think his condition should have been diagnosed before he was nearly four, and could the setting's attempts to communicate with his parents have been handled more sensitively? Did the informal referral help or hinder the situation? Consider how you could have handled such a situation in your setting.

Conclusion

This chapter has placed the focus on the potential for EYGPs/EYTs to act as *leaders* rather than as managers, modelling good practice and supporting teams within settings. Literature, theories and research initiatives that support this concept have been explored, and you have been asked to identify with and reflect upon practice evidence supplied through various scenarios. Three key questions were examined.

What strategies are needed to ensure that effective working partnerships with children and their families are valued and embedded in practice in order to promote children's well-being, learning and development?

In attempting to answer the above question, consideration of what 'the family' means in contemporary Britain and its impact on children's learning and development was discussed. The need for practitioners to reflect on their own values and beliefs in order to develop meaningful and inclusive partnerships that value the diversity of children and their families was shown to be underpinned by considerable research into working in partnership with parents. This section established the need for practitioners to avoid a 'deficit' model of parents' abilities and instead recognise and celebrate them as being children's first and most enduring educators.

The need for EYGPs/EYTs to lead and support practice in establishing authentic partnerships with parents means going beyond a surface structure that simply cajoles parents into supporting various practitioner-instigated activities within and beyond the setting (for example, by narrowly defined tasks to 'take home'). Empowered parents should be involved in decision-making and policy issues, and should be welcomed by practitioners as co-constructors of their children's learning and development. It is the practice leader's responsibility to lead his/her staff away from situations in which information about children moves uni-directionally from staff to parents, and rarely in the opposite direction, to a situation in which practitioners and parents work together authentically, communicating effectively to share the care and education of the children.

What strategies can help EYGPs/EYTs to build and lead teams in early years practice?

Traditional roles of the leading practitioner within early years practice were examined, along with the need to develop more modern and democratic approaches. Theories and research underpinning concepts around effective leadership were examined; for example, Goleman's (2000) ideas on the links between emotional intelligence and successful leadership. The findings of the Effective Leadership in the Early Years Sector (ELEYS) project undertaken by Siraj-Blatchford and Manni (2006) were also considered, as was Edgington's (2004) and Belbin's (2010) research on teams. Whitaker offers a concise and realistic definition of the complexity of a leader's work:

> Leadership is concerned with creating the conditions in which all members of the organisation can give of their best in a climate of commitment and challenge. Leadership helps an organisation to work well.
>
> (Whitaker, 1992, p. 74)

There is always a need for early years practice leaders to be proactive in encouraging reflection on the part of staff, encouraging them to recognise their interdependence as well as their independence, and in ensuring that practitioners feel valued as individuals while working in an effective collaborative team.

In what ways can the EYGP/EYP lead practice to ensure that multi-agency teamworking is understood, valued and used effectively in supporting children's particular needs, both among professionals and within the setting and external agencies?

This section considered the benefits and challenges of multi-agency working, in particular overcoming professional barriers to achieve a common aim (extending from the concepts in chapter 3), while simultaneously developing the day-to-day work of core specialist teams. We considered the comments of Frost (2005) on the complexity of creating a successful 'organisational climate' in contemporary early years practice given the diversity of settings and the roles of the workforce within them. Finally, we considered a complex example of multi-agency working, which also required sensitive interaction with a family where the need to engage with both cultural diversity and English as an additional language was part of the process. In this way, we highlighted the leading practitioner's role as a bridge between the child, the staff within the setting, the multi-agency staff and the family.

We hope you will take some of the examples raised in this chapter forward into your consideration of the Reflections raised in chapter 9, which follows, in order to resource your professional development not only as a practitioner, but additionally as a leader of practice.

Recommended reading

Anning, A., Cottrell, D., Frost, N., Green, J. and Robinson, M. (2010) *Developing Multiprofessional Teamwork for Integrated Children's Services: Research, policy and practice* (2nd Edn). Milton Keynes: Open University Press.

Brock, A. and Rankin, C. (Eds) (2011) *Making it Work for the Child: Professionalism for the early years interdisciplinary team*. London: Continuum.

Hadfield, M., Jopling, M. and Needham, M. (2015) *Practice Leadership in the Early Years: Becoming, being and developing as a leader*. Milton Keynes: Open University Press.

Rodd, J. (2007) *Leadership in Early Childhood* (3rd Edn). Maidenhead: Open University Press.

Siraj-Blatchford, I. and Manni, L. (2006) *Effective Leadership in the Early Years Sector (ELEYS) Study*. London: Institute of Education.

References

BBC (2014) Children's social work to have new set of standards. Retrieved from: www.bbc.co.uk/news/education-29836897 27th July 2015.

BBC (2015) Change to poverty definition will 'cast children adrift', says Alex Neil. Retrieved from: www.bbc.co.uk/news/uk-scotland-scotland-politics-33665443 27th July 2015.

Belbin, M. (2010) *Management Teams: Why they succeed or fail*. Abingdon: Routledge.

Bourdieu, P. (1977) Cultural reproduction and social reproduction, in J. Karabil and A. Hasse (Eds) *Power and Ideology in Education*. New York: Oxford University Press, pp. 487–511.

Brock, A. and Rankin, C. (Eds) (2011) *Making it Work for the Child: Professionalism for the early years interdisciplinary team*. London: Continuum.

C4EO Archive (2015) *The Parents Involved in their Children's Learning (PICL) Approach*. Retrieved from: http://archive.c4eo.org.uk/themes/families/vlpdetails.aspx?lpeid=414 27th July 2015.

Centre for Social Justice (2010) *The Centre for Social Justice Green Paper on the Family*. London: Centre for Social Justice

DfE (2012) *A Know-How Guide: The EYFS progress check at two*. Retrieved from: www.gov.uk/government/uploads/system/uploads/attachment_data/file/175311/EYFS_-_know_how_materials.pdf 27th July 2015.

DfE (2015) *Downward Mobility, Opportunity Hoarding and the 'Glass Floor'*. Retrieved from: www.gov.uk/government/uploads/system/uploads/attachment_data/file/447575/Downward_mobility_opportunity_hoarding_and_the_glass_floor.pdf 27th July 2015.

Edgington, M. (2004) *The Foundation Stage Teacher in Action*. London: Paul Chapman.

EPPE (2004) Available at: http://eppe.ioe.ac.uk/eppe/eppeintro.htm

Frost, N. (2005) *Professionalism, Partnership and Joined-Up Thinking in Frontline Children's Services*. Totnes: Research in Practice Series.

Ghate, D., Hazel, N., Creighton, S., Finch, S. and Field, J. (2002) *A National Study of Parents, Children and Discipline*. London: Policy Research Bureau.

Goleman, D. (2000) *Leadership that Gets Results*. Retrieved from: www.haygroup.com/downloads/fi/leadership_that_gets_results.pdf 7th December 2015.

Lave, J. and Wenger, E. (1991) *Situated Learning: Legitimate peripheral participation*. Cambridge: Cambridge University Press.

Malaguzzi, L. (1997) quoted in H. Penn, *Comparing Nurseries: Staff and children in Italy, Spain and the UK*. London: Paul Chapman.

Prime Minister's Office (2015) *PM Speech on Opportunity*. Retrieved from: www.gov.uk/government/ speeches/pm-speech-on-opportunity 27th July 2015.

Reay, D. (1998) *Class Work: Mothers' involvement in their children's primary education*. London: University College Press.

Rinaldi, C. (2005) *In Dialogue with Reggio Emilia*. London: Routledge.

Rodd, J. (2007) *Leadership in Early Childhood* (3rd Edn). Maidenhead: Open University Press.

Siraj-Blatchford, I. and Manni, L. (2006) *Effective Leadership in the Early Years Sector (ELEYS) Study*. London: Institute of Education.

Siraj-Blatchford, I., Sylva, K., Muttock, S., Gilden, R. and Bell, D. (2002) *Researching Effective Pedagogy in the Early Years*. Report No RR356. London, DfES. Retrieved from: https://www.ioe.ac.uk/REPEY_research_report.pdf 7th December 2015.

Southworth, G. (1998) *Leading Improving Primary Schools*. London: Falmer Press.

The Guardian (2015) Tories have redefined child poverty as not just about having no money. Retrieved from: www.theguardian.com/society/2015/jul/01/tories-redefined-child-poverty-no-longer-finances 27th July 2015.

Whalley, M. (2005) *Leadership and Management in the Early Years*. Derby: Pen Green.

Whalley, M. (2007) *Involving Parents in Their Children's Learning*. London: Paul Chapman.

Whitaker, P. (1992) *Managing Change in Schools*. Milton Keynes: Open University Press.

Wigfall, V. and Moss, P. (2001) *A Study of a Multi-Agency Childcare Network*. Retrieved from: www.jrf.org.uk/report/study-multi-agency-childcare-network 7th December 2015.

Section 3

Wider perspectives in early years leadership

9 Continuing professional development

Jonathan Doherty and Pam Jarvis

CHAPTER OVERVIEW

This chapter will consider the historical context for continuing professional development (CPD), moving on to consider the background to professional training and CPD specifically for Early Years Teachers (EYTs) and Early Years Graduate Practitioners (EYGPs), focusing upon the current situation in England. We will consider the recent recognition of the need to develop highly qualified practitioners to lead practice within the early years arena. We argue that a more 'joined up' approach to CPD involves understanding the roles and functions of the range of professionals within the children's workforce, leading to a more inter-professional 'multi-agency' approach. This book is, in itself, an example of such an approach, with chapters written not only from the perspective of teaching and everyday practice in classrooms and other early years settings, but also from the perspectives of child psychology, social work, the sociology of childhood and the family, and consequent policy development.

Recent routes in CPD will be unpicked and discussed in the frame of vocational practitioner routes, qualified teacher routes and academic qualifications. The chapter will then turn to the practical issues surrounding CPD, including the use of journaling and portfolio building, which will include reference to online and interactive portfolios and blogs. The term 'setting' will be used within this chapter to cover the multitude of environments in which EYGPs/EYTs operate, including school classrooms. However, readers do need to take into account the fact that much of the research that has taken place with respect to CPD that most directly relates to early years practice has been focused upon teachers in classrooms.

The chapter will address the following questions:

✔   What is continuing professional development and why is it of such importance?
✔   What are the stipulated professional expectations of Early Years Graduate Practitioners and Early Years Teachers in England?
✔   How can I make the most of my CPD activities?

The recommended reading list at the end of this chapter will introduce readers to a range of texts and online resources to further explore these topics.

Introduction: What is continuing professional development and why is it of such importance?

In recent years the area of professional development has emerged as one of much interest for educators working across the age span. There is now much interest in how the activities associated with CPD impact upon standards of teaching and learning, and upon the quality of practice as a whole. The fast pace of change in education through the acceleration towards academisation for primary and secondary schools, the emergence of Teaching School Alliances, and a surge in school-to-school support sees us currently in a place where professional development has entered a new and potentially positive era. There is much CPD activity within schools and between school alliances that is highly effective. With the demise of the central CPD system set up under the New Labour Government (1997–2010) (see chapter 4) through the Primary National Strategies, a localised model of activity has now emerged. Where this works well, schools are operating co-ordinated approaches to professional development which meet the specific needs of teachers very effectively, across clusters of schools. This is a mixture of in-house expertise typically led by Specialist Leaders in Education (SLEs) and other experienced educators including external consultants, thereby giving schools a central role in developing a self-improving and sustainable school-led system. Linked to National Standards and performance management, CPD is now a professional entitlement for all teachers. In such a climate, the children's workforce is required to work more closely together – early years practice, education, social care, health and the range of support services can engage in collaborative CPD. We borrow the phrase 'inter-professional education' from Aubrey (2011), and interpret it in the widest sense. Linked to one's own sense of professional identity (Brock, 2012), working together requires that we share practice to the extent that the whole children's workforce is aware of what each branch of these professional services has to offer and has an understanding of how these services benefit children and their families. Leading practitioners should develop a core knowledge of how services can be effectively integrated, along with the skills to work effectively with other professionals. Such a process requires that we explore our own individual professional training needs in order to self-manage our own continuing professional development.

It is ironic that, in a world which celebrates a continual 'transforming of practice', clarity in what is actually meant by terms like 'continuing professional development' or 'professional learning' remains elusive. Fullan and Hargreaves commented on 'how little systematic attention has been devoted to understanding the topic' (1992, p. 1). We can start from the descriptions of Bell and Gilbert (1994), who described what they considered to be key features of teacher development, comprising two aspects:

- Input of theory and new teaching suggestions
- Trying out ideas, evaluating practice of these over time in a collaborative situation where teachers receive support and feedback and where they are able to respond critically.

Although this reference is 20 years old, it still represents the core that lies beneath the drive for continuing professional development within teaching and teaching-related professions.

Commenting upon this, Evans (2002) sees this interpretation of teachers' behaviour change as a longitudinal process involving their personal, professional and social development. As authors, we use the terms CPD, professional learning and professional development almost interchangeably for convenience in this chapter, but take the stance that professional *learning* supersedes the rather more generic concept of professional development, because the process of professional learning better reflects the kinds of experiences that are effective. In the most positive situations, such learning becomes a catalyst for new knowledge, and introduces activities that transfer directly into early years practice (Timperley *et al.*, 2007).

High-quality professional development is much sought after internationally. The Organisation for Economic Co-operation and Development (OECD) states that 'at the level of the education system, professional development of teachers is a key policy lever' (OECD, 2005). In England, the profession has seen a massive drive towards accountability linked to the Standards agenda and the measurement of pupil achievement. Teachers in other countries are also experiencing a trend to increased professionalisation. Singapore provides structured routes into as well as progression through teaching. South Africa is moving its 'barefoot teachers' who had a vocation but no qualifications or training into teacher training courses to fast track their professional learning (Villegas-Reimers, 2003, p. 19). The Step by Step programme (SbS) (International Step by Step Association, 2010) was a very different approach to early childhood within the old Eastern Bloc nations that involved practitioners in more democratic approaches to teaching, besides introducing the concept of professional development in a very different, less prescriptive format than teachers had been used to in the past. Closer to home, Huw Lewis, the Welsh Minister for Education and Skills, speaking at the National Assembly for Wales proposed a Welsh Model of Professional Learning (2014). He emphasised that in order to secure world class education and deliver learner outcomes, the role of effective professional learning is crucial. This new model, designed to improve the quality of professional practice, is to be shaped by professionals for professionals, and is aimed squarely at delivering national priorities of improving literacy and numeracy and breaking the link between poverty and educational attainment. Lewis points out that a commitment to high-quality professional learning should be part of the professional experience of every practitioner and support their career-long progression, whatever their aspirations. He stated that in return for better access to high-quality professional learning and support, there is an expectation that practitioners will take more responsibility for their own development and share their practice with others, a feature of any high-status profession (Lewis, 2014). This type of attitude from government requires that teachers and practitioners define their own requirements for professional development, rather than have it imposed upon them by governments with political agendas, hopefully igniting a focus on research- and practitioner-informed CPD within the early years arena. Chapter 10 considers such agendas further, with a focus on international comparison.

Given its importance, what then does effective teacher professional learning look like? In an Ofsted survey in 2006, inspectors found that the best schools had a clear and accurate view of what they needed to achieve and planned varied activities to support whole-school development, systematically managed to achieve intended outcomes. In the very best schools, outcomes were then rigorously evaluated to inform the next cycle of planning. The cyclical nature of this process reflects the action research methodology, which you can read about below. Overall, CPD was found to be most effective in the schools where senior managers fully understood the connections between each link in the chain and gave it a central role in planning for improvement. Teachers and support staff in these schools enjoyed high-quality CPD, which had been well chosen from a wide range of possible activities to meet individual and school needs. Kempton (2013) proposes the following as indicative of quality professional development for teachers: it maintains a focus on pupil learning needs with ongoing rigorous evaluation of outcomes; it contributes to whole-school development; it is collaborative and driven by teachers themselves; it is sustained over a period of at least two terms; it involves regular external expert input that builds on the best practice and understanding. In 2015 the Sutton Trust reported that through quality professional development, real improvements in teaching and achievement can take place. The report recognised the need for teachers to have both subject and pedagogical knowledge on entry, and to be set upon a pathway that recognises that their professional development should be nurtured throughout their career.

Liz Francis, Director of the Workforce Strategy for the Teaching and Development Agency, in her presentation on the role of professional development in redefining the place of primary teachers (2009) alluded to a changing future that emphasised the importance of professional development and its evolving nature. She stated that the professionalism of the school workforce is the key to what happens within schools. She proposed that this is increasingly delivered through groups of schools working collaboratively, and that this approach offers new opportunities for professionals to take control of the process of change with less top-down control and a greater say for front-line staff. Public service professionals are best placed to innovate from a platform of consistent high quality, in which the agenda is set by the professionals themselves. Underpinning principles for CPD include:

- Using evidence-based approaches
- Organisational and individual development occurring in tandem
- Giving consideration to the 'team around the child'
- Balance between work-based learning and external expertise
- Identifying impact measures from the outset
- Engaging children and young people with priorities

- Addressing cultural and practical issues – time is the most significant barrier
- Working in partnership with schools, settings and other agencies.

Clearly then, at an organisation level, collaboration is key in sustainable networks of quality-assured cluster-based professional development provision central to the organisation of the school system, and the model for the future. Consider the list of nine characteristics of high-quality professional development below from Stoll *et al.* (2012).

Case study: nine characteristics of high-quality professional development

1   Effective professional development starts with the end in mind.
2   Effective professional development challenges thinking as part of changing practice.
3   Effective professional development is based on the assessment of individual and school needs.
4   Effective professional development involves connecting work-based learning and external expertise.
5   Effective professional learning opportunities are varied, rich and sustainable.
6   Effective professional development uses action research and enquiry as key tools.
7   Effective professional development is strongly enhanced through collaborative learning and joint practice development.
8   Effective professional development is enhanced by creating professional learning communities within and between schools.
9   Effective professional development requires leadership to create the necessary conditions.

Reflection
- What do the above characteristics mean to you within the situation of your current professional role?
- Is there one statement in the list that is top priority for you? Why is this?
- Do you think that the priorities are likely to change as you progress in your career?

We move logically now to professional development at an individual level and refer initially to Schön's concept of 'reflection in action' (1983, p. 128), which raised the desirability of a climate within education where teachers individually engage in deeply reflective practice; for example, Tripp (1993), McGill (2000), Roach and Kratochwill (2004), DeSchon Hamlin (2004), Talbot (2002) and Kuit *et al.* (2001). McGill (2000, p. 2) strongly advocated that the development of a 'habit of mind' employing critical evaluation at the start of a teaching career will predispose the trainee to develop into a truly proficient practitioner.

There are several reflective techniques that have been trialled with both experienced and trainee teachers. McGill (2000) used anecdotal story writing, Kuit *et al.* (2001) list several techniques including action research, critical incidents and storytelling, Henderson *et al.* (2003) used significant event analysis (SEA) and Talbot (2002), DeSchon Hamlin (2004) and Tripp (1993) used critical incident analysis (CIA). Other authors outline detailed programmes to assist the individual in critical reflection. Jay and Johnson (2002) advocated the division of reflection into descriptive, comparative and critical categories, while Larrivee (2000) outlined a set of underpinning requirements for reflective practice, including the need for allocation of professional time for solitary reflection and the ability and confidence to question conventional practice 'wisdom'. From this she developed a 'personal filtering' model, where the individual is led to recognise the impact of his/her past experiences, beliefs, assumptions, expectations, feelings, mood, personal agendas and aspirations upon the process of reflection.

Weiss and Weiss (2001) designed a detailed 'reflective supervision model', which outlines a schedule of activities for trainee teachers, purpose-designed to cultivate critical reflection. This schedule includes extensive experience of collaborative activities with inexperienced and experienced colleagues and parents. These researchers also advocated that teachers in initial teacher training should be taught action research techniques (see below). McArdle and Coutts (2003) took a different approach, considering the perceived qualities possessed by good teachers, thence defining the target 'product' that teacher trainers should be creating. Such qualities include strength, confidence and the ability to make skilful discriminating judgements, added to stability and maturity. These authors proposed: 'implicit in notions of reflection is the idea that experience can be abstracted from a situation ... it may be more relevant to suggest that the core of qualities affects the situation in a more holistic way in each situation that is encountered' (McArdle and Coutts, 2003, p. 232).

Pillay and McCrindle defined the nature of professional expertise as:

> The ability to combine domain knowledge with appropriate professional tools and strategies to solve problems within the socio-cultural context of the profession. With increasing expertise, the individual is able to bring sufficient knowledge and experience to deal with more complex and novel situations.
>
> (Pillay and McCrindle, 2005, p. 67)

Case study: critical incident analysis

Critical incident analysis (CIA) is designed to support trainee teachers and other practitioners in reflection upon real, personally experienced events. It is unfortunately named, as it sounds as though the term should apply to an emergency situation, but in fact it describes relatively mundane events within the classroom which are 'rendered critical through analysis' (Tripp, 1993, p. 25). The classic CIA process involves the following steps:

- The identification of an issue of interest within a teaching/practice session, which may be positive, negative or neutral, mundane, dramatic, funny or sad. The key point is that the issue captures the attention of the teacher, to the extent that s/he continues to contemplate it after the session has ended.
- A more formal, concentrated focus is then exerted upon the issue, considering how practice may be developed as a result of this reflection.
- Practice is subsequently developed, and the practitioner continues to reflect upon the result.

This process is essentially 'dialogic' (Wolfe and Alexander, 2008, online); that is, it engages professionals in authentic dialogue, using concepts generated from personal experience, and discussion through digital interfaces offers a further window of opportunity to learn through these: 'digital tools offer ... opportunities to rehearse argumentation skills, and learn in less formal, more personal ways' (Wolfe and Alexander, 2008, online, and see e-portfolios, below)

Reflection

It is very easy to pilot the critical incident analysis technique for yourself. The type of incident that you should be looking for is the sort of event that you keep thinking about, even after it has concluded. It could be a conversation with a child, parent or colleague, something you observed in the setting, or an activity that you planned that went unexpectedly well, or badly. Write a detailed description of your incident, how you felt about it at the time, how you feel about it now, and, after reflection, what you might do differently next time. It is in essence learning by experience, but with a more formal consideration of how you might move your practice along in the light of this example.

What are the stipulated professional expectations of Early Years Graduate Practitioners and Early Years Teachers in England?

The Early Years Graduate Practitioner

In October 2005, the Early Education Advisory Group (EEAG) in England agreed that the organisation and management of early years education and care services needed to be reviewed and reshaped. Their focus was to produce a role that, while it retained many of the very positive features of the existing nursery teacher role, also encompassed the multi-agency practitioner leadership of a child care and education team in the new children's centres and extended schools, which would also provide services for children under three and their families. The other aspect that the advisory group wished to address was that services for children under three were, at that time, most frequently led by staff who, whilst typically possessing high levels of practitioner competence and dedication, had not received education and training at the university or higher education (HE) level. Many recent high-profile early years research projects, in particular the British-based Effective Provision of Pre-School Education (EPPE) project (Sylva *et al.*, 2004), made a clear finding that outcomes for children, particularly those from a background of disadvantage, were improved when the practice in the setting was led by a graduate.

The decision that the EEAG came to was to create a new graduate early years role, the Early Years Professional (EYP), somewhat similar to the role of Danish pedagogue, but with some of the same skills and duties as the English Nursery Teacher. The difference between the EYP and the Nursery Teacher was that EYPs were trained to work with children aged between birth and five and their families within a multi-agency team and in non-school-based practice, while Nursery Teachers were trained principally to work in schools and nursery schools, specialising within the three to seven age range. The Early Years Professional programme ran from 2006 to 2013; however, following the change of direction for Children's Centres initiated by the Coalition government of 2010–15 (see chapter 4) and the advent of initiatives to place children in schools from the age of two years (BBC, 2014), it was subsequently replaced by the Early Years Teacher initiative. At the time of writing there are still many debates ongoing about these changes, in particular the lack of parity between Early Years Teachers and Nursery Teachers in terms of Qualified Teacher Status (QTS) and subsequent pay and career prospects.

The key issue to emerge from these events is the firm agreement between professionals and politicians that practice in early years should be led by a graduate. Since advances in our knowledge of neuronal development in the early 2000s (see chapter 2) we now fully recognise the huge importance of the early years, and the breadth and depth of development that takes place between birth and the seventh birthday. Although changes to the administration of professional roles within the sector are still ongoing, *all* graduate practitioners in English early years settings – and within the settings of the other UK nations – are recognised as a crucially important workforce in terms of nurturing the healthy mental and physical development of the youngest people in society.

Such recognition applies as much to graduate practitioners who have not yet decided upon a route to a formal professional role as it does to those who have already attained their professional status. It is possible for a graduate in Early Childhood Studies to seek out further development in academic study; for example, through a master's degree. However, given the word limits of the current chapter, we have chosen to focus our most detailed overview on the current routes to the different professional statuses that are conventionally required to lead practice in early years settings, particularly within schools. Readers should, however, note that nations differ quite widely in this respect, and while we do not have room to cover the full range of variations, we have provided one clear alternative example from another nation for you to reflect upon.

Case study: the Danish pedagogue

The concept of 'pedagogue' is specific to Denmark. Most pedagogues work in early years settings, but some may work with adults with special needs, or the elderly. The pedagogue's most important role is to address the social, emotional and physical care of the people with whom they work. Those who work with children are expected to be emotionally in tune with children's needs, to show interest in the ideas that the children bring to them, and to support children's development of self-confidence, social skills and emotional security.

The Danish National Federation of Early Childhood Teachers and Youth Educators proposes that the role of the pedagogue is to help children to:

> become capable of acting socially responsible and through this contribute to ensure and develop the social coherence in society. To summarise it is about what children are and how they become active participants in decisions concerning them as citizens in a democratic society. Pedagogues are responsible for enabling children to actively, responsibly and constructively take part in social life and by this contribute to promote solidarity, democracy and humanity in society.
>
> (Danish National Federation of Early Childhood Teachers and
> Youth Educators, 2006, online)

Reflection

The role of the Early Years Professional was far more similar to the Danish pedagogue than the role of the Early Years Teacher that replaced it. Standards relating to the support of children's social and emotional well-being were eclipsed by those that required those being awarded the status to demonstrate knowledge of curriculum, phonics and early numeracy. What do you think about this? Make sure to bring your knowledge of child development into your consideration. You can read more about the work of Danish pedagogues in chapter 10.

Early Years Teacher Status

A main driver for this book has been to argue the case that well-qualified professionals are vitally important in the privileged work they do with our youngest children on a daily basis, and the associated need for graduate leadership. The Government is committed to raising the quality of early years provision by encouraging graduate leadership. This, however, as Moss (2000) argues, is a quantum leap from a poorly qualified and poorly paid workforce to one on a par with professionals in schools, and as such, taking young children as seriously as we take school-age children. This debate was the platform for the development of the Early Years Teacher Status (EYTS) initiative.

The introduction of EYTS in September 2013 built on the foundations of Early Years Professional Status (EYPS). It aimed to raise the prominence of the early years workforce and the difference is made explicit in the title, in that it presents the high-status role of 'teacher' broadly across the range of early years settings, not only within schools. The change of title and greater focus on formal teaching activity was introduced under the banner of raising the status of leading practitioners working with children from birth to five in the full range of settings. There are, however, several underlying issues here. Criticisms have been made of these changes, in particular the lack of clarity regarding the status of those holding EYTS compared with Early Years Teachers with QTS in terms of potential career trajectories, questions which at the time of writing (mid-2015) still need to be resolved. One important lack of clarity arises from the ways in which pay scales are determined for different 'grades' of professional. Schools have traditionally worked on the basis of different scales for employees who hold QTS and those who do not. It is currently argued by the DfE that QTS and EYTS are different but equal statuses, which makes the distinction between the two pathways into early years teaching quite opaque. This is further complicated by the fact that pay and conditions for practitioners working in early education and childcare settings outside maintained (that is, local authority-administered) schools are determined locally by employers, and this situation is also in a state of flux as schools joining academy chains move outside the maintained sector.

Nutbrown and Clough (2014) extend this point, arguing that until there is sufficient funding for further and higher education programmes and the will of political parties to invest, then issues of pay, status and conditions for practitioners in the early years sector will continue to be a point of conflict, and that while this is the case, the core goal, high-quality provision for all children in early years care and education settings in England will not be realised (2014, p. 178). EYTS is however a major initiative which holds the potential to make a real difference to early years education and care. These graduate leaders will be trained to understand early childhood development and the EYTS standards reflect the specialist role that they will have in working with children under three as well as with children from three to five years old. Whether their status is EYTS or QTS (Early Years), all EYTs enter the profession in the expectation that they will continue their professional learning throughout their careers. For example, the National College for Teaching and Leadership states:

> Early Years Teachers make the education and care of babies and children their first concern. They are accountable for achieving the highest possible standards in their professional practice and conduct ... They have strong early development knowledge, keep their knowledge and skills up-to-date and are self-critical.
>
> (National College for Teaching and Leadership, 2013)

EYTS is awarded to graduates who have been judged to have met all of the Teacher Standards (Early Years) from birth to five years old. All applicants must have GCSE qualifications in maths, English language and a science (grade C or above) and must have successfully passed the Professional Skills Tests in English and maths before entering the programme. There are four routes into this:

- Graduate Entry Mainstream route (12 months full-time for those already holding a degree at honours level)
- Undergraduate Entry route: trainees will attend an early childhood-related degree blended with preparation for EYTS (three years full-time)
- Graduate Employment Based route, to encourage the professional development of graduate staff employed as early years practitioners, and to encourage employer engagement in the EYTS project (12 months part-time)
- Assessment Only route (three months part-time for experienced, leading graduate practitioners employed within the early years sector).

The Early Years Teacher's Standards can be found at: www.gov.uk/government/uploads/system/uploads/attachment_data/file/211646/Early_Years_Teachers__Standards.pdf

Information about routes to EYTS can be found at: https://getintoteaching.education.gov.uk/become-an-early-years-teacher

Information on the Professional Skills Tests, and some practice material can be found at: www.teacherstalk.co.uk/resources/qts-practice-test.php

Qualified Teacher Status

There are two routes to QTS (Early Years), either through an undergraduate route, which will comprise a three- or four-year BA(Hons) in Education Studies with QTS, or through a Postgraduate Certificate in Education with QTS. For graduate programmes of Early Years Initial Teacher Training (EYITT), all entrants must hold a first degree from a UK higher education institution or equivalent qualification. They must have GCSE qualifications in maths, English language and a science (grade C or above) and must have successfully passed the Professional Skills Tests in English and maths before entering the programme. The Teachers' Standards (QTS) can be found at: www.gov.uk/government/uploads/system/uploads/attachment_data/file/301107/Teachers__Standards.pdf

Those seeking the postgraduate route may choose to undertake this through a programme offered by a university, or through 'on the job' training directly within a school, which is overseen by the DfE's School Direct initiative. Information about all routes to QTS may be found on the DfE website at: https://getintoteaching.education.gov.uk/explore-my-options/primary-training-options

The role of the graduate leader

Throughout this book the authors have argued that the quality of early education and childcare provision is higher when practice is led by graduates who have been specifically trained in child development theory and early years practice. Nutbrown (2012) made it clear that there is a need to increase the number of teachers in England with specialist early years knowledge to lead practice in settings and use their pedagogical knowledge to support young children's play, learning and development. In the review *Foundations for Quality* (2012), she speaks of rigorous qualifications so that employers have confidence in the credentials of staff, with graduate leaders of practice who are supported by teams of practitioners who hold at minimum a Level 3 ('A' level equivalent) qualification that has been rigorous and challenging. She states that all who work in early years settings, graduate and non-graduate, should take pride in their work and demonstrate that they are 'continually seeking to extend and develop their knowledge and skills' (2012, pp. 10–11). She proposes that reflective graduate leaders should be responsible for facilitating and leading high-quality professional practice in settings with a range of partners, with their main impact being upon daily practice with children under five. This makes them ideally placed to fulfil the needs of employers for high-quality care and education of babies and young children.

Practitioners who are qualified only to the Level 3 standard may still undertake professional training that will eventually lead to the award of EYTS, by undertaking part-time study towards a Foundation Degree in Early Years, followed by a 'top-up' to honours degree status and EYTS training on the Employment Based pathway. Information on such routes should initially be sought from the university nearest to home. The equivalent of the Foundation Degree exists in Scotland as the Diploma of Higher Education in Childhood Practice, and there are likely to be equivalent qualifications in most European nations; the Bologna process is currently aligning higher education standards across the European Union (European Commission, 2015).

Case study: EYTS

Kathryn, who leads the EYT Employment Based route in a university in the north of England, comments that with the introduction of the 'two year old offer' (BBC, 2014), many schools now urgently require graduate leaders with knowledge and expertise working with very young children, and in particular those from socio-economically deprived backgrounds. The role of Early Years Teacher was created to address this need, and achievement of the status offers clear career development opportunities for graduate practitioners. Read the brief transcript below of an interview with Sally, a newly qualified EYT, sharing her views on the EYT programme she has just completed.

Interviewer: What attracted you to the EYT programme in the first place?
Sally: I did a degree in Early Childhood Studies and I just loved my placements during the course. I got to work with the very youngest children and loved being involved in helping them learn. On the course we did a module on babies and how they learn and I found this very interesting.

Interviewer: Can you tell me a little about the actual course last year?
Sally: It is quite intensive! I did the Employer Route which means I also work and so balancing a full-time job in a nursery with study was hard. But rewarding too. I could see real changes in my practice very soon. The sessions at the university were a lot of theory but also practically based too. New ideas you could take into the setting the next day. Really great.

Interviewer: Would you recommend the course to others then?
Sally: Very much. Do it for sure.

Interviewer: What then would be the biggest selling point for the EYT course, do you think?
Sally: Mmm. Making a difference to children's lives really. Yes.

Interviewer: What difference do you think you have personally made after doing the course?
Sally: I think I have and early on too. You can see it. When a child does something for the first time it is such a great feeling of achievement. Not only for the child but for me. I think, 'I have helped do this'. I saw a lot of that, and understanding what to look for meant you really know what is going on. Child development was the key for me. You can see huge differences in learning and development week after week in settings. It's like I said, a difference to children's lives.

Reflection

Sally sees success very much through the positive results she achieves with the children, rather than in terms of salary or career prospects. This is quite typical of teachers and practitioners working within early years settings. While this clearly reflects very positively upon their professionalism, some would trace such attitudes through to the current situation in which those working in the early years arena, particularly with the youngest children, are less well paid and have lower professional status than those working with older children.

This situation is further exacerbated by the emerging status differences between teachers with QTS 3-7 and teachers with EYTS, which focuses on the younger birth to five age range. This can be especially the case for practitioners who work in private daycare settings. Consider how this situation might be addressed, without the loss of the depth of professionalism that Sally personifies. You will be able to gather more information to help you with this reflection in chapter 10, where you will consider some more detailed international comparisons.

How can I make the most of my CPD activities?

Communities of Practice and storytelling

One way for EYTs/EYGPs to continue their professional learning is through Communities of Practice, a concept that was initially developed by Lave and Wenger (1991). These are relevant to the range of early years and school settings because as Wenger (2000) argues, the success of organisations ultimately depends upon their ability to form as a learning system and, at the same time, take part in a range of extended learning opportunities within broad arenas, including in partnership with other closely associated professions. Wenger recommended periods of reflection and information-sharing following CPD and maintains that teachers' professional development should always refer to their classroom practice, which reflects our earlier assumption that CPD activity must be relevant to the day-to-day practice that is undertaken in settings. Those who work in settings where multi-agency engagement is routine can especially benefit from this approach, as here there will be meetings between different Communities of Practice, and a potential for blending people in different roles within the children's workforce into a new multi-agency Community of Practice. See for example, the work that practitioners do in multi-agency teams that is outlined in chapter 3. The process of storytelling (Kuit *et al.*, 2001) is also relevant here, as people in different roles tell their professional stories to audiences from other areas of the children's workforce, broadening and deepening understanding of the range of practice undertaken with children and families.

In line with Communities of Practice is the idea of Professional Learning Communities (PLCs). Common to these are shared beliefs and values amongst participants, supportive leadership, collective learning and shared reflective practice (Hord and Sommers, 2008), which corresponds with the professional development needs of the EYGP/EYT community. Teachers' energies can be renewed when a PLC is used to invigorate collective learning, which includes personal development, and is not merely a tool to implement mandatory change. The key word here is alignment - where there is aligning across settings and schools, and between practitioners, sometimes in different roles within the children's workforce, through meeting and storytelling in order to share ideas and refresh each others' practice. McKibben and Pawson (2014) make a strong case for having trusting relationships when forming PLCs. In their view professional development is in no way a selfish pursuit but an essential element necessary to develop a community that values the learning process. The concept of Communities of Practice is based upon the view that learning and work are intrinsic to each other. If EYGPs/EYTs espouse this concept, then learning underpins everything that goes on in the workplace. Sharing practice outside one's own place of work with colleagues and in turn listening to their stories enriches practice, regardless of whether the workplace in question is a nursery, play group, daycare setting or school.

Action research

Cordingley (2007) in an informative report entitled *Sauce for the Goose* stated that in the past the main source of CPD activity was one-off courses and 'one size fits all' Inset (Inservice Training) days. Thankfully, the situation is changing, as we explored in the introductory section to this chapter, and we now have a much deeper evidence base to substantiate the recent advances made in CPD. Activities typically include: peer support to encourage experimentation and enable teachers to interpret goals in their own programmes; activities to structure dialogues that encourage review and reflection; support for evaluating learning through the lenses of individual hopes and aspirations; and using personally selected starting points, with CPD time allocated to support such development. Other activities for individual development and for learning communities include: professional development meetings and professional development items in staff and team meetings; conference attendance; lesson/practice observations; and discussions with colleagues to reflect on working practices. We expand on some of these examples in the text below.

Burnett (2014) explains the links between research and continued professional development, arguing that research activities linked to personal practice allow new insights, build confidence to refine or innovate and even generate evidence to justify why you should continue to do what you are already doing! She reflects that engaging in research is similar to the existing processes of collecting evidence and drawing conclusions that already take place in busy settings; research just makes it more systematic. It is also about communicating what has been discovered to a larger audience. 'Action' research is about the piloting of ideas to increase knowledge. Cochran-Smith and Lytle (1993) argued that action research has the potential to prompt educational change, transform teachers' perceptions of themselves as professionals and contribute to the generation and critique of knowledge about teaching and learning. As the name suggests, action research is about taking action, making decisions about one's own actions that inform future practice. This type of research is designed and undertaken by practitioners in their own professional settings to inform and improve aspects of their own practice, or to focus on the ways in which particular practices are structured within the setting as a whole. It can also take the form of professional learning projects that are undertaken to benefit the setting and may involve collaboration between small groups of practitioners. Collaboration provides an ideal forum for professionals to share questions and ideas relating to practice and enhance the professional development of the enquiry; such co-construction of ideas may be particularly productive in a multi-agency collaboration.

Bell *et al.* (2010) proposed that the nature of the support provided by external specialists was an important element in practitioners' engagement in and/or with research. These researchers found that peer collaboration and critical friendship emerged as an essential support and motivator for those carrying out the research. The use of interventions went beyond knowledge acquisition into the development of the pedagogical understanding and skills needed to change practice, and involved the application of new or different approaches to teaching and learning. Research carried out by Poet *et al.* (2010) asked how teachers used research or enquiry to inform their teaching. These researchers' findings indicated that teachers valued the opportunity to become involved in research. Teachers who had been involved in a higher number and wider variety of professional development activities in the last 12 months were also more likely to have a positive view about the potential of research to improve their teaching. These findings provide some very positive reasons to engage in research as part of your CPD. Furthermore, if you undertake a postgraduate qualification in any career route that relates to working with children and families, you will usually find that you are required to both formally reflect upon your own practice, and undertake a research activity to focus on a particular topic, in which you may opt to undertake an action research approach.

The basis of the action research methodology is rooted within identifying an aspect of practice that you think you can improve, followed by planning and operationalising a small change in your practice, evaluating its effects, and on the basis of this evaluation, making a further small change and evaluating again (Figure 9.1).

The cycle can go on for as long as the practitioner feels that it is producing positive results. The evaluation of impact can be quite an eclectic process, and may involve a range of investigation techniques. A technique that will help you to more comprehensively evaluate effects is to use more than one method of investigation and then compare what you find from each. For example, you could carry out observations of children, interviews/surveys with parents and staff, and formal tests of progress made with both children and staff. Using a range of investigations and co-ordinating the results in this way is called triangulation.

- Areas of *agreement* between the different sets of data can help you pinpoint further issues and subsequently to move forward to the next investigation.
- Areas of *disagreement* may raise interesting points for reflection. For example, some recent research (see http://digest.bps.org.uk/2013/05/engaging-lecturers-can-breed. html) found interesting indications that 'star performer' university lecturers who make their subject seem easy, while receiving very positive feedback, may conversely elicit less enhanced performance from students than those who are more rigorous and less entertaining!

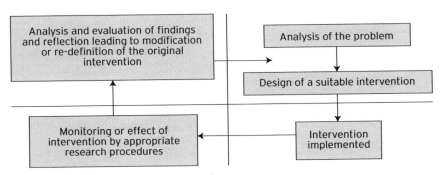

Figure 9.1 A diagrammatic view of action research

Source: Opie, C. and Jarvis, P. (2012) Introduction to methodology, in P. Jarvis, S. Newman, W. Holland and J. George (Eds) *Research in Early Years: A step by step guide*, p. 61 © Pearson Education Ltd 2012.

If action research is carried out thoroughly and with a willingness to engage 'in depth' it has the dual benefit of producing a more thoughtful, effective practitioner, and a more vibrant, innovative setting. The aim should be to engage in *gradual*, research-informed development of practice. This technique can be equally applied both to your own practice and to the practice of more junior practitioners for whom you are providing leadership.

Reflection

Veteran practitioner–researcher Angela Anning proposes that the following should be deeply considered before embarking on a practitioner research project:

- The paramount importance of confidentiality in observing, listening to and reporting on the behaviours of young children and their parents.
- The need to understand the sensitive nature of using cameras and when deciding what to write in field notes.
- The need to be very sensitive to the ways in which researchers attempt to engage in dialogue with very young children and in interview processes with early years workers.
- The impossibility of getting fully informed consent to be a research participant from a child under the age of seven.
- The need to reflect on potential conflicts between a professional role serving the needs of children, families and communities and the researcher's role in 'objectifying' the objects of enquiry.
- The potential for the research processes to influence/change relationships with colleagues. (For example, what if they express an opinion that is highly antithetical to your own? What if they exercise their right to withdraw from your research?)
- Are practitioners always able to be non-judgemental about practice in their setting? (For example, when assessing a rota system that has previously caused the researcher a lot of personal inconvenience.)
- What will be the results of honestly sharing your findings with your colleagues? Might this sometimes create issues within the setting, in certain circumstances?

Anning warns: 'the brutal fact is that your position as a professional gives you power over your community; but is it justifiable to use this power as a researcher as well, without serious thought and preparation?' (Anning, 2010, p. 190).

Reflection

If you have previously carried out a research project, did you consider the points that Anning makes above? Reflect on this in your journal (see below), and then consider how you might bring these ideas into your own ongoing research activities and in supporting colleagues in your setting who are engaging in research for various qualifications.

The role of the journal and portfolio in reflective practice

You will be asked to keep a professional journal and/or a professional portfolio at an early point in any professional training in early years teaching or practice. This will involve writing a reflective record of your practice activities, and archiving plans and resources for practice, which may include, for example, lesson plans, plans for whole-class and small-group activities, plans for continuous provision and (carefully anonymised) child observations.

Tripp (1993), McGill (2000), Roach and Kratochwill (2004), DeSchon Hamlin (2004), Talbot (2002), Kuit *et al.* (2001) and McGill (2000, p. 2) all strongly advocated the need to understand and utilise critical evaluation at the start of the career, drawing upon Schön's concept of 'reflection in action' (1983, p. 128). The professional journal is where much of the reflection engendered by action research is carried out. It is where a practitioner contemplates the information that s/he collects through the evaluation stage of action research, in an ongoing professional conversation with the self. The idea is that the practitioner engages in 'reflection in action' (Schön, 1983, p. 128).

The full portfolio should not only contain the journal; there should also be extensive notes relating to resources and practice plans, cross-referenced to the journal. Jay and Johnson (2002, p. 73) proposed that over many years of extensive evaluation, the value of such reflection has 'become generally accepted', while Pellicone *et al.* (2005, p. 527) explained 'the growing support for portfolios (either paper-based or electronic) is due to the fact that many ... see the benefits of their use as pedagogical, learning and reflection tools' with the ultimate goal being 'authentic tracking of growth over time'. The professional development portfolio, at the heart of which lies a reflective journal, has a relatively long history in teacher training, being widely used as a tool for student teacher reflection from the 1960s. Prior to this time, the term 'portfolio' was more generally used to refer to a collection of professional work; for example, by an artist or writer (Chatham-Carpenter *et al.*, 2010).

There are many formats in which you may be required to structure journals and portfolios, so we will not give you narrowly directive guidelines through a case study here. However, we do offer a reflection on how you might *use* a journal productively, not just to submit for assessment on a programme of learning, but as an ongoing professional development activity.

Case study: using your professional journal to reflect on learning

Initially, what you need to do is to produce a basic introduction to your setting and your role within it. This will need to be revised when inevitable changes occur (you move to a different role, move settings, etc.). You should try to write an entry at least every three or four days, focusing on aspects of your work-based experience that caused you to reflect upon and develop your practice. Incidents that form the basis for your reflections should be judged on the same basis as critical incidents – those that have made you think, and that you have continued to contemplate. You should not have to share your whole journal at any time (as this may inhibit the scope of your reflection), but it is useful from time to time to share edited extracts with fellow students, tutors and colleagues. *Do* make sure that your journal text is safely anonymised, particularly if you are storing it electronically (see below) – it is surprisingly easy to unwittingly stray outside the data protection legislation if you use full, real names for colleagues, children and locations!

Alongside your reflective journal, you should also maintain a CPD portfolio where you keep records of training courses attended, job reviews/appraisals, possibly some samples of children's work (with their permission) and associated planning from activities you designed that went particularly well, letters/cards expressing thanks from parents and carers (you could even keep communications of complaint with associated notes relating to how you rectified the relevant issues!) and any other materials that you feel serve to document your continuing development as a practitioner.

Reflection

If you were to start your professional journal and portfolio right now, what do you think would be the most important ideas and resources that you could put into it?

The next stage of reflective practice: shared reflection through the e-portfolio

By the early 1990s, the concept of the electronic (e-) portfolio emerged, principally from those who were considering decreasing reliance on paper as 'a tool to enhance learning, conduct assessments, meet standards and increase employability' (Chatham-Carpenter *et al.*, 2010, p. 438). Barrett (2013) proposed that the traditional qualities of portfolios, such as collecting and reflecting, can much more easily evolve into storytelling and collaborating through technology-based sharing, thereby enabling the user to become more focused on an ongoing process than on construction of a static store of paper documents.

Barbera (2009) found that where peer feedback was part of a student blogging process ('blogging' is a term derived from the original concept of a we*b-log*), students were significantly more likely to revise and improve their work, although they did not consciously recognise this effect. As we have discussed above, the input of another professional to the reflective practice can shed light upon and freshen ideas, and help to move on a process that has become 'stuck in a rut'. The ability to share parts of a journal easily through online interaction can help to make it far more reflective than the solitary construction of a diary-style document where there is no infiltration of other voices, raising alternative ideas to move reflection along, and to make learning through journaling less formal and more personally relevant (Wolfe and Alexander, 2008). It is therefore proposed that at the heart of every e-portfolio should be a reflective blog created by the user. As such, the e-portfolio can encompass storage of supporting materials, which may include plans for practice, details of resources and additionally, a body of evidence relating to practice/formal assignment work that has been formally assessed. Due to the nature of digital storage, these do not have to be limited to printed/written documents, and even the blog may contain recordings of spoken reflections, rather than be simply limited to text. The e-portfolio may also contain video recordings of practice (although users do have a legal and ethical responsibility to ensure that they have all necessary permissions to store images of children in a repository that is personally owned and maintained).

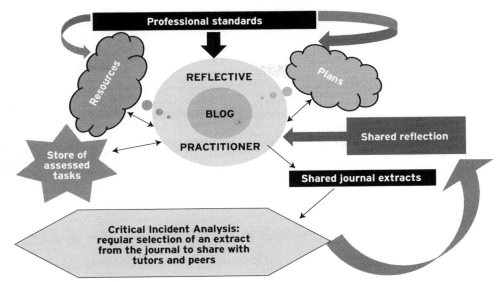

Figure 9.2 The practitioner e-portfolio

E-portfolios therefore have several advantages over the paper-based alternative, being more versatile in terms of storage, less unwieldy to physically manage and easier to organise, particularly with respect to the owner choosing which elements to share, with whom and when. The variety of artefacts that can be gathered are appropriate to a world where education processes are becoming increasingly digital; for example, the use of video and audio materials in teaching and learning. The e-portfolio allows the blog-based journal to seamlessly interface with other artefacts underpinning professional development, such as resources, plans and, where a practitioner is studying for further qualifications, assignment work, as these can be stored as digital files within the same 'space' and linked in flexible combinations by the user.

In the Web 1.0 environment that existed in the early days of the personal computer, digital resources were prone to catastrophic destruction/loss due to their location on individual drives; however, the advent of Web 2.0 (Underwood, 2008) introduced a range of online 'cloud' storage opportunities, with the additional advantage of potentially infinite capacity. As such, an online store can easily be set up to belong to an individual rather than to an institution, portfolios can be infinitely added to as careers develop, and taken from training provider to training provider. Barrett (2013) makes the additional point that engagement with an online e-portfolio also provides the user with a source of digital citizenship and an ongoing interface that supports proficiency in the most up-to-date technological developments in the field of practice, a source of personal development that grows with the practitioner and may eventually link across to aspects of social/professional online networking.

Case study: why use an electronic portfolio in Early Childhood Studies?

Watch this video of Dr Lynn Worden explaining why her department at the University of Delaware has developed an e-portfolio process:

www.youtube.com/watch?v=Th-5I-QKJK4

Claire Fellows, a student at the University of Surrey, uses an e-portfolio system called 'PebblePad'. Here she talks about her experiences:

> PebblePad has been a key part of my life now for nine months. I am currently on placement and have found it to be an invaluable tool. I have made a webfolio specifically about my placement and created pages that illustrate my different projects. I regularly update specific blogs about the work I am doing, the things I am learning and how I am developing. Tagging my thoughts has proved extremely helpful! I recently wrote an interim placement report outlining what I have learnt so far; this could not have been easier! All I had to do was skim through the thoughts I had tagged and then had an endless list of skills and abilities but also specific examples I could refer back to! This will be a life-saver when it comes to the next CV or application form I write!
>
> I also use PebblePad to store examples of the work I have actually produced. At the start of my placement I designed a flyer advertising an event the organisation was holding, which I uploaded to have access to at a later stage. I recently compared it with a current design. The difference was quite astounding! A key example of how much I have developed throughout the placement so far, yet without having a resource such as PebblePad, this important realisation would have been lost. I would not have had a record of my past work or skills and so would not be able to make a comparison to my current situation. The things that I now take for granted as common procedures were not originally as obvious to me but this would have been long forgotten! ...
>
> Overall PebblePad is making me more employable as I am developing both personally and professionally and I am sure there are other ways it can help me which I am yet to discover! ... Having granted my manager access to my webfolio, we use PebblePad as a mentoring tool.
>
> (Fellows, 2010, online)

Reflection

You can access free e-portfolio software at http://foliofor.me

Ideally in collaboration with colleagues or fellow students, set up an account and begin to build your e-portfolio, starting with a journal. There are instructions on the website, and particularly if you are able to share this experience, you will probably find it easier than you think.

Mentoring

We have indicated above our belief that CPD activity should involve interaction with individual colleagues within our day-to-day professional environment and with external networks, with a view to creating learning organisations. Aubrey (2011) ably makes the point that if mentoring becomes integral to early years settings there are greater chances that the organisation will become a learning community (much as the PLC section describes earlier).

Mentors are usually well-established practitioners, ideally with some experience of leadership. They are likely to be people who are established in the profession in which the mentee is seeking to develop their skills. The role of the mentor is to provide encouragement and to act as a sounding board, supporting finding solutions rather than giving 'instruction' or solving problems for the mentee. They can also help mentees to reflect upon possible gaps in their current knowledge and point them towards opportunities that exist where the mentee can obtain the additional experience that they may currently lack. This should include the consideration of options within or external to the setting, and may involve shadowing other professionals, both within the same area of the children's workforce and in others. It is very possible (and often productive) to be both a mentor and a mentee at the same time, which results in a cascade of professional knowledge and skills.

The associated culture then becomes one where 'learning, the development of oneself and others through reflective conversations become the norm' (Aubrey, 2011, p. 89). Professional settings that are learning communities increase their staff's focus on learning and development as the critical means of ensuring high-quality practice. They identify the key skills needed for individuals to operate successfully within their setting, and create mentors and mentoring programmes to support the professional development of their staff. In such organisations, the aim would be to facilitate mentoring that is focused upon supporting staff to manage their own learning to maximise potential, develop their skills, improve their performance and enable them to become who they want to be in the professional sense (Parsloe and Wray, 2000).

Clearly, the social aspect of mentoring is highly important. Aubrey (2011) discusses possibilities for mentoring that include learning through study groups, action research and sharing experiences in support groups. Mentoring can assist in linking personal and professional growth. Mentors are agents of help. They are role models who use their experience and expertise for positive influence. They can create new opportunities and solve problems for mentees. They challenge and coach and provide feedback that enables development. Mentoring in an educational context has been described as a 'learning conversation' (DfES, 2005) and the idea of honest conversations between mentor and mentee is critical to the process. These conversations will vary according to the needs of the individual and the aims of the mentoring programme.

Four stages in the mentoring process identified by Thomson (2006) may be helpful in framing the mentoring development journey. The initial stage is *establishing rapport*. Here the mentor and mentee will work out the relationships and the ways of working. This is the time to agree and set the ground rules. They will also agree a contract which will set up protocols for future meetings. The second stage is *direction setting* in which a diagnosis of the mentee's needs takes place. Goals and priorities are identified and clarity given on the ways of working throughout the agreement. Stage 3 is *progress making* in which you create a forum for progressing the mentee's development by sharing each other's expertise. At this stage there is likely to be recognition of achievements to date and monitoring of progress. The final stage of *moving on* allows the relationship to conclude or evolve. There should be a review of the learning and personal growth that has taken place during the mentor–mentee relationship and the opportunity to discuss a next phase or the end of the process.

Case study: mentoring relationships

It is customary to separate mentoring from performance management, as the power balance between mentor and mentee should be less hierarchical and directive than that between manager and employee. While the mentor may be more experienced, s/he acts as a listener and enabler for development that the mentee has chosen to undertake, rather than as a judge or evaluator. If you find that you are uncomfortable with what is deemed 'mentoring' within a professional environment, it is worth reflecting upon this point, and possibly further discussing your concerns with an individual within the relevant setting who has the power to change the way that mentoring is structured.

Reflection

Put yourself in the role of mentee, from the perspective of your own current professional situation. Imagine you are having a meeting with your mentor.

- What would constitute an ideal mentoring session for you?
- What would you want from a mentoring relationship?
- What would you expect from a mentoring relationship?
- What do you believe the boundaries of a mentoring relationship are?

Explore the implications if, for example, your mentor was a senior manager in your organisation.

Action Learning Sets

It is also possible for a form of mentoring to take place between equals, in an 'Action Learning Set' (ALS). These sets work through peer mentoring, and combine features of mentoring and action research. A typical ALS process would be structured as in the case study below.

Case study: Action Learning Sets

A group of six to eight people meet regularly over the period of one academic year, usually around once each half term. One member of the group acts as a facilitator, ensuring that ground rules are established and adhered to, that the members engage in effective listening and develop trust in one another ('what is said in the room remains in the room' is a very important ground rule in this respect) and acts to move the analysis of issues beyond the shallow or superficial, which may sometimes involve reflection upon the processes within the group itself.

It is up to each ALS to establish its own operational processes, but here is a very general set of guidelines for meetings that occur after the ground rules have been agreed:

- Each member updates the others on the 'headlines' of what has happened to them over the time between the last meeting (in a first meeting, this would involve introductions and discussions of the reasons for joining the ALS).
- The members then take it in turns to talk about a situation that they currently wish to explore. The ground rules will have determined how long each member 'holds the floor', and facilitators may use a timer for this purpose.
- When the issue has been presented, the members ask the presenter open questions to help the presenting member develop his/her reflection on the situation. Issues raised may include potential solutions, attitudes to issues and the potential for different types of behaviour. The facilitator needs to ensure that these are presented as open options rather than in the frame of 'if I were you, I would …'.
- The facilitator needs to ensure that individuals' issues are not 'swamped' by other members passing judgement, telling anecdotes from their own experience or diverting the discussion onto their own issues; the conversation must stay focused on the issue raised by the presenter.
- The presenter reviews the options that s/he considers feasible and decides upon his/her next action within the situation.
- The focus then moves to the next presenter.
- At the end of the session, the members reflect together on the various discussions, and how these have inputted to their own individual practice learning.
- Each member then actions the solution that they have decided upon in their workplace.
- Each member then reports on the results of this action at the next meeting, which leads in turn to further discussion and further plans for action.

Reflection

The processes of the ALS sound simple on paper, but in reality the role of the facilitator can become quite complex as some individuals 'clam up' in such a situation, and others either over-disclose or talk at length about problems that they present as insoluble, consequently rejecting all suggestions for action.

Consider the group of colleagues with whom you work. Do you think an ALS process would work for you? Consider the reasons for your response to this question, and whether there might be anything you could change to make success more likely.

Conclusion

This chapter has explored a range of questions that focus on the changing role of continuous professional development or, as we prefer to call it, professional learning. In a fast-changing world the need for professionals from early years, social care and health services to work together is more urgent than ever. As authors and as teachers and trainers of students on EYTS, QTS (Early Years) and academic, inter-disciplinary Early Years/Childhood Studies degrees, we hope this is reflected in a new era of inter-professional education (Aubrey, 2011) in which more collaborative ways of working occur, enhancing individual professional learning.

What is continuing professional development and why is it of such importance?

High-quality professional development for those who work with young children is much sought after within the UK nations, and within a wider international arena. Aspirations for a world-class education system must include continuing professional learning so that practitioners can access high-quality, internationally recognised continuing professional development pathways at all stages of their professional lives. From early piecemeal approaches to CPD, we are moving into a new era in England where collaboration though school alliances, school-to-school support, multi-agency collaborations and informal clusters of settings offer bespoke CPD activity. Collaboration both with EYTs and EYGPs in a range of settings, and across multi-agency boundaries, is a key feature for organisational development. Parallel to this at an individual level, we discussed the importance of reflection and outlined several reflective techniques – story writing and storytelling, action research and critical incident analysis were raised as useful tools to develop relevant professional knowledge and skills.

What are the stipulated professional expectations of Early Years Graduate Practitioners and Early Years Teachers in England?

A key issue is the general recognition that practice in early years should be led by a graduate. Since advances in our knowledge of neuronal development in the early 2000s we now fully recognise the huge importance of practice in the early years, and the breadth and depth of development that takes place between birth and the seventh birthday. The Danish pedagogue model was discussed, as was the new initiative of the Early Years Teacher (EYT) which replaced the previously successful Early Years Professional (EYP), and their relationship with Qualified Teacher Status (Early Years). Whilst EYTS is still relatively new, there are encouraging signs of the effectiveness of the programme nationally, building on the previous initiative of Early Years Professional Status, and the impact of EYPs and EYTs upon children's lives. The need for the value of graduate early years leaders to be better recognised in terms of pay and status was discussed, and it is hoped that readers of this book will pick up this mission in order to progress the situation of this still new profession. For more information on this point, visit the Prospect website www.prospect.org.uk/index?_ts=1

How can I make the most of my CPD activities?

In contrast to some practice in the past, we now have a deeper evidence base to substantiate the recent advances made in CPD. Activities include various ways of structuring 'communities of practice' of EYTs/EYGPs to extend their professional learning peer support to encourage experimentation and enable EYGPs/EYTs to collaboratively interpret their own goals, in both uni- and multi-professional groups. We considered various activities to structure dialogue that encourage review and reflection and support for evaluating learning through the lenses of hopes and aspirations, using personally selected starting points, and the need for allocated professional time to support such learning. Links between research and continuing professional development were discussed in the chapter, alongside the role of the portfolio/e-portfolio in action research and reflective practice. The professional journal is where much of the reflection engendered by action research is carried out. Professional development portfolios, at the heart of which lie these reflective journals, have a relatively long history in teacher training; however, the e-portfolio is a relatively new innovation. We proposed that the next stage for the reflective journal will be focused upon ongoing shared reflection through such e-portfolios, and to conclude, the chapter discussed different forms of mentoring as a further tool to enhance professional learning with dialogue, reflection and collaborative working integral to this process.

Recommended reading

Brock, A. (2012) Building a model of early years professionalism from practitioners' perspectives. *Journal of Early Childhood Research.* 11(1), 27–44.

Brock, A. (2014) *The Early Years Reflective Practice Handbook*. Abingdon: Routledge.

Cordingley, P. and Bell, M. (2012) *Understanding What Enables High Quality Professional Learning: A report on the research evidence*. CUREE and Pearson School Improvement. Available at: http://www.curee-paccts.com/files/publication/1297423037/Practitioner%20Use%20of%20Research%20Review.pdf

Ofsted (2010) *Good Professional Development in Schools*. London: Ofsted.

Wenger, E. (2000) *Communities of Practice: Learning, meaning and identity*. Cambridge: Cambridge University Press.

Whitehouse, C. (2011) *Effective Continuing Professional Development for Teachers*. London: Centre for Education Research and Policy. Available at: https://cerp.aqa.org.uk/sites/default/files/pdf_upload/CERP-RP-CW-19052011.pdf

Williams, K., Woolliams, M. and Spiro, J. (2012) *Reflective Writing*. London: Palgrave Macmillan.

Websites

Action Research Tips: www.jeanmcniff.com/ar-booklet.asp

Association for Coaching Tips for Action Learning Sets: www.associationforcoaching.com/media/uploads/coachinginorganisations/ACHGuide6.pdf

Association for Professional Development in Early Years: http://tactyc.org.uk

Coaching Network website: www.coachingnetwork.org.uk

Early Years Foundation Stage Forum: http://eyfs.info/home

International Professional Development Association: www.ipda.org.uk

Professional Development in Education (journal): www.tandfonline.com/loi/rjie20#.VbgMtPnff4U

References

Anning, A. (2010) 'Research' in early years settings: a pause for thought. *Early Years: An International Journal of Research and Development.* 30(2): 189–91.

Aubrey, C. (2011) *Leading and Managing in the Early Years* (2nd Edn). London: Sage.

Barbera, E. (2009) Mutual feedback in e-portfolio assessment: an approach to the netfolio system. *British Journal of Educational Technology.* 40(2), 342–57.

Barrett, H. (2013) *Classroom 2.0*. Retrieved from: www.slideshare.net/eportfolios/classroom20 4th August 2013.

BBC (2014) *Schools Urged to Take Two Year Olds into Nurseries*. Retrieved from: www.bbc.co.uk/news/education-26031574 24th July 2015.

Bell, B. and Gilbert, J. (1994) Teacher development as professional, personal, and social development. *Teaching and Teacher Education*. 10(5), 483–97.

Bell, M., Cordingley, P., Isham., C. and Davis., R. (2010) *Report of Professional Practitioner Use of Research Review: Practitioner engagement in and/or with research*. Coventry: CUREE, GTCE, LSIS & NTRP. Available at: www.curee-paccts.com/node/2303

Brock, A. (2012) Building a model of early years professionalism from practitioners' perspectives. *Journal of Early Childhood Research*. 11(1), 27–44.

Burnett, C. (2014) Teaching, research and further qualifications., in T. Cremin and J. Arthur (Eds) *Learning to Teach in the Primary School*. Abingdon, Routledge.

Chatham-Carpenter, A., Seawel, L. and Raschig, J. (2010) Avoiding the pitfalls: current practices and recommendations for ePortfolios in higher education. *Journal of Educational Technology Systems*. 38(4), 437–56.

Cochran-Smith, M. and Lytle, S. (1993) *Inside/Outside: Teacher research and knowledge*. New York: Teachers College Press.

Cordingley, P. (2011) *Sauce for the Goose: Learning entitlements that work for teachers as well as for their pupils*. Coventry: CUREE.

Danish National Federation of Early Childhood Teachers and Youth Educators (2006) *The Work of the Pedagogue: Roles and tasks*. Retrieved from www.bupl.dk/iwfile/BALG-7X4GBX/$file/The%20work%20of%20the%20pedagogue.pdf 12th July 2015.

DeSchon Hamlin, K. (2004) Beginning the journey: supporting reflection in early field experiences. *Reflective Practice*. 5 (2), 167–79.

DfES (2005) *National Framework for Mentoring and Coaching: What is leading teaching?* London: DfES.

Early Education Advisory Group (EEAG) (2005) Annex 3, Paper 05/5/9, Item M.

European Commission (2015) *The Bologna Process and the European Higher Education Area*. Retrieved from: http://ec.europa.eu/education/policy/higher-education/bologna-process_en.htm 24th July 2015.

Evans, L. (2002) What is teacher development? *Oxford Review of Education*. 28(1), 123–37.

Fellows, C. (2010) *Student Perspective*. Retrieved from: www.pebblepad.co.uk/pp2010/ss04.pdf 10th January 2015.

Francis, F. (2009) *The role of professional development in redefining the place of primary teachers*, NaPTEC Annual Conference, Oxford, September.

Fullan, M. and Hargreaves, A. (1992) Teacher development and educational change, in M. Fullan and A. Hargreaves (Eds) *Teacher Development and Educational Change*. London: Falmer, pp. 1–9.

Henderson, E., Hogan, H., Grant, A. and Berlin, A. (2003) Conflict and coping strategies: a qualitative study of student attitudes to significant event analysis. *Medical Education*. 37, 438–46.

Hord, S.M. and Sommers, W.A. (2008). *Leading Professional Communities: Voices from research and practice*. Thousand Oaks, CA: Corwin Press.

International Step by Step Association (2010) *Competent Educators of the 21st Century: Principles of quality pedagogy*. Budapest: ISSA.

Jay, J. and Johnson, K. (2002) Capturing complexity: a typology of reflective practice for teacher education. *Teaching and Teacher Education*. 1(18), 73–85.

Kempton, J. (2013) *To Teach, To Learn: More effective continuous professional development for teachers*. London: CentreForum.

Kuit, J., Reay, G. and Freeman, R. (2001) Experiences of reflective teaching. *Active Learning in Higher Education.* 2(2), 128–42.

Larrivee, B. (2000) Transforming teaching practice: becoming the critically reflective teacher. *Reflective Practice.* 1(3), 294–307.

Lave, J. and Wenger, E. (1991) *Situated Learning: Legitimate peripheral participation.* Cambridge: Cambridge University Press.

Lewis, H. (2014) Oral Statement. *A National Model of Professional Learning.* The Record of Proceedings. National Assembly for Wales, Cardiff, June.

McArdle, K. and Coutts, N. (2003) A strong core of qualities – a model of the professional educator that moves beyond reflection. *Studies in Continuing Education.* 2(25), 225–37.

McGill, M. (2000) *A Sting in the Tale: Use of anecdote as a research tool*, Retrieved from: www.aare.edu.au/data/publications/2000/mcg00120.pdf 24th July 2015.

McKibben, J. and Pawson, G. (2014) Early years teachers as influential leaders, in J. Johnson (Ed.) *Becoming an Early Years Teacher.* Maidenhead: Open University/McGraw Hill.

Moss, P. (2000) *Workforce Issues in Early Childhood Education and Care.* Retrieved from: www.childpolicyintl.org/publications/Workforce%20Issues%20in%20Early%20Childhood%20Education%20and%20Care_Peter%20Moss.pdf 24th July 2015.

National College for Teaching and Leadership (2013) *Teachers' Standards (Early Years).* London: NCTL.

Nutbrown, C. (2012) *Foundations for Quality: The independent review of early education and childcare qualifications.* Final Report. London: DfE.

Nutbrown, C. and Clough, P. (2014) *Early Childhood Education: History, philosophy and experience* (2nd Edn). London: Sage.

OECD (2005) *Education at a Glance: OECD indicators 2005.* Paris: OECD Publishing.

Ofsted (2006) *The Logical Chain: Continuing professional development in effective schools.* London: Ofsted.

Parsloe, E. and Wray, M. (2000) *Coaching and Mentoring.* London: Kogan Page.

Pelliccione, K., Dixon, L. and Giddings, G. (2005) *A Pre-Service Teacher Education Initiative to Enhance Reflection through the Development of e-Portfolios.* Retrieved from: http://cms.ascilite.org.au/conferences/brisbane05/blogs/proceedings/60_Pelliccione.pdf 28th May 2013.

Pillay, H. and McCrindle, A. (2005) Distributed and relative nature of professional expertise. *Studies in Continuing Education.* 1(27), 67–88.

Poet, H., Rudd, P. and Kelly, J. (2010) *Survey of Teachers 2010. Support to improve teaching practice.* London: NFER/GTC.

Roach, A. and Kratochwill, T. (2004) Evaluating school climate and school culture. *Teaching Exceptional Children.* 1(37), 10–17.

Schön, D.A. (1983) *The Reflective Practitioner: How professionals think in action.* London: Temple Smith.

Stoll, L., Harris, A. and Handscomb, G. (2012) *Great Professional Development which Leads to Great Pedagogy: Nine claims from research. Research and development network national themes: Theme two.* Nottingham: National College for School Leadership.

Sutton Trust (2015) *Developing Teachers. Improving professional development for teachers.* London: The Sutton Trust.

Sylva, K., Melhuish, E., Sammons, P., Siraj-Blatchford, I. and Taggart, B. (2004) *The Effective Provision of Pre-School Education (EPPE) project.* Retrieved from: www.ioe.ac.uk/RB_Final_Report_3-7.pdf 11th July 2015.

Talbot, M. (2002) Reflective practice? New insights or more-of-the-same? Thoughts on an auto-biographical critical incident analysis. *Reflective Practice.* 3(2), 225–9.

Thomson, B. (2006) *Growing People: Learning and developing from day to day experience.* Oxford: Chandos.

Timperley, H., Wilson, A., Barrar, H. and Fung, I. (2007) *Teacher Professional Learning and Development: Best evidence synthesis iteration (BES).* Wellington, New Zealand: Ministry of Education. Available at: http://www.oecd.org/edu/school/48727127.pdff

Tripp, D. (1993) *Critical Incidents in Teaching.* London: RoutledgeFalmer.

Underwood, C. (2008) *What is Web 2.0?* Retrieved from: http://collaborationevangelist.com/about-underwood-partners/what-is-20 7th August 2013.

Villegas-Reimers, E. (2003) *Teacher Professional Development: An international review of the literature.* Paris: UNESCO, International Institute for Educational Planning.

Weiss, E. and Weiss, S. (2001) Doing reflective supervision with student teachers in a professional development culture. *Reflective Practice.* 2(2), 125–54.

Wenger, E. (2000) *Communities of Practice: Learning, meaning and identity.* Cambridge: Cambridge University Press.

Wolfe, S. and Alexander, R. (2008) *Argumentation and Dialogic Teaching: Alternative pedagogies for a changing world.* Retrieved from: www.robinalexander.org.uk/wp-content/uploads/2012/05/wolfe alexander.pdf 5th August 2013.

10 The child, the family and the state

International perspectives

Pam Jarvis

CHAPTER OVERVIEW

This chapter will outline some of the principal contemporary international debates relating to the provision of care for young children. The emphasis will not be upon providing readers with a set of 'answers', but upon encouraging them to engage with the issues and to come to their own considered position. It is very possible that you will decide that there are *no* conclusive answers to some of the debates identified. The chapter will address the following questions:

✔ How do we provide education and care for young children in contemporary societies?
✔ What are the dominant contemporary models of the child and of society?
✔ What are the debates relating to the role that early years education and care should play in contemporary societies?
✔ What is the 'schism' between the provision of early years education and care for children under and over three?

The recommended reading list at the end of this chapter will introduce readers to a range of texts and online resources in which to read further on these topics.

Introduction: How do we provide education and care for young children in contemporary societies?

In 2008, UNICEF published the Child Care Transition Report, which reflected:

> A great change is coming over childhood in the world's richest countries. Today's rising generation is the first in which a majority are spending a large part of early childhood in some form of out-of-home child care ... Whether the child care transition will represent

an advance or a setback – for today's children and tomorrow's world – will depend on the response.

(UNICEF, 2008, p. 1)

The report was prepared from the perspective of rolling cultural change for families throughout the western world. From the perspective of putting women back into the home, and men into paid labour that had been prevalent in the mid-twentieth century, the emphasis had moved towards the expectation that the typical family budget must depend upon earned income from both parents. Barbara Tizard, a psychologist who worked closely with John Bowlby (see chapter 2), remembers:

> Soon after the end of the Second World War ... there was a big movement to get women, in many ways liberated by their wartime work experiences, to stay at home. Professional women like myself ... became worried that they would damage their children by returning to work even on a part-time basis, and those who worked full-time were widely criticised.

(Tizard, 2009, p. 902)

However, the employment rate for women in the UK continued to rise over the years that followed, illustrated in Figure 10.1, which indicates a very rapid pace of change in the ten years between 1985 and 1995.

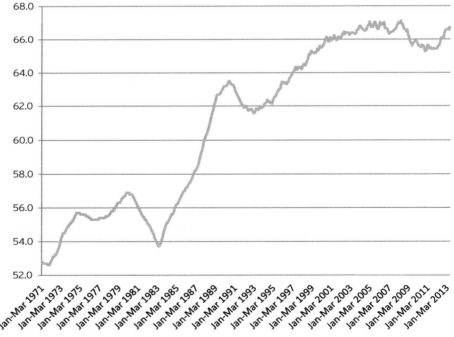

Figure 10.1 UK female employment 1971–2013

Source: Data drawn from Office for National Statistics (2013).

This was a demographic development that was mirrored across the western world (Cohen, 2012). This chapter will explore how various nations dealt with this situation, and the debates that arose relating to the care and education of young children, many of which are still 'live' today. A key question revolves around the balance between parental leave and subsidised childcare and how this corresponds to the age of the child. In terms of parental leave, there are huge differences between nations (see Table 10.1).

Table 10.1 International comparison of childcare leave

Nation	Length of leave	% wages paid
United Kingdom	52 weeks	90% for the first six weeks; thereafter £139.58 or 90% of wage if lower for the next 33 weeks. The last 13 weeks are statutory but unpaid
United States	12 weeks	No national programme – some states offer a small sum. If the mother works for a company with under 50 employees, she does not have any automatic right to the 12-week leave period either
Iceland	12 weeks	80%
Germany	14 weeks	100%
Japan	14 weeks	67%
Malta	14 weeks	100%
New Zealand	52 weeks	100% for 14 weeks, then 38 weeks are statutory but unpaid
Switzerland	14 weeks	100%
Belgium	15 weeks	82% for the first 30 days, then 75% for the remaining time
Finland	15 weeks	70%
Austria	16 weeks	100%
France	16 weeks	100%
Netherlands	16 weeks	100%
Spain	16 weeks	100%
Greece	17 weeks	50%
Australia	18 weeks	100% for 18 weeks only per child, but each parent can take up to 12 months leave
Italy	5 months	80%
Ireland	26 weeks	80%
Czech Republic	28 weeks	60%
Norway	46 weeks	100% for 36 weeks, 80% for the remaining 10 weeks
Canada	52 weeks	55% for 17 weeks. The remaining time can be taken by either parent, and payment depends on the provincial policy
Denmark	52 weeks	100%
Sweden	60 weeks	80%

Source: Data drawn from *The Huffington Post, Canada* (2012, online).

Calculating the amount of support that different nations offer to families, and how it is offered can be quite complex. The amount of maternity leave offered, and how it may be split between both parents is only the beginning of the story. The level of subsidy offered for childcare is also important. Traditionally, the Scandinavian nations have offered the highest subsidies for childcare, while the Anglo-American nations, the US in particular, have offered the least. For example, in 2014 in Sweden, parents were expected to contribute 3% of their gross income up to a maximum cost of £113 per month per child, with reductions for sibling pairs and groups. In the US there are no national subsidies for childcare, although some states run programmes for low-income families, and some employees in large companies may have access to childcare places subsidised by their employers. The US government has recently shown a desire to move on in this respect in its passing of the Child Care and Development Block Grant Act in 2014. Ongoing information can be found on this topic on the US Office of Child Care website: www.acf.hhs.gov/programs/occ.

The cost of childcare has been a topic of ongoing concern in many western nations. In 2015, the Family and Childcare Trust found that, in the UK, it cost families approximately £115.45 on average for a child aged under two attending a childcare setting for 25 hours a week, which works out at £6,003 per year. They concluded that 'the reality is that for far too many families it simply does not pay to work' (Rutter, 2015, p. 3).

Whether this will be remedied by the Conservative Government elected in May 2015 remains to be seen. On 13th May, David Cameron promised that he would fast-track legislation to ensure that children over three were eligible for 30 hours of free childcare a week (Lepper, 2015). This was further cemented in the Queen's Speech at the opening of the new Parliament on 27th May 2015 (BBC, 2015). However, this does not deal with the issue of care for children between one and two years of age. Issues relating to the provision of care for children under three arise in many nations, and will therefore be revisited below.

International comparisons of the costs of childcare to families as a percentage of their family income indicate that families in the UK are in a poor position in comparison with other families in the western world, paying 33% of their household budget towards childcare in comparison with 6% in Sweden, 8% in Denmark, Norway and Germany, and 11% in France. Even US parents pay less at 19%, and the European Union average is 12% (Think Left, 2011). When child-linked benefits and tax reductions are taken into account, UK parents also fare poorly in comparison with other nations, having to pay more for childcare with less eligibility for tax deductions (Full Fact.org, 2103).

In 2002, a meeting of the EU states in Barcelona set targets for the provision of care for children in the EU nations, proposing that by 2010, in all EU nations, there would be provision for 90% of children over three and for 33% of children under three. By 2010, the UK had hit both targets, although in both cases this related to part-time rather than full-time care, while in the Scandinavian countries, most of which began from the position of full target compliance, the provision was far more likely to be full-time (European Programme for Employment and Social Solidarity, 2014).

Some nations had made very little progress, such as the Czech Republic; however, this related to the singular Czech approach to parental leave:

Following the period of maternity leave, Czech parents are entitled to parental leave. After parental leave, there is no guaranteed return to exactly the same job but the employer is obliged to offer a position corresponding to the parent's qualifications up to the child's third birthday. According to 2011 data from the Ministry of Labour and Social Affairs of the Czech Republic, only 1.8% of Czech fathers take parental leave.

(Europa, 2015, online)

This might lead us to wonder whether, rather than juggling complicated figures relating to benefits, taxation rates and payments to childcare settings, it would be easier to follow the Czech example. However, while an entitlement to three years of 'parental leave' from the workplace might seem to be a measure which empowers parents to choose home-based care for children under three, it has led to some reluctance amongst Czech employers to employ women of child-bearing age, and a subtle pressure on mothers (but not fathers) to become full-time carers; this can be illustrated by the tiny number of Czech fathers who take parental leave (Sokačová, 2011). This evokes the situation that Tizard (2011) describes emerging from the immediate post World War II milieu in the UK: increasing gender discrimination, threatening hard-won rights and magnifying psychological and societal pressures upon mothers of young children.

 Case study: funding childcare

Australia has recently published an extensive review into the provision of services for young children, which came to the following conclusion:

> The Australian Government should combine the current funding for Child Care Rebate, Child Care Benefit and the Jobs Education and Training Child Care Fee Assistance to support a single child-based subsidy, to be known as the Early Care and Learning Subsidy (ECLS). ECLS would be available for children attending all mainstream approved ECEC services, whether they are centre-based or home-based.
>
> (Australian Government Productivity Committee, 2014, p. 44)

Reflection

How do you think your nation should fund care for children below the school starting age, and why? Consider:

- Length of maternity leave and percentage of earnings to be paid
- Subsidies for childcare and education for children under three
- Subsidies for childcare and education for children over three
- The roles of both mothers and fathers in the pattern of parental leave.

What are the dominant contemporary models of the child and of society?

You will have found the term 'children as human capital' used throughout this book. This describes a concept rooted in measuring the worth of children via a projection of the extent to which it is presumed that they will be able to contribute to society in the future, in terms of creating wealth in a culture dominated by international movements of capital between people, companies and nations.

Childcare provided on a commercial basis becomes an integral part of this system, and consequently, providers are expected to offer 'value for money'. In the UK and US in particular, this translates to an environment in which children's cognitive skills become the overwhelming focus, to enable them to progress academically and become 'school ready' in the sense that they will be able to successfully 'jump through the hoops' presented to them in regular standard tests, to eventually fill an employment role that will amass capital for themselves, their employer and their nation. Campbell Barr (2012, p. 424) comments that 'future returns are based on the acquisition of human capital (principally in the form of laying the foundations for later learning) and the contribution that this can make to the knowledge economy'.

In a literature review focused on early years education undertaken for the Scottish Parliament, Stephen (2006) proposes that justification of practice from a perspective of future development is rejected by many education theorists as a politically dominated approach. In 2014, Jarvis *et al.* elaborated upon this topic, commenting:

> It is important to support every generation of children in their development of transferable skills and independent learning abilities so that they can keep abreast of ongoing societal developments. No Western generation following the industrial revolution has ever been able to fully predict the world in which their children are going to live as adults.
>
> (Jarvis *et al.*, 2014a, pp. 294–5)

The 'children as human capital' approach focuses on children as human resources in society; in the sense of sociological theory, it is a *functionalist* approach, rejecting the concept of human beings as autonomous, self-determining individuals. The explanation given for this approach by governments is generally that of breaking cycles of deprivation to make children fit for employment; however, if we cannot accurately predict what that employment is going to be, it can be argued that this is a risky strategy. The other, more obvious issue is the potential violation of rights of self-determination that signatory nations to the United Nations Convention on the Rights of the Child (UNCRC) have promised their child populations (see chapter 4). Ken Spours, writing in *The New Statesman*, comments:

> The abiding metaphor of education is now a race, a global race in which every country and every person has to become ever more competitive. The best nursery, followed by the best school, the best university all to get the highest paying job. Along the way we learn to compete and to be in debt. Our children and their teachers become stressed and anxious in this arms race that can never end.
>
> (Spours, 2015, online)

The original meaning of the Latin 'educere' which gave rise to the English word 'education' was to 'lead out' (related to the modern English term 'educe'). This describes a concept that constructs a learner as a person who has inherent individual talents and skills which can be nurtured towards independence and self-determination, particularly in young children, who need sensitively judged support as their personalities and preferences emerge. Such ideas can be found at the heart of the philosophies espoused by the pioneers in early education you read about in chapter 1; for example, Pestalozzi, Froebel, McMillan and Isaacs. A comprehensive review of early primary education was undertaken by British education policy expert Bridget Plowden in 1967, who had been immersed within such ideas during her own training. Her stated position was that the child, not a politically dominated curriculum, should be 'at the heart of the educational process' (Gillard, 2004, online). Such views are most closely related to the sociological approach of *interactionism*, which views society as comprised of individuals, all with their own unique personalities and talents. The provision of services for children and their families can still be viewed as an integral element of society from this perspective; however, the focus is, in this frame, upon giving every child an equal chance to develop his/her individuality within a safe environment in which his/her health and well-being are protected, alongside developmentally and individually appropriate enrichment.

A key difference between these two models of the child emerges from the ways in which measurements of 'success' or 'failure' are constructed within the resulting education systems. If a child is expected to fit quite a narrow niche through the inculcation of a highly defined skills set, it is relatively easy to develop standard tests to measure their progress towards this. If, on the other hand, the goal is to nurture individual development of skills and talents, the imposition of standard testing is far more difficult; moreover, within a culture of individual development, such testing is unlikely to be such a central element of the process. Rogoff and Toma (1997) describe rigid curriculumisation as 'transmit and test', while Oberhumer (2001) proposes that such frameworks arise within the context of public accountability for producing workers who will be able to compete within a global economy – what we have called 'the production of human capital' throughout this book.

Within such a highly cost-and-benefit driven culture, some western governments, particularly those of the UK and US have developed a culture that constructs young human beings as 'standard models' expected to develop along a standard trajectory; this has also brought in its wake a culture of blame with respect to teachers and practitioners, who are seen to be doing their jobs poorly if their pupils do not 'tick the boxes' at pre-designated times. James Hempsall, National Support Director for Achieving Two Year Olds, comments on the *Nursery World* website:

> If school readiness means we support children to develop their key skills in communication, speaking, listening and questioning, social and emotional well-being, and physical development, then count me in. If it is about producing learning robots trained to comply with a rigid and inflexible education system, then I am less keen on the idea.
>
> (Hempsall, 2014, online)

The 'school readiness' issue sits at the heart of the most compelling contemporary early years debate, and it is now moving outwards from the UK and US into the developing nations.

Reflection: school readiness

British researchers Whitebread and Bingham commented:

> It is not **whether** a child is ready to learn, but **what** a child is ready to learn … The model of 'readiness for school' is attractive to governments as it seemingly delivers children into primary school ready to conform to classroom procedures and even able to perform basic reading and writing skills. However, from a pedagogical perspective this approach fuels an increasingly dominant notion of education as 'transmission and reproduction', and of early childhood as preparation for school rather than for 'life'.
>
> (2011, pp. 2–3)

- How do you construct the term 'school readiness? Do you agree with Whitebread and Bingham's criticism?
- Do you think having to comply with standard assessments has had some influence on the way you think about children's learning?
- Has reading this chapter so far helped you to question some of the ideas that you previously took for granted?

What are the debates relating to the role that early years education and care should play in contemporary societies?

The nursery as the engine of human capital production

It can be argued that the production of human capital is currently the dominant discourse of state-funded education in nations such as the UK, France and the US. In the US, the national initiative 'Race to the Top' (RTTP) controls state funding to schools on the basis of their adherence to nationally decreed standards, which is measured through standardised testing (The White House, 2009). This created an outcry when some states proposed that they were going to routinely test children under five; writing in *The Slate* Dana Goldstein comments 'What could be crazier, after all, than the prospect of a kindergartner gripping a No. 2 pencil in his tiny fist, looking down in confusion at a Scantron sheet he couldn't hope to decode, and bursting into tears?' (Goldstein, 2011, online). France integrated its pre-school system into primary schools in 1989, and French early years education based in their *école maternelle* system is highly 'school readiness' influenced; children are closely trained in particular skills – especially literacy and numeracy – with a view to performance on later standard testing. There is currently growing interest in developing a French curriculum for children under three due to concern relating to 'parental competencies' (Rayna, 2010, p. 121).

In the UK, the 2015 election outcome of a Conservative-led majority in England, and an overwhelming Scottish National Party majority in Scotland, is likely to make for a growing disparity between the early years education and care systems within these nations over the next five years. It is likely that Scotland will follow Wales' early lead in developing a rights-based, social-justice-oriented approach in early years education (see Chapter 5), while English Conservatives are set upon further formalisation of the early years environment, pursuing the top-down school readiness agenda that has been infiltrating from the 'transmit and test' mainstream state education culture over the past two decades, under a succession of Conservative, New Labour and Conservative-Liberal Democrat Coalition governments.

> Today's fixation on testing and the requirement to design curricula around its requirements is historically unprecedented in any early childhood education philosophy. No longer is the child the centre of the pedagogy; rather, the approach is reversed, with adult-imposed subject matter relentlessly driving the goals of education to create a different landscape for childhood in this present generation ... Qualitative educational practices structured on research results that document favourable long-term effects are replaced with short-term targets of arbitrary assessment scores, delineated in identifiable categories.
>
> (Jarvis *et al.*, 2014b, p. 60)

The assessment regime for young children under the current English Early Years Foundation Stage and Key Stage 1 curriculum is, in summary, as follows:

- The average school entry age of four and a half is one of the earliest in the world. Schools focused on children's 'performance' in standard testing now exert pressure for all children in a specific school year to start in the relevant September. In the past, 'summer-birthday' children more commonly started in the calendar year in which they became five. Some children may therefore be admitted to school only a few days after their fourth birthday.
- The Early Years Foundation Stage has 17 early learning goals against which a progress report must be made at two, and a summative assessment must be made at transfer to Year 1.
- The government is currently moving towards formal testing of children's skills in literacy and numeracy on their entry to reception – 'baseline testing', which is an especially onerous prospect for summer-born children.
- There is also a test of reading skills in Year 1, which use words devoid of meaning to assess children's mechanical reading skills (decoding of phonics). This is reminiscent of the pre-industrial approaches to literacy instruction which were rejected 200 years ago by Pestalozzi and Owen (see chapter 1).

The school-readiness culture of early years education has now moved far beyond the UK and US. Baker (2015) describes a focus on meeting academic goals and accountability in Abu Dhabi, a nation which is currently developing its early years education system through a drive to blend western and Arabic cultures, with a firm emphasis on literacy and numeracy rather than play: 'drill and fill ... there isn't enough time for play in an academic curriculum' (p. 30). Frewen *et al.* (2015) found a similar situation in Singapore, proposing that the context of the economy is important for moulding early years education, reflecting upon 'a need to rethink traditional assumptions regarding parenting practices' (p. 46). They propose that contemporary 'parents prefer kindergartens that they believe will give their children the skills necessary to cope with a rigorous primary education curriculum' (p. 42), with many additionally enrolling their children in supplementary 'enrichment' classes. Ying Hu *et al.* (2015) correspondingly found intense competition between parents in China for admission into top-quality early years public provision, which is disproportionately found in urban areas. This issue tends to be rather circular, given that as in England, a poor inspection grade leads to loss of enrolments, which impacts on funding levels, with the risk of public funding being withdrawn. Miyahara and Meyers (2008) additionally list Cambodia, Fiji, Lao, Mongolia, The Phillipines, Thailand and Vietnam as nations developing their early years education regimes from the perspective of a human capital/school readiness approach.

The nursery as an instrument of social justice

The Scandinavian approach to early years education is rather different, rooted in a culture which prizes social justice and consequently constructs early years education as an enabling endeavour that gives every child the opportunity to develop in an individually enriching environment. You have met this approach before in chapter 1, in the ethos of many of the pioneers. In this frame, children are not viewed as future generators of capital, but as people whose holistic development is to be nurtured. There is a particular emphasis on social skills, and children as rights-bearing citizens both in the present and the future.

This tradition is particularly strong in Denmark, in which publicly subsidised childcare has been available for nearly a century, since 1919. Brostrom and Hansen (2010) comment that Danish early years practitioners, known as pedagogues, actively reject the label of 'teacher'. The emphasis of their practice is upon 'independence and a sense of connectedness' (p. 89). Danish early years education is not administered through the Education Ministry but through the Ministry of Social Affairs, as a decentralised process with no national framework. Brostrom and Hansen (2010) describe Danish early years practice as highly focused on children's individual needs, with the practitioners engaging in 'reflection, theory on phenomena that concern teaching, upbringing, care, plus possible effects and impacts' (p. 206). These researchers comment that the Danish Social Service Act (1998) requires that pedagogues facilitate experiences and activities likely to stimulate imagination, creativity and linguistic skills, providing each child with space and opportunities to play, learn, investigate, engage in physical exercise and socialise with each other.

Early years practice traditions in the other Scandinavian nations are very similar. Greve and Solheim (2010, p. 161) describe the early years education tradition in Norway as 'built on a social pedagogical foundation more than on preparing for school' but raise concerns that under the influence of dominant Anglo-American culture 'this tradition is maybe at a changing point'. Hannikainen (2010) comments that in Finland, the early years education tradition involves intertwining dimensions of care, education and teaching depending on the age of the child, promoting positive self-image, expressive, interactive skills and development of thinking, while Johansson and Emilson (2010) propose that Swedish early years education is based on a model of the child as a vulnerable individual, who nevertheless has his/her own particular areas of competence and individual rights as a citizen of the Swedish nation. Pre-school experience is, through this lens, seen as the human right of every child in Sweden, and as a consequence, 46% of one-year-olds and 90% of two- to three-year-olds attend Sweden's heavily subsidised pre-schools. The prime adult responsibility for young children is viewed as holistic socialisation towards eventual citizenship, with all adults considered to be collectively responsible in this endeavour, not just the child's family and/or a delegated 'teacher'.

The move into primary education also comes later in the Scandinavian nations, at seven in Finland and Sweden, and six in Denmark and Norway, and is not dominated by a formal or centralised curriculum even at this stage. The incompatibility of the Scandinavian social justice culture of education with the Anglo-American production of human capital orientation cannot be over-emphasised, with the result that suddenly transporting a Scandinavian early years regime into a contemporary English or US environment would be unlikely to succeed.

The early years education ethos in Scandinavian nations is, however, similar to that advocated in the UK a century ago by Margaret McMillan, at the dawn of the development of modern early years education; this extends to Scandinavian development of open-air pedagogies through their Forest School projects (McCree and McCree, 2012). McMillan used her position as first president of the fledgling Nursery School Association to publicise the social justice driven practice in her South London nursery as the most beneficial approach for both children *and* their families, providing not only education but sustenance and facilities that were not available to economically deprived urban families. However, she was unable to overcome the opposition to this model both from those in government, who raised concerns about the expense to taxpayers, and from those in her own association who felt that a focus upon the development of cognition rather than socialisation should be the main purpose of early years education (Jarvis and Liebovich, 2015). McMillan was still engaged in heated public debate about this issue at the time of her death in 1931. Had she been able to continue, and win more influential people to her way of thinking, the UK early years education and care system might have developed more securely along a social-justice-oriented trajectory.

Case study: the Swedish nursery

www.youtube.com/watch?v=ecinNaR32Qs
www.youtube.com/watch?v=cmdHvkcMhZ4
www.youtube.com/watch?v=eo1AJWqClww

These three links will take you to a video made by Teacher's TV and now housed on YouTube, which follow the everyday practice of a Swedish pre-school, including the nature of the considerable public subsidies that fund its holistic provisions for the children.

Reflection

It would be a good idea to take notes as you watch, reflecting on the difference between your everyday practice and that of the Swedish practitioners. It should be noted that this video was made in the early 2000s, and that some of the practice may have changed since then. As such, it would be a good idea to follow up with some research on contemporary Swedish pre-school practices, to consider how they have changed. You may possibly find some evidence that suggests some recent infiltration from contemporary Anglo-American concepts.

What is the 'schism' between the provision of early years education and care for children under and over three?

A marked 'stage difference' between services provided for children aged between birth and three, and three and six, can be detected in most western nations. In England, this is quite strongly represented in the generic entitlement to free hours of childcare only *after* the third birthday. At the time of writing, this is for 15 hours per week for 38 weeks a year, but the newly elected Conservative Government has pledged, in its election manifesto, to double this to 30 hours, from 2017. There are, however, problems looming, given that nursery owners and managers have previously claimed that the hourly rate paid by the government is not sufficient to cover their costs; therefore, they have had to raise the price for those hours of care for which parents have to pay. So it would seem, if state-subsidised hours of care are doubled and the per-hour rate paid remains the same, the resulting lack of funding will create a supply crisis:

> Claire Schofield, NDNA's (National Day Nurseries Association) director of policy, membership and communications, said: 'NDNA has long campaigned for nursery funding reform to address the chronic shortfalls experienced by our nursery members across the country ... NDNA research shows that 85 per cent of nurseries in England are making losses on the current 15 hours per week free childcare, an average of £809 per year for each funded child'. Ms Schofield believes that 'more funded hours without a better hourly rate for providers would be a disaster for nurseries and would lead to bigger financial losses and even closures'.
>
> (Learner, 2015, online)

This issue will no doubt be the source of more negotiation and headlines as the situation unfolds over the next two years. One possible outcome could be that childcare costs for children under three might greatly increase in order to make up the shortfall, which will create a different crisis, for parents of younger children. In pursuit of an alternative, less publicly damaging solution, the Conservatives have already attempted to reduce ratios of adults to children during the 2010–15 Coalition government, which was swiftly vetoed by their Liberal Democrat partners. The Conservative Minister for Children at that time, Elizabeth Truss, used French early years policy and practice as a model for her proposals, commenting that French teachers were supervising large groups of young children using structured instruction: 'We want children to learn to listen to a teacher, learn to respect an instruction, so that they are ready for school' (*The Guardian*, 2013, online). This again raises the English school readiness culture that now stands to be fully unleashed under a government in which Conservatives are in complete control.

The lower status of education and care for under threes is also a feature in Norway, which is reflected in a 'schism' within early years practitioner training, in which those who work with over threes are expected to reach a higher academic level than those who work with under threes (Greve and Solheim, 2010). Other nations also report lower status for practitioners working with children under three. For example, Hannikainen (2010) clearly illustrates this situation in her finding that there are very few Finnish doctoral dissertations focusing on practice with under threes as compared with those focusing upon practice with over threes.

This situation is also mirrored in France, in terms of a dearth of early childhood departments in French universities, and very few French publications on play-based learning; however, there is growing French interest in research with under threes ongoing in other nations (Rayna, 2010). French infants under three are most typically cared for by their families, or in daycare centres under the management of paediatric nurses in which a care rather than education culture is paramount.

Italy recently developed a policy for under threes through a 2007 expansion programme, although services remain patchy and variable. Musatti and Picchio (2010) report that while 96% of over threes attend *Schola dell'infanzia* (Italian nursery schools), the Nido service for under threes reaches only 10% of children in this age group, and parents pay around a quarter of the costs.

In the latter years of the Coalition government, England had a heated discussion about the provision of daycare for children between two and three, in which the dominant Conservative faction proposed that two-year-olds, particularly those from disadvantaged backgrounds, would benefit from school attendance. The Chief Inspector of Schools, Michael Wilshaw, said:

> Too many of our poorest children are getting an unsure start because the early years system is letting them down. What children facing serious disadvantage need is high-quality, early education from the age of two delivered by skilled practitioners, led by a teacher, in a setting that parents can recognise and access. These already exist. They are called schools.
>
> (McArdle, 2014, online)

The reference to 'high-quality education' evokes the formal, 'school readiness' construction of Elizabeth Truss (*The Guardian*, 2013), which brings us back to education as the production of human capital agenda. Wilshaw's proposed solution has already been applied by the French government through the admission of a small number of two-year-olds, largely from disadvantaged backgrounds, to their highly formal early years education system (Le Bouteillec et al., 2014). Rayna (2010) additionally reports a French interest in developing services for children under three whose parents are judged as lacking in competency, which suggests a similar deficit approach to that taken by David Cameron in his targeting of English Children's Centres towards 'problem families' (see chapter 4). It is interesting to note the social construction dominating both nations: that such 'inadequacy' needs to be addressed in a narrow drive to make young children cognitively 'school ready' rather than by dealing with the range of complex social, emotional and cognitive issues that emerge within families as a whole as a consequence of restricted access to culturally appropriate material resources.

In an article outlining a range of evidence that points to the vital requirement for children under three to build social skills in informal interaction, Jarvis commented:

> Schooling infants is ... commensurate with placing a young animal in a cage. Human beings evolved in a niche in which the requirement to learn how to engage in complex

spontaneous interaction is paramount. Taking short cuts in early childhood in pursuit of processing human beings into units of human capital as quickly as possible risks the production of 'damaged goods'. The question for the English government should not be how to find funds to build more schools and put more teachers into more classrooms to deal with an increasing number of ever-younger pupils. Instead, it should be about supporting families and local communities to care for and educate young children within environments that are most appropriate to their biologically evolved needs.

(Jarvis, 2015, online)

A recent Australian government review into the provision of education and care for young children came to a similar conclusion, proposing 'Early intervention programs to address the development needs of children from disadvantaged backgrounds should be underpinned by research' (Australian Government Productivity Committee, 2014, p. 47).

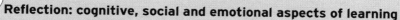

Reflection: cognitive, social and emotional aspects of learning

What do you think? Should the emphasis of early years education for children under three be principally upon the development of 'school readiness' cognitive skills in a highly adult-directed environment, or upon the development of social and communication skills in a child-led environment? Or might there be a middle way? You can use the Recommended reading at the end of this chapter to help you research this question.

Case study: an alternative viewpoint

On 27th April 2015, Vanessa Olorenshaw wrote on *The Huffington Post* blog:

> There is such an imbalance in popular debate that there has been article after article about 'free hours', celebrating the dawn of a new consensus: each political party engaging in a one-upmanship contest on the issue. That contest neglects families who wish for one parent to be in with a chance of staying at home with their children...
>
> So far this election season, it seems that no mention is being made of children outside of a nursery environment ... the media is airbrushing parental care out of debate and policymakers are clapping their hands with glee – keen for everyone to be an economic drone ... yet it is seen as a victory that more and more mothers are being forced by financial pressures to enter the workplace, and a victory that all main political parties are unanimously pursuing childcare ...
>
> The way in which political parties are ignoring the wishes of many families, and the way the media enables and feeds this agenda, is fundamentally undemocratic.
>
> (Olorenshaw, 2015, online)

Reflection

What do you think, if we consider Olorenshaw's views with respect to children under three? Do you think she is right, or that her ideas are outdated and anti-feminist? We have seen earlier in the chapter that, in the Czech Republic, national policy aimed at children being cared for in their own homes until their third birthday resulted in a situation that damaged women's career prospects, although it was not implemented with this idea in mind. We have also seen that the agenda of the post war government in the UK resulted in a huge burden of guilt for mothers of young children who chose, or were economically impelled, to engage in paid labour outside the home. But has the pendulum now swung too far in the opposite direction, with mothers who choose to remain at home being stigmatised?

Conclusion

This chapter has explored a range of questions that focus on some of the key issues emerging from some contemporary societies across the world relating to the provision of education and care for young children. It does not seek to cover all possible issues; if it did, the length would increase to the extent that it could fill a large book just upon this one topic. For example, we have not given consideration to the way that traditional childcare proceeds in pre-industrial societies, of which there are still several around the world, although in ever decreasing numbers. We have also not explored specific early years frameworks, some of which you have met elsewhere in the book, for example the US Head Start project's High Scope, northern Italy's Reggio Emilia framework, and New Zealand's Te Whariki, to which you will find links in the Recommended reading section of this chapter. We hope, however, that we have covered some key aspects which impact upon your everyday practice, and given you some examples that have helped you to reflect and consider your own position towards issues arising.

How do we provide education and care for young children in contemporary societies?

We have found over the past two or three decades that young children are increasingly cared for in professional settings, while the stay-at-home parent (who was traditionally the mother) has become an increasingly out-dated concept. Most western nations offer some support for parents seeking care for their young children while they engage in paid employment, but the ways in which this is administered vary considerably from nation to nation. An attempt by the European Union in 2002 to set a minimum standard for the provision of care and education for young children met with variable results (European Programme for Employment and Social Solidarity, 2014). The ways in which care is provided are greatly affected by the construction of the young child in the specific nation.

What are the dominant contemporary models of the child and of society?

These models exist as a dichotomy that can be simplified to child as human resource versus child as citizen. The nations that view children as human resources have a culture of 'channelling' children through highly formal 'transmit and test' education systems to fill existing roles in society that they believe will ultimately protect their population's comparative economic performance in the future. Nations that view children as citizens have a principally rights-based perspective. Their model of the child is that of a vulnerable human being with as yet undeveloped potential, skills and talents that should be individually nurtured. In such societies, formal education starts later, and is not dominated by heavily prescribed curricula. It can be difficult to definitively measure the ultimate results of different cultures of care and education; however, children in the Scandinavian nations report the greatest sense of well-being in the EU, and children in the UK are amongst the most troubled. The most recent rankings of nations in terms of well-being are listed in Table 10.2, with respect to children's educational well-being.

Table 10.2 Ranking of educational well-being, 2012

Ranking
Netherlands
Belgium
Germany
Finland
Slovenia
Norway
Denmark
Hungary
Poland
Iceland
Sweden
Czech Republic
Estonia
Canada
France
Switzerland
Ireland
Portugal
Lithuania
Latvia
Slovakia
Luxembourg
Austria
United Kingdom
Italy
Spain
United States
Greece
Romania

Source: Data drawn from *Child Well-Being in Rich Countries* (UNICEF, 2012).

What are the debates relating to the role that early years education and care should play in contemporary societies?

The nations that look upon children as future human resources (or 'capital'), in a society based on the movement of capital between nations, companies and individuals, tend towards 'transmit and test' mainstream education systems, and focus on 'school readiness' in the early years, with a view to developing quite narrow employment-ready competencies to produce commercially competitive populations. Nations that view children as citizens with individual needs tend to take a rights-based, enabling approach to education, focused upon inculcating transferable skills. They put a much greater emphasis on a social justice agenda, developing social skills and concepts of citizenship within the youngest children, and upon the provision of publicly funded services for families to address the human rights of all, both adults and children within societies of autonomous but collaborative individuals.

What is the 'schism' between the provision of early years education and care for children under and over three?

While there seems to be relatively general international agreement that some amount of collective care and education should be provided for children over three, there is less agreement about the 'place' of children under three. Some nations, such as the Czech Republic, make their position quite clear; in this case, that children under three should be cared for within their immediate families, while in the case of Sweden an alternative approach is taken in the provision of a comprehensive, publicly funded care and education system for children from the first birthday onwards. Other nations such as Italy, France and the UK appear to be in transition with respect to the provision of care for children under three, with England and France demonstrating a common ambition to absorb two-year-olds into the existing schools system to begin 'school readiness' training at an earlier stage, rather than creating developmentally appropriate provision. In the UK, the debates around this issue look set to continue into the new Parliament elected in 2015, in the shape of a potentially widening gap between early years policy proposals in Conservative-led England and Scottish National Party-led Scotland.

What might the future be for early years education and care in the UK?

Within the UK, the future of early years care and education is likely to become increasingly diverse between nations, given the considerable political differences that are emerging between the four nations, England and Scotland in particular. While the left-leaning Scottish administration is more in tune with the Scandinavian social justice approach (which, interestingly, is mirrored in recent policy developments within the Scottish youth justice system; for example, effective raising of the age of criminal responsibility), England seems set upon a similar 'school-readiness' trajectory to the US, with increasing privatisation on the one hand, and national target setting on the other. The Anglo-American 'children as future economic capital' culture is also being increasingly transported to nations that are currently developing early education and care services (Baker, 2015; Frewen *et al.*, 2015; Ying Hu *et al.*, 2015; Miyahara and Meyers, 2008).

A major clue we can rely upon to help us predict what is likely to happen with respect to future developments in early years education and care systems within various nations is that they will inevitably mirror the societal culture in which they are immersed. Over the last few decades this has become more of an issue for very young children, as international practice has largely moved towards placing them in collective education and care settings at an earlier stage in development. How this will impact upon these children as individuals and upon society as a whole is not yet clear, but as UNICEF (2008, pp. 8–9) warn, 'there is a clear danger that the child care transition may follow a course that is determined by the needs and pressures of the moment, uninfluenced by long term vision or choice'. This is not a situation into which we as an international community should be 'sleepwalking', and we hope that this final chapter has given you a basis for some reflection on and consideration of this most important of issues, for society as a whole, not only those engaged in early years practice.

Reflection: developing national policy

If you were asked to work on a committee to improve the early years education and care system in your nation, what would you identify as the most important issues to address?

● Make a list and then narrow it down to three key priorities.
● How would you go about changing/enhancing policy in order to achieve your goals?

Recommended reading

Dahlberg, G. and Moss, P. (2005) *Ethics and Politics in Early Childhood Education*. Abingdon: Routledge.

Einarsdottir, J., and Wagner, J. (2006) *Nordic Childhoods and Early Education: Philosophy, research, policy and practice in Denmark, Finland, Iceland, Norway, and Sweden*. Charlotte, NC: Information Age.

Georgeson, J. and Payler, J. (2013) *International Perspectives on Early Childhood Education and Care*. Milton Keynes: Open University Press.

Hall, K., Horgan, M., Ridgway, A., Murphy. R., Cunneen, M. and Cunningham, D. (2010) *Loris Malaguzzi and the Reggio Emilia Experience*. London: Bloomsbury.

High Scope Website: www.highscope.org

Iorio, J. and Parnell, W. (2015) *Rethinking Readiness in Early Childhood Education*. London: Palgrave Macmillan.

New Zealand Ministry of Education (1996) *Te Whariki Early Childhood Curriculum*. Available at: www. education.govt.nz/assets/Documents/Early-Childhood/te-whariki.pdf

Journals

Early Years: An International Journal
International Journal of Early Childhood
International Journal of Early Years Education

References

Australian Government Productivity Committee (2014) *Childcare and Early Childhood Learning. Productivity Commission Inquiry Report: Overview and recommendations*, Inquiry Report No. 73. Canberra: Commonwealth of Australia. Retrieved from: www.pc.gov.au/inquiries/completed/childcare/report/childcare-overview.pdf 29th May 2015.

Baker, F. (2015) Challenges presented to personal theories, beliefs and practices of play in Abu Dhabi kindergartens: the English medium teacher perspective. *Early Years: An International Journal*. 35(1), 22–35.

BBC (2015) *Queen's Speech 2015: Childcare access to double*. Retrieved from: www.bbc.co.uk/news/uk-politics-32896284 28th May 2015.

Brostrom, S. and Hansen, O.H. (2010) Care and education in the Danish creche. *International Journal of Early Childhood*. 42, 87–100.

Campbell-Barr, V. (2012) Early years education and the value for money folklore. *European Early Childhood Education Research Journal*. 20(3), 423–37.

Cohen. P. (2012) *Converging Towards Equality: Female employment from 1964 until today*. Retrieved from: www.theatlantic.com/sexes/archive/2012/11/converging-toward-equality-female-employment-from-1964-to-today/264625 9th June 2015.

Europa (2015) *Czech Republic: Supporting parental care in early childhood and protecting children's rights*. Retrieved from: http://europa.eu/epic/countries/czech-republic/index_en.htm 27th May 2015.

European Programme for Employment and Social Solidarity (2014) *Use of Childcare in the EU Member States and Progress towards the Barcelona Targets*. Brussels: RAND Europe. Retrieved from: http://ec.europa.eu/justice/gender-equality/files/documents/140502_gender_equality_workforce_ssr1_en.pdf 27th May 2015.

Frewen, A., Chew, E., Carter, M., Chunn, J. and Jotanovic, D. (2015) A cross-cultural exploration of parental involvement and child-rearing beliefs in Asian cultures. *Early Years: An International Journal*. 35(1). 36–49.

Full Fact.org (2013) *Childcare in the UK: The tightest and most expensive?* Retrieved from: https://fullfact.org/factchecks/childcare_costs_ratios-28918 27th May 2015.

Gillard, D. (2004) *The Plowden Report*. Retrieved from: www.infed.org/schooling/plowden_report.htm 27th May 2015.

Goldstein, D. (2011) *Kindergartners, Put Down Your Pencils*. Retrieved from: www.slate.com/articles/double_x/doublex/2011/11/obama_s_race_to_the_top_goes_to_kindergarten_is_standardized_testing_for_5_year_olds_a_good_idea_.single.html#pagebreak_anchor_2 27th May 2015.

Greve, A. and Solheim, M. (2010) Research on children in ECEC under three in Norway: increased volume, yet invisible. *International Journal of Early Childhood*. 42, 155–63.

Hannikainen, M. (2010) 1 to 3-year-old children in day care centres in Finland: an overview of eight doctoral dissertations. *International Journal of Early Childhood*. 42, 101–15.

Hempsall, J. (2014) *School Readiness: An issue for children, parents, providers and schools*. Retrieved from: www.nurseryworld.co.uk/nursery-world/opinion/1144141/school-readiness-issue-children-parents-providers-schools 27th May 2015.

Jarvis, P. (2015) It's against human nature to send two year olds to school. *The Conversation*. Retrieved from: https://theconversation.com/its-against-human-nature-to-send-two-year-olds-to-school-37180 27th May 2015.

Jarvis, P. and Liebovich, B. (2015) British nurseries, head and heart: McMillan, Owen and the genesis of the education/care dichotomy. *Women's History Review*. Retrieved from: www.tandfonline.com/doi/abs/10.1080/09612025.2015.1025662?journalCode=rwhr20#.VUZripPff4U 27th May 2015.

Jarvis, P., Newman, S. and George, J. (2014a) Play, learning for life: in pursuit of 'well being' through play, in A. Brock, P. Jarvis and Y. Olusoga (Eds), *Perspectives on Play* (2nd Edn), pp. 269–94. Abingdon: Routledge.

Jarvis, P., Newman, S. and Swiniarski, L. (2014b) On 'becoming social': the importance of collaborative free play in childhood. *International Journal of Play*. 3(1), 53-68. Retrieved from: www.tandfonline.com/doi/pdf/10.1080/21594937.2013.863440 27th May 2015.

Johansson, E. and Emilson, A. (2010) Toddlers' life in Swedish preschool. *International Journal of Early Childhood*. 42, 165–79.

Learner, S. (2015) *Nursery Leaders Call on New Conservative Government to Honour Childcare Funding Review Promise*. Retrieved from: www.daynurseries.co.uk/news/article.cfm/id/1568927/nursery-leaders-conservative-government-childcare-funding 27th May 2015.

Le Bouteillec, N., Kandil, L. and Solaz, A. (2014) *Who Are the Children Enrolled in French Daycare Centres?* Retrieved from: www.ined.fr/fichier/s_rubrique/21857/population.societes.2014.514.nursery.france.en.pdf 28th May 2015.

Lepper, J. (2015) *Government Plans to Fast-Track 30 Hour Childcare Pledge*. Retrieved from: www.cypnow.co.uk/cyp/news/1151357/government-plans-to-fast-track-30-hour-childcare-pledge 27th May 2015.

McArdle, L. (2014) *Ofsted Chief Blames Early Years Providers for School Readiness Failings*. Retrieved from: www.cypnow.co.uk/cyp/news/1143215/wilshaw-blames-providers-school-readiness-failings 27th May 2015.

McCree, J. and McCree, M. (2012) *A Brief History of the Roots of Forest Schools in the UK*. Retrieved from: www.outdoor-learning.org/Portals/0/ForestSchoolAssociation/H60.Author.version.FSHitory.pt1.pdf 4th June 2012.

Miyahara, J. and Meyers, C. (2008) Early learning and development standards in East Asia and the Pacific: experiences from eight countries. *International Journal of Early Childhood*. 40(2), 17–31.

Musatti, T. and Picchio, M. (2010) Early education in Italy: research and practice. *International Journal of Early Childhood*. 42, 141–53.

Oberhumer, P. (2001) International perspectives on early childhood curricula. *International Journal of Early Childhood*. 37(1), 27–37.

Office for National Statistics (2013) *Full Report: Women in the Labour Market*. Retrieved from www.ons.gov.uk/ons/dcp171776_328352.pdf 9th June 2015.

Olorenshaw, V. (2015) *This Political and Media Childcare Consensus Is Burying the Voice of Parents and Annihilating the Needs of Children from Debate – and It Is Entirely Undemocratic*. Retrieved from: www.huffingtonpost.co.uk/vanessa-olorenshaw/parenting-election_b_7147150.html 27th May 2015.

Rayna, S. (2010) Research and ECEC for children under three in France: a brief review. *International Journal of Early Childhood*. 42, 117–30.

Rogoff, B. and Toma, C. (1997) Shared thinking: community and institutional variations. *Discourse Processes*. 23(3), 471–97.

Rutter, J. (2015) *Family and Childcare Trust Childcare Costs Survey 2015*. London: Family and Childcare Trust. Retrieved from: www.fct.bigmallet.co.uk/sites/default/files/files/Childcare_cost_survey_2015_Final.pdf#overlay-context=annual-childcare-costs-surveys 27th May 2015.

Sokačová, L. (2011) *The Czech Republic: Gender Studies O.P.S in comparative analysis of the work/life balance situation in the Czech Republic, Poland, Germany and Slovakia*. Retrieved from: www.genderstudies.cz/download/AnalysisEN.pdf 27th May 2015.

Spours, K. (2015) *Forget the Global Race. Education is about more than that*. Retrieved from: www.newstatesman.com/politics/2015/03/forget-global-race-education-about-more 27th May 2015.

Stephen, C. (2006) *Early Years Education: Perspectives from a review of the international literature.* Edinburgh: The Scottish Executive. Retrieved from: www.gov.scot/Resource/Doc/92395/0022116.pdf 27th May 2015.

The Guardian (2013) *Childcare Minister Elizabeth Truss Attacks Unruly Nurseries.* Retrieved from: www.theguardian.com/education/2013/apr/22/childcare-minister-elizabeth-truss-nurseries 28th May 2015.

The Huffington Post, Canada (2012) *Maternity Leaves Around the World.* Retrieved from: www.huffingtonpost.ca/2012/05/22/maternity-leaves-around-the-world_n_1536120.html 27th May 2015.

The White House (2009) *Fact Sheet, Race to the Top.* Retrieved from: www.whitehouse.gov/the-press-office/fact-sheet-race-top 27th May 2015.

Think Left (2011) *A Bold Approach to Childcare.* Retrieved from: http://think-left.org/2011/08/16/a-bold-approach-to-childcare/ 27th May 2015.

Tizard, B. (2009) The making and breaking of attachment. *The Psychologist.* 22(10), 902-3.

UNICEF (2008) *The Child Care Transition: A league table of early childhood education and care in economically advanced countries.* Retrieved from: www.unicef-irc.org/publications/pdf/rc8_eng.pdf 28th May 2015.

UNICEF (2012) *Child Well-Being in Rich Countries.* Retrieved from: www.unicef.org.uk/Images/Campaigns/FINAL_RC11-ENG-LORES-fnl2.pdf 9th June 2015.

Whitebread, D., and Bingham, S. (2011). *School Readiness; a critical review of perspectives and evidence,* Occasional Paper 2. TACTYC Conference, Birmingham: 'Ready for School? Research, Reflection and Debate'. 11-12 November.

Ying Hu, B., Vong, K.I. and Chi Kuan Mak, M. (2015) An evaluation of China's kindergarten quality rating system through the Chinese early childhood rating scale - the Zhejiang case. *Early Years: An International Journal.* 35(1), 50-66.

Index

Note: Page numbers in *italics* represent *tables*
Page numbers in **bold** represent **figures**

Printed in Great Britain
by Amazon